UNLIKEABLE FEMALE CHARACTERS

The Women Pop Culture Wants You to Hate

Anna Bogutskaya

sourcebooks

Copyright © 2023 by Anna Bogutskaya
Cover and internal design © 2023 by Sourcebooks
Cover design by Sara Wood
Cover images © CSA Images/Getty Images
Internal design by Laura Boren/Sourcebooks

This publication is designed to provide accurate and authoritative information in regard to the subject matter covered. It is sold with the understanding that the publisher is not engaged in rendering legal, accounting, or other professional service. If legal advice or other expert assistance is required, the services of a competent professional person should be sought. —*From a Declaration of Principles Jointly Adopted by a Committee of the American Bar Association and a Committee of Publishers and Associations*

Published by Sourcebooks, an imprint of Sourcebooks
P.O. Box 4410, Naperville, Illinois 60567-4410
(630) 961-3900
sourcebooks.com

Cataloging-in-Publication Data is on file with the Library of Congress.

Printed and bound in Canada.
MBP 10 9 8 7 6 5 4 3 2 1

PRAISE FOR *UNLIKEABLE FEMALE CHARACTERS*

"Fascinating, insightful and kick-ass. This book is a super smart and deeply personal addition to the canon. All hail the unlikeable female!"

—Emma Jane Unsworth, internationally best-selling author of *Grown Ups* and *Animals*

"Anna Bogutskaya's beautifully written *Unlikeable Female Characters* takes a deep dive into bitches, sluts, trainwrecks, psychos—and more—to prove that bad girls make good films and even better TV. A necessary read for all Harley Quinn fiends, Fleabag aficionados, *Promising Young Woman* stans, and Shonda Rhimes fans, *Unlikeable Female Characters* blows apart the myth of likeability and reveals the female liberation (and male fear) of girls gone wonderfully bad."

—Chelsea G. Summers, author of *A Certain Hunger*

"For me, being vilified on a global Netflix show in the height of a pandemic didn't come with a guidebook. But oh, I wish it had—and I wish it would have been this brilliant masterpiece breaking down the tired tropes of reality television and beyond. Time's up for the archetypes outlined by Bogutskaya. We're here for the unleashing of brilliant, ambitious women who are three-dimensional, complex, and gracing us with their whole selves."

—Aparna Shewakramani, author of *She's Unlikeable* and star of *Indian Matchmaking*

"Anna Bogutskaya's *Unlikeable Female Characters* is a sweeping, celebratory journey through the tropes of unacceptable femininity, saluting the unladylike and improper and creating a fresh lens through which to appreciate notions of strength and independence. A how-to guide as much as a pop cultural history, Bogutskaya captivates and activates in equal measure."

—Alexandra Heller-Nicholas, author and film critic

"Not only is this a smudged eye-liner written love letter to the perfect imperfection of unlikeable women on screen, but a searing and essential analysis of decades of iconic characters. Packed with smart observations and laugh out loud asides, Anna Bogutskaya's *Unlikeable Female Characters* is a wry and constantly entertaining history of the mean girls, angry women, psychopaths, and weirdos we let into our hearts. Prepare to see your watchlist with new eyes. I didn't want it to end."

—Louise Blain, writer and broadcaster

"There's a certain alchemy to Anna's writing—what looks like a book about the fates of women on screen turns out to really be a book about how women have always been forced to perceive themselves through mirrors built by other people's presumptions. *Unlikeable Female Characters* is part-cultural exposé, part-Taylor Swift album. An illuminating read and a true comfort for any woman who's ever been called a slut, bitch, shrew, or weirdo."

—Clarisse Loughrey, Chief Film Critic at *The Independent*

"Anna Bogutskaya grapples with the dichotomies of being a long-time film nerd and a staunch feminist in this acerbic, searing analysis of on-screen female stereotypes. From the Slut to the Bitch (via the Psycho), we are invited to take another, harder look at the women we have watched for decades on screen and wonder why we have accepted them in such broad terms for so long. Anna's writing perfectly expresses her passion for cinema; her enthusiasm is evident in every line in this book but she is unafraid to confront some hard truths about some of our favorite and (let's face it) most hated female characters. Her explorations invite the reader to come to their own conclusions about why we have been conditioned to mark out such limiting parameters around these roles in pop culture, but Anna gives us the tools in this book to see how it has been done and what is needed to break out of this cycle. Reclaiming the word 'unlikeable' has never felt so good."

—Rhianna Dhillon, film critic and broadcaster

For Ruby,
a most likeable female character

CONTENTS

"It's super-exciting to not care if you're liked, and to watch someone's face as they realize that. It's fun defying expectations about me. It's a nice secret weapon."

AMY POEHLER, ACTRESS

"Make me out to be the villain if that helps you sleep at night."

ANNALISE KEATING, *HOW TO GET AWAY WITH MURDER*

Foreword

The year is 2022 and as the final chapter of this book says, it "really shouldn't exist." Hey, don't stop! Where are you going? I didn't say it needn't exist, but that it *shouldn't*. I mean, come on: surely it shouldn't. It's 20-Actual-22, society has (by some accounts) made progress and yet here I am writing a foreword to a book called *Unlikeable Female Characters*. One of the very first books to consider the non-nice girls on screen. And here you are, reading it.

Both of us—you and me—know though that it's entirely, absolutely needed. And Anna Bogutskaya—programmer, writer, broadcaster, activist, and glorious champion of women who are committed to film and those who work to commit others—is the one to write it. To consider and weigh and articulate the arguments that have raged for generations and continue today.

For it's a note that I still know echoes around writers' rooms and boardrooms alike; the furrowed brow of an exec who's trying to put it any other way than the way he finally has to put it: **but is she...*likeable*?**

What do we, what do *they*, mean by likeable? It's been said that likeability means relatability. And that relatability is what a female character needs in a film or TV show for that film or TV show to succeed commercially.

I call bullshit on two fronts: firstly, this book forms a long, *long* list of successful films with unlikeable protagonists. And secondly, most, if not all, women I know can relate to an unlikeable woman. For—whisper it—we often *are* unlikeable women. Whether men (and some women) *want* an unlikeable woman on screen is another question entirely.

Because to me, likeability means palatability. And specifically, how palatable these characters are to a patriarchal world that in many cases still like its women—both fictional and otherwise—to be supine and silent.

We are to be nice. To be good. To be soft and yielding. To say we like it when we absolutely don't. To be grateful and gracious. To swallow our anger and resentment. We aren't to resist or fight, attack, or confront. We shouldn't violate the social codes and norms that have offered a blueprint—really, a straitjacket—for women for generations.

This book traces how, from the early days of Hollywood and after the first golden age of the unlikeable character, that straitjacket was tied tightly by the studio system, critics, producers, and even audiences.

How the decades since then imprisoned the unlikeable character. And now, how releasing her offers freedom, not just to those female characters but to women in the real world.

And there are those who would argue that we've never had it better than now. That on-screen representation has never been healthier. And to be sure, in my twenty years of writing, we've travelled some distance. But how far exactly? That's the question Anna rightly asks.

We've had Villanelle and Fleabag and Annalise Keating and Amy Dunne and Cassie Thomas. Flawed, sometimes-but-not-always fucked-up women who fight and kill and shag and manipulate. Who are about as far from the "nice, good girl" as it's possible to be.

This "rise of the unlikeable woman" on screen has seen these female characters move front and center. They're winning awards and critical recognition, as are their creators. It feels as though audiences finally, fully recognize that complex, flawed, *human* female characters enrich our screens. They're no longer a reason *not* to watch (if they ever truly were).

And so with a forensic, expert eye, Anna explores the nine tropes that make-up our unlikeable female characters on screen: the Bitch, the Mean Girl, the Angry Woman, the Slut, the Crazy Woman, the Psycho, the Trainwreck, the Shrew, and the Weirdo. None are without complication, without problem. All have contributed to the landscape as it exists today.

Harnessing the language and arguments that have so often been used against us as women—in life, in fiction, and everything in between—she unpicks our progress and the state of contemporary film and TV. Her opinion shifts as she studies and probes and challenges. And you may well find that yours does too. I know mine did.

I ask myself: are we fully there yet, and by "there," I mean on an equal footing with men? Taking up space next to them in a world where adulterers, sociopaths, and psychopaths are not just be tolerated but admired, revered, lusted-after, liked (hi Don

Draper, Walter White, Tony Soprano, and the rest of your merry band of bad brothers).

Men can be liked for being bad, but can women? Should we even aspire to the same: to be liked? After all, likeability, in whatever form it takes is still, surely, a trap.

Maybe, in fact, the ultimate act of the unlikeable woman is to be recognized and seen, shown to be alive—as in the pages of this book—but to say, after careful consideration, fuck it and fuck you. To stay true to her name, to remain proudly unlikeable. Maybe that's what freedom really feels like. For them, for me and for you.

—Terri White, writer, columnist,
author, and screenwriter

How Not to
Be a Girl

When I was a teenager, my parents gave me a book titled *How to Be a Girl*. Not the Caitlin Moran memoir—it was a Russian-language how-to guide for teenage girls on how to behave, how to dress, how to move, how to attract boys, how to be proper. It was a manual on what the appropriate behaviors were for a teenage girl, mainly aimed at pleasing parents and boys. I remember promptly throwing it away and experiencing a feeling of disgust that I could not yet articulate. What were these rules? Who wrote them? And why was I expected to abide by them?

The lessons in that book, which I never really read, would haunt me well into my adult life, my career, and the writing of this book. Books like that—which have existed since the Victorian era, when titles such as *Practical Hints to Young Females: On the Duties of a Wife, a Mother, and a Mistress of a Family* were commonplace—are just one of the ways women have been presented with rulebooks on how to behave and how to please everyone else.

"Proper" or "ladylike," among other gendered terms, are concepts imbued with the multitude of unspoken rules that women are expected to learn and abide by. You should be pretty, primped, and polite. Read: be fuckable enough to merit attention, but don't enjoy the attention too much. You should wear makeup and take care of yourself. Caution: not too much, lest you appear to be vain and superficial. You should be smart and well read. But beware: never disagree or have opinions that contradict or are more informed than any man's. Be approachable and have a personality, lest you be branded basic. But, you know, not too much of a personality. Be girly—but not too feminine, because then you seem vapid. Be ambitious—but not so much that it makes men uncomfortable. Be nice—because, more than anything, you need to be liked. Smile—because you look prettier that way.

Every time I failed to abide by these rules, every time I was chastised for stepping outside the bounds of what was "ladylike," I wondered if there was something fundamentally unlikeable about me. I would then remember that book and the expectations that came with it. With every personal and professional rejection, every disappointment, every failure, I'd think of my perceived lack of likeability. Of course I was failing—I'd literally thrown away the rule book and failed to learn the rules.

In pop culture, I was always drawn to the women who were unapologetically angry, horny, ambitious, and even bad, who got away with cons and murders, acting out and misbehaving. I didn't know I was looking *for* them. Sometimes, I hated them. At other times, I was afraid of them. But I remembered them and was drawn to them, drawn to their hunger. In music, I was drawn to the messy women of punk, like Courtney Love, Kathleen Hanna, and Brody Dalle, who screamed coarsely and earnestly about their experiences. They *shouted*, they were loud, they had voices and bodies and faces that did not look like those of the girls I was told I should aspire to look like. On my tiny square TV screen, which lived in my room and with which I learned English through subtitled movies, I watched the manipulative, rich, mean girl Kathryn Merteuil of *Cruel Intentions*. Although I knew I was supposed to hate her, I liked her more than the prissy protagonist (even more so when I graduated to the adult adaptation of the novel *Dangerous Liaisons*, in which the Marquise de Merteuil is played by Glenn Close). As I entered the professional sphere, I yearned to have the ballsy, naked ambition of Bette Davis characters (and much later, of Miranda Priestly in *The Devil Wears Prada*, who created a new blueprint) but was swiftly chastised for it.

I've always been more eagerly attuned to my shortcomings than to my positive attributes. Even these were often turned into negatives through everyday experiences, passive aggressive "negs," and outright insults, not just from others but often from myself. My own inner monologue was shaped by warning signs, which were in turn shaped by pop culture as much as by real-life experiences: "Too smart for your own good," "Too intense," "Too ambitious," "Too much." "Too" being the operative word. I come back to the behind-the-scenes stories of defiance of actresses like Bette Davis—who was, in her own words, "too much," both onscreen and off—much more often than I do those pretty, polite, and primped stories that resonated so very little with me or any woman I have ever known.

Before I even understood the layers contained in these words, I was drawn to these extreme characters, these difficult women. When I worried about being too pushy at work, I'd think back to these fictional women, think of how they would have handled the situation. As I write this, I keep asking myself: Why am I so taken with these unlikeable women? Am I defending them? Do I want to redeem them? Do I applaud their transgressions? Do I see myself in them? Do I want to be like them?

Working as a film programmer, participating in those discussions in which decisions were made concerning what was written about, what was screened, what was acquired for distribution, or what was programmed for a festival, I often thought about the question of "likeability" and about these women that I continued to be drawn to. Before I knew anything about criticism, film theory, or film history, I was drawn to these women who didn't look, behave, or talk like the blueprint of a "good woman." They swore, they fucked, they robbed, they killed. They lived fantastic, over-the-top lives and did not apologize for it. When they succeeded, they didn't downplay their achievements, and they dominated any room they went into. When they fucked up and failed, they owned it and moved forward. They were the center of their own stories, the drivers of them. They went after the things they wanted, and I thought, even before I had the awareness or the language to articulate it, that if they could do all those things, maybe I could too. And if I messed up, I could just get back up again and not be ruined. It's not about relatability; it's about permission to fail and be flawed.

The thing is, though, it's not about me at all. I'm just tired of trying so hard to pretend to be superhuman, of bending in incongruous ways to try to fit into a box that was not designed for me, or any woman, to begin with—but who isn't?

Like the complicated, often contradictory demands of being a woman, being unlikeable implies being both too much of something and not enough of something else. What the "something" is will always vary, mutate, and slip away before being understood, with some other unlikeable quality taking the place of the first one.

The silent implication of being unlikeable is that it's a free pass to be dismissed, disrespected, and disempowered. If you are deemed unlikeable, you have refused to be a part of the machine of femininity, so you are fair game. You can, and perhaps should, be punished, taught a lesson, put in your place. Unlikeable women—we are told by decades of pop culture—need a valid excuse to be so unlikeable, or else they need to be punished for going against the rules. Only a woman's intense suffering can justify her unlikeability.

We are now living in a cultural reckoning of the stories we had accepted as canon, questioning the rules and empathizing with the characters we had point-blank considered villainous or unlikeable. We're finally asking ourselves the question: *Why* do I consider her unlikeable? These stories, these roles that fall under the catchall term "unlikeable female character," are important because they open up the type of narratives that women can inhabit.

In her book of essays *Too Fat, Too Slutty, Too Loud*, Anne Helen Petersen hits the nail on the head when she ties the 2016 U.S. presidential election (specifically the criticism directed against Hillary Clinton) to the deep-rooted societal distrust of any woman who bends the unspoken rules of likeability: "There have been unruly women for as long as there have been boundaries of what constitutes acceptable 'feminine' behavior: women who, in some way, step outside of the boundaries of good womanhood." While Petersen is talking about women in general, and women in the public sphere in particular, this applies to women on the screen too.

The term "unlikeable" is a very particular one. It's a word that means everything and nothing at the same time. Likeability implies both affection (Do I like spending time with this person?) and moral approval (Are they a good person?). It's incredibly nebulous and hard to define, yet any woman who hears it understands instinctively the baggage of connotations it carries. Every time I speak this word out loud to another woman, there is a nod of recognition. The rules defining what makes you "likeable" are so obscure they're almost impossible to abide by.

In June 2019, I presented a curated program of films and events at the British Film Institute that drew a lot of attention. It was dedicated to exploring the trope of the onscreen Bitch, the ultimate unlikeable female character, and it was titled Playing the Bitch. This ten-film repertory season caused a debate that reached much further than the niche but very loud domain of "Film Twitter." And in retrospect, it was all because of the use of the "B word" by a big cultural institution. Before the program, the more I researched and thought about it and spoke to people about it, the more I thought about a particular type of female character that exists in cinema and TV, mostly in the English language, that didn't quite have a PG name yet. When writing the copy for the program, a male copy editor tried to change my use of the word "unlikeable" to "disagreeable" because grammatically the word made more sense, but the connotations implicit in it went completely over his head. The fact that he didn't understand the baggage of that word just proved my point. That project was the genesis of this book. The conversations I had with people during that project wormed their way into my brain.

Movies are fantasies. They are, and always will be, an imaginary retreat. They're a place to relax when I'm tired of trying to fit in. How can we relax, though, if even movies are feeding us a superhuman ideal? And these characters, these women... I want to know more about them. Film fans, and film obsessives (like me), live in a world stuck between the often grim reality of filmmaking and the emotional dreamland of the films themselves. Thinking of these characters deemed unlikeable, I'm not thinking about which bits of myself I can see in them—I'm living out a fantasy in which I don't care whether people like me or not. I have a problem with boxes. I want the world to be complicated, layered, and flawed; I want to make mistakes and have the possibility of learning from them. I want this for myself, for my friends, colleagues, and all women, and I want it for these characters.

Disliking someone is a visceral reaction. An instant judgment of character. You know when you feel it; sometimes it's a first impression, other times an icky feeling that develops over time. But this gut feeling, this "There's just something about her I don't like" shouldn't be a rule book that only women follow. What happens, then, when that dislike is systematized, combined with social stereotypes, ingrained in systems of oppression and an industry based on sexual and emotional voyeurism? Movies and

TV series, the images and stories that pop culture creates, feed into our own construction of womanhood. They matter because they create blueprints for what's acceptable and what's possible for us in the real world. The stranglehold pop culture has on us lies in its cyclical nature: it is both a mirror and an influence. There's a reason moral panics have happened because of books, films, music videos, and video games. The stories and characters we see onscreen, the ones we grow up with, the ones that we enjoy publicly, and the ones that we secretly think are only ours to understand—all those stories influence how we see the world and how we see ourselves.

The history and evolution of unlikeable female characters tells us about the characters that screenwriters were interested in writing and that actors were willing to play and about what the industry was ready to fund and reward with golden statuettes. Fundamentally, though, it tells us about the types of women that people are willing to accept in real life. How audiences and critics respond to these characters, whether they are embraced or not, and how harshly we judge them tells us so much about what we're willing to embrace in women.

For women, for girls, for anyone who's not the default main character, this is especially important. We seek out the stories that validate us, that move us, that make us feel just a little bit better about our place in the world. When we see ourselves being punished onscreen, we take this as a lesson. We get used to seeing our suffering, and we internalize what we need to do to avoid it. Even though I threw away that rule book on how to be girl, I couldn't escape the rules.

Pop culture is the stories that we tell ourselves about

ourselves. It's our folklore. The manner in which cinema and television are made and received by audiences is a cultural thermometer, a reflection of a time and a place. It is also our framework for deciding what is acceptable, or normal, and is vital in forming our ideas of behaviors and social norms. Some books, films, or TV shows become such cultural touchstones that they integrate themselves into our language and descriptions of each other ("You're such a Carrie/Samantha/Charlotte/Miranda!"). I can see the choices being made by screenwriters, directors, casting directors, editors, and—crucially—actors. Every raised eyebrow, every pursed lip—a deliberate choice. Here, I want to acknowledge the actresses who play these characters. The makeup, hair, and costume design are a collaboration between performer and designer that fleshes out a character wordlessly. These characters are theirs as much as they are the writers', the directors', and ours. Pop culture has created and perpetuated the platform for these tropes and stereotypes to coalesce—but they are never set in stone. These tropes are in constant evolution, both fueled by and creating ideas around "acceptable" womanhood. They are cultural constraints placed on womanhood, supposedly for our own good, so we're not led astray by "bad role models." I don't want to be like these characters, but I do envy them. All this to say, I've been thinking about what makes a woman likeable because I've always been afraid of being unlikeable.

No one should need a film studies degree to read this book. I'm going to use pop culture to explore these intersecting questions: What makes a good woman? What does it mean to be likeable? What does likeability tell us about being good? How do women claim power within the stories that are designed to keep them disempowered? How have the limits of likeability changed? And why, gradually and then suddenly, has being unlikeable become a selling point?

These questions have been at the heart of cultural conversation and criticism in one way or another. Anne Helen Petersen calls it "unruliness"; Rachel Vorona Cote dubs it "too muchness"; Elizabeth Wurtzel calls it "villainy"; Angelica Jade Bastién has written extensively about the "madwomen" of cinema. Since I'm going to be talking about movies, TV series, and pop culture, I'll use the word that has been linked to the entertainment industry since its inception: "unlikeable." It's a limited—and limiting—word, one that I'd like retired, but as it is, it's one that keeps rearing its head.

Throughout the history of pop culture, we've seen the rise of unlikeable female characters, their demonization, and we are now living through an era of cautious acceptance, even trying to monetize the very idea of unlikeability in the same way pop culture monetized feminism. This rise is contemporaneous with an increased number of female creators (screenwriters, directors, producers, showrunners), an increase in the visibility of female critics (professional and amateur alike), and a new form of online fandom (social media, memes, merchandise). We're just getting used to seeing unlikeable female characters take center stage and propel the narrative forward instead of being relegated as the supporting characters to difficult men. We're also seeing the commercial tide swing in favor of unlikeable women, the marketing of these stories emphasizing their wickedness (think of *Cruella*, which was sold to us with the tagline "Brilliant. Bad.

And just a little bit mad"). While tacky, this does feel momentous. The screen industries have been mostly dominated by men and whiteness; this means that male characters are considered to be the relatable ones and that whiteness is assumed to be the universal experience. Everyone in the audience who is not a man (and by "man" I mean, ordinarily, a white, cis, able-bodied, straight man) is meant to project themselves onto the screen, to find an entry point to connect to the story, all at the expense of their own experience. While flawed male characters have been rewarded and praised, entering the pantheon of cultural immortality, female characters plagued with flaws have been outliers. The actresses playing them, when they've dared risk their reputations, have sometimes been rewarded with professional recognition for their so-called bravery, but they've just as often been typecast, branded as "difficult," or made to disappear from the industry altogether. So when female villainy is being used as a springboard for stories and marketing, we're being told that it's commercially viable. Being unlikeable has become *a selling point*.

I couldn't—not in a thousand pages—write a complete history of the unlikeable female character. To be truly comprehensive, such a history would need to be a list of thousands of entries, spanning films and series from all over the world, taking into account cultural nuances and different notions of femininity. I will have missed a lot of titles that are relevant or fitting, but my aim is to use accessible and recognizable titles that might be an entry point for people not as intensely obsessed with films as I am. I've tried to pick the films and shows that have been, for better or worse, lightning rods in pop culture. The sort of productions that can create a moral panic, new slang, and new fashion

trends. The kind that become a point of comparison for everything produced over the next decade. Despite my deep love for
horror, exploitation, and underground cinema, I've avoided any
titles that are too niche. Horror cinema has always been ahead of
the curve, a Trojan horse of a genre with its own thorny relationship to women that is a subject for another book entirely. There
are a myriad of examples; some have been watched and loved by
many fans, but few have actually shifted the cultural dial. What
I'll use are watershed characters who became, for lack of a better
word, *iconic*; those whose influence can be felt and traced in the
pop culture products that are capturing our imaginations today.

I'll weave together nine tropes of unlikeable female characters:
the Bitch, the Mean Girl, the Angry Woman, the Slut, the Crazy
Woman, the Psycho, the Trainwreck, the Shrew, and the Weirdo.
Consider this not a history but a taxonomy of unlikeability.

Before I dive in, I'd like to address the language that will per-
meate this book. These words I'm using are confrontational.
Some of them are downright ugly. All of them have been used
as insults, specific and gendered attacks designed to put down,
dehumanize, and minimize women, to diminish our sense of
self. I have been called some of these words myself, and I understand the weight they carry and how they are wielded against
us, day in, day out. I chose these words deliberately to illustrate
character archetypes that have tried to do the same. This is not
an act of reclamation but one of acknowledgment. Each of these
tropes describes a woman who is stepping out of the norms of
moral acceptability and appropriateness. Each chapter will trace
the evolution of a trope: how it was born, how it responds to
and has evolved in tandem with women's access to power in

the media landscape. In this way, each chapter will show how contemporary film and TV have built on these foundations to create complex characters that are, if not empowering, relatably human. The book will also talk about the way that audiences, especially women, have engaged with unlikeable female characters, how female creators and audiences have not only learned to unpack these harmful words and the tropes but have embraced these characters. I hope to give them value, warts and all, and to foster a sense of empathy. Behind unlikeability lies humanity, which is flawed by default and necessity. There's nothing interesting or grounded about being perfect. It's a trap that's been set for women throughout centuries, in very real, very dangerous ways and through the padded, creatively insidious fictional worlds that we inhabit for entertainment. The unlikeable female character is liberating for all of us: directors, showrunners, writers, actors, and audiences alike.

Because just like them, I am done with being likeable.

A Brief and Incomplete History of the Unlikeable Female Character

"Likeability," as a term, is intrinsically linked to the entertainment industry and is quietly gendered. It's not sexist in an obvious way, in a way that needs to be caveated with a side note on its "problematic" nature. And yet there are no synonyms for it that carry the same invisible weight. It's not usually applied to men unless it's as a positive. But when a woman is characterized as "unlikeable," there's a cold shudder of recognition. A little side-eye wrapped in fear. Like a secret code, the word "unlikeable" causes a specific tenseness. The word itself may not be gendered, but the layers of implications and connotations it carries are.

There is a fine line between being "likeable" and "unlikeable," and each one of us is always tiptoeing around breaking one or more of the many invisible rules of likeability that apply to women in the real world as well as the fictional one. The question of women's likeability in popular culture has gone from a quiet rumble on niche Reddit threads, to a hot topic in the press, to the subject of a confirmed cultural renaissance.

In her 2014 essay about likeability for Buzzfeed, author Roxane Gay writes that "when a girl is unlikeable, a girl is a problem." We know this in our bones. We might not be able to pinpoint what the problem is exactly, but there's "something about her" that just isn't clicking. When that amorphous something isn't working, a girl is undoubtedly in trouble. The fear that's instilled in us is that when a girl is a problem, she is a problem without a solution. I remember the sting of being asked—as a girl who was most definitely a problem—"Who's gonna want you with that attitude?"

The same year that Gay's essay was published, the David Fincher–directed and Gillian Flynn–scripted adaptation of Flynn's literary blockbuster *Gone Girl* hit the screens. Only a year later, *Mad Max: Fury Road* was released with Charlize Theron as Furiosa, a rabid, violent character (more recognizable than the titular leading man himself) who became a fan favorite. Also that year, *Jessica Jones*, a Marvel series centered on a prickly PI struggling with alcohol and a history of abuse, premiered on Netflix to critical acclaim. *UnREAL*, a Lifetime series about two cutthroat reality TV producers whose job it was to manipulate everyone around them to make addictive television, became a ratings hit.

A year later, 2016 saw the first big-screen adaptation of comic book fan favorite Harley Quinn, played by Margot Robbie in *Suicide Squad* (she'd reprise that role twice in later years, in *Birds of Prey* in 2018 and *The Suicide Squad* in 2021—more on her later). That same year, Emily Blunt played an alcoholic unreliable witness to a murder in *The Girl on the Train*, and Samantha Robinson played a witch who enamors and then violently disposes of men in *The Love Witch*. Lena Dunham and Jenni Konner's show *Girls* was coming to an end in 2017, after six seasons that had evolved into a collective hate watch.

The tide was changing, and the press was noticing: *Bitch Media* published "In Defense of Unlikable Women" in 2016; *Screen Rant* published "How Netflix Is Ruling TV with Unlikable Female Leads," and *Esquire* printed "The Characters in *The Girl on the Train* Aren't Likable—But That's the Point"; in 2017, *Little Whites Lies* wrote about "The Mick and the Art of the Unlikable Female Character." Writers like Flynn and showrunners like Lena Dunham were asked ad nauseum to defend their unlikeable female characters, and by virtue of having depicted them they became, themselves, emblems of female unlikeability.

And then, something bigger than the movies happened.

NASTY WOMEN

In November 2016, Democratic nominee Hillary Clinton lost the U.S. presidential race to Donald J. Trump after a political campaign of many controversies. Most pertinent to this book was the constant debate around Clinton's "likeability" and the moment, during a live-broadcast presidential debate, when Trump called her a "nasty woman." This insult would be swiftly reclaimed by women everywhere; whether they were fans of Clinton or not was a moot point. Endless opinion pieces, essays, and entire books were written trying to pinpoint exactly what was so nasty about Clinton—and whether these were traits that were unique to her or shared by many other women. What that moment did was pinpoint the nebulous question of likeability. The point was bigger than Clinton, although that particular presidential race crystallized it. There was always going to be the invisible ceiling of likeability to break through, and once Hillary was labeled a "nasty woman," there was no precedent for a correct response. The real question at the heart of this reclamation of the insult hurled at Clinton was: Do we avoid being nasty or do we lean into it?

Less than a year later, in October 2017, the biggest cultural reckoning concerning sexual assault and harassment was coming to a head. *New York Times* and the *New Yorker* both published investigative reports exposing the hugely successful film producer and Hollywood power player Harvey Weinstein, who had been accused by more than a dozen women of sexual harassment, sexual assault, and rape. This became the igniting flame for what has been dubbed the #MeToo movement, following a tweet actress Alyssa Milano posted asking people: "If you've been sexually harassed or assaulted write 'me too' as a reply to this tweet." This was the second iteration of the movement initiated by activist Tarana Burke in 2006 on MySpace advocating for empathy with sexual assault victims, particularly women of color. A decade later, Hollywood did as Hollywood does best and magnified the movement by adding the power of celebrity to the mix, which kick-started a global shift in consciousness raising.

After these seismic cultural shifts started happening, our visual pop culture transformed the aftershock into cultural products and the media continued pushing the conversation. After the U.S. election, critic Inkoo Kang wrote about the need for inclusivity in culture because "art and entertainment are how many of us simply stay sane, but they also play a huge role in how we're groomed to look at the world." Kang is right, but these events not only shifted power and capital; they also shifted the way we looked at and talked about pop culture. They forced us to look at pop culture history and rethink how we treated women, both onscreen and off.

BIG UNLIKEABLE ENERGY

In 2018, three critically acclaimed films starring major A-list actresses were released, all of them garnering substantial atten-tion, all of them with deeply unlikeable leads: *The Favorite*, about the scheming three-way dynamic between two noble-women vying for the favor of Queen Anne; *Can You Ever Forgive Me?*, based on the real-life Lee Israel, a struggling writer with an alcohol problem and an acidic personality who turned to literary forgery to make ends meet; and *Destroyer*, with Nicole Kidman in the leading role as LAPD detective Erin Bell, an aggressive, depressed woman who is dealing with a murder and a gang she infiltrated years back with a commitment that borders on suicidal. That same year, on the small screen, *Buffy The Vampire Slayer* producer and *UnREAL* co-creator Marti Noxon premiered two series with difficult women as the lead: the first, *Dietland*, centered on a fed-up, fat agony aunt writer who gets caught up in a feminist cabal flirting with terrorism, and Noxon also spearheaded the adaptation of Gillian Flynn's bleak first novel *Sharp Objects*, about a self-hating journalist following a murder case into her hometown, which became an acclaimed HBO limited series directed by Jean-Marc Vallée and scripted, once again, by Flynn herself. In this year, the tide that had started turning slowly, cautiously reached a pop culture zenith: the #MeToo reckoning was referenced directly at the biggest events in sports, music, and film; Frances McDormand, during her Best Actress acceptance speech, faux hyperventilated onstage before diving into a speech invoking inclusion riders and asked all the female nominees to stand up in unison. People were talking about women in film and were willing to throw money and roles at them. All of these roles starred A-list actresses, all of whom were lauded for their performances and recognized with industry awards.

The tide had, seemingly, fully turned.

In the coverage of these films and shows, all of them disparate in genre, style, and ambition, there is one thing in common that made journalists and audiences lump them together: the unlikeable female character.

Whenever there is a coincidence of themes, the press deems it a trend. A headline in the *Guardian* talked about "the new wave of 'unlikeable' women in film." *Washington Post* wrote, "'Unlikable' women suddenly dominate films." *Harper's Bazaar* covered "the rise of the female antiheroine" and tried to find economic reasons to explain it.

The majority of these pieces also quoted the same Roxane Gay essay that I've quoted and have been rereading ad nauseum during the process of writing this book. She writes about the importance of unlikeable female protagonists as an uncomfortable mirror wherein we can see women in glorious complexity who not only refuse to pander to expectations placed on them but also accept the consequences of their own morally question-able actions. Ultimately, Gay argues, they make for more com-pelling characters, which is, to put it in blunt terms, the whole fucking point. Why are we talking about whether a character is likeable or not when we should be talking about whether they are *interesting*. The burden of likeability had so far been shouldered mostly by the female characters, and while the male protago-nists were praised for their problematic or extreme complexities, complicated women were villainized, punished, or used as cul-tural warning signs.

Gay, it should be said, was writing mostly about literature, which has had to reckon with a similar questioning but ulti-mately is an entirely different business model from that of film and television. Books do not require the sponsorship of a huge machine, and they do not rely on actors to embody characters (they leave that up to us, the readers).

Movies and television have a distinct pathway into existence that needs more than one voice. They are not ever the work of a sole person, no matter how much the auteur theory tries to convince us otherwise. Films and shows are made by commit-tee; need to be sponsored by the industry in order to reach as many people as possible; feed from and into the star system; get press coverage, eyeballs, and awards; and garner other markers of success that will then enable their makers to move on to bigger things with more resources and more creative free-dom. In the best-case scenario, there is an overarching creative visionary (usually the director, or the showrunner in the case of television), but it is nigh impossible to determine who is actu-ally responsible for each individual choice that makes a film possible. Filmmaking is beautiful chaos. And when a film is finished and released into the world, it no longer even belongs to the filmmakers: it becomes part of popular culture, ready to be ripped apart, analyzed, reinterpreted, reclaimed, and presented back to the filmmaker.

That is to say, even when a film is done, even at the highest level, with all the talent, producers, publicists, consultants, and advertising that money can buy, there is no hard science that's able to predict how it's going to be received and talked about. Every film is a prototype, and even if something similar has succeeded before, there's no way to secure success via imitation. It's a beautiful vicious cycle that is both pregnant with creative possibility and vicious in its capitalistic cannibalism.

I believe wholeheartedly that a film belongs to the audience as much as it does to the people who made it. The way an audience responds to a film, and more precisely to its characters, tells us a lot about the culture at large. To be even more precise—our response to female characters tells us a lot about what we find acceptable in women in real life. Film, as the most populist of art forms, is a great litmus test for behaviors we consider reputable (and even aspirational) versus those we deem unacceptable or even deviant. Unlike real life, films allow us to see bad behaviors *punished* and good behavior *rewarded*.

THE BIG BAD MEN OF PRESTIGE TELEVISION

Narratives led by antiheroes make our relationship with the work that much more complicated—and that much more delicious. It makes the whole process of watching a piece of work an active conversation, a negotiation with ourselves as to what we're willing to accept, what we relate to, and what it says about us. While the attributes that make up a hero are generally universal and aspirational—courage, honesty, integrity, selflessness—the antihero is a slippery figure who is both the hero's opposite and also much more human. A good antihero demands good writing and a good performance, so it's unsurprising that television started attracting high-caliber talent away from the movies and onto the small screen, where actors had the opportunity to develop a character over hundreds of hours instead of just two. The usual career path for filmmakers (starting in low-budget films or TV work before moving into cinema) was reversed, with established, acclaimed filmmakers taking the weight of their names to TV. High-profile directors who've made their name in film will set the visual tone for the series in the first few episodes, lending the work the artistic credence of their reputation and publicity by association: Martin Scorsese created and set the visual style for shows like *Boardwalk Empire* and *Vinyl*; David Fincher did the same for *House of Cards*; Jane Campion directed *Top of the Lake*; Steven Soderbergh directed *The Knick*; The Wachowski Sisters made *Sense8*; even Michael Bay, not strictly considered a beacon of quality filmmaking, lent his name to *Black Sails*, a show much more nuanced than the entirety of Bay's filmography.

Much has been written about the rise of the antihero over the last twenty-odd years, during which time TV series became prestigious cultural mainstays that hold a quartet of series featuring difficult men as their kingpins: *The Sopranos*, *The Wire*, *Breaking Bad*, and *Mad Men*. Tony Soprano, Omar Little, Stringer Bell, Jimmy McNulty, Walter White, and Don Draper were critically acclaimed characters who became pop culture icons during the original run of these shows and even more so since they went off the air. These shows would, in turn, inspire a whole slew of high-budget prestige shows like *Ozark, Dexter, Mr. Robot, True Detective, House,* and a pick'n'mix of other wannabe antihero-driven shows. But I'm not here to add to that conversation; there are plenty of excellent books and articles written about them and I don't need to write more words about men who've got enough Reddit threads and podcasts dedicated to them.

Alongside these difficult men were equally difficult women. They were not center stage of these shows, but their characters were demanding, knotty beings who pushed beyond expectations of what "the wife" character could be. But while their fictional hubbies were elevated to iconic status, there were hardly any pins or T-shirts being made with the likeness of Carmela Soprano, Skyler White, or Betty Draper. While entire books were written about the protagonists, the female characters in those shows were either dismissed, disliked, or downright hated. Carmela Soprano, Tony's headstrong wife, was shrill; Betty Draper was boring; and Skyler White was a killjoy and became one of the most hated characters on television. Meanwhile, people were dressing up as Walter White for Halloween. Of course, this reverential take on the male antihero and the dismissal of the antiheroine wasn't universal while the shows were airing—there were defenses of these characters from journalists, and the actresses playing them received industry accolades (Edie Falco won three out of the six Primetime Emmy Awards she was nominated for while playing Carmela; January Jones received two Golden Globe and a Primetime Emmy Award nomination for playing Betty Draper; and Anna Gunn won two out of her three Primetime Emmy Award nominations for her work on *Breaking Bad*). It has always been quietly fascinating to me that while the big bad husbands (who were liars, cheaters, drug dealers, or straight-up murderers) became beloved pop culture icons and Funko Pop figurines,[1] their wives, girlfriends, or partners were judged and smirked at. Was it because the evilness of the male antiheroes was too abstract, too big and dramatic to be seen as real? Or maybe it was because we wanted them to be bad, because being bad meant they were interesting and watchable? And yet, the reaction to their female counterparts seemed to defy this logic. If they stepped out of line, they were lambasted by audiences for allowing, accepting, or indulging the bad behavior of their partners. Why was it so much easier to hate the more quotidian immorality of the antiheroines? While audiences hope that the male antihero might eventually improve, their female counterpart is irredeemable. As these totem shows have continued to expand their reach beyond their original runs, especially once they arrived on popular streaming services, these characters have also been revisited and reappraised as richly flawed antiheroines, trapped in some ways, complicit in others.

THE RISE OF THE ANTIHEROINE

Something has changed in recent years, though. We have embraced the antiheroine, the unlikeable female character, and, in fact, increasingly build narratives around her. Female

---

1 There is yet, as of 2022, no Funko Pop of Skyler White. I'm waiting.

unlikeability has become a marketing tool. The once negative tropes have been expanded and deepened to create memorable, complicated, intensely human characters. Bitches, Trainwrecks, and Sluts are dominating pop culture. Creators have embraced the messy reality of being a woman, expanded on distinctively gendered shades of cruelty, and run with it, telling stories placed in fantasy worlds, contemporary scenarios, and imagined alternatives to our world. Fleabag, Cersei Lannister, Shiv Roy, Claire Underwood, Villanelle—these characters have become fan favorites, household names, clear markers in the zeitgeist. Acclaimed actresses like Meryl Streep, Charlize Theron, Viola Davis, Robin Wright, and Laura Linney are lending their gravitas and star power to play them, likeability be damned, and up-and-coming actresses are seeking them out. There are countless think pieces, video essays, works of fan art, listicles, and merchandise inspired by them. They win Emmys, Golden Globes, and Oscars. Their success feels like our collective success. The image of writer-performer Phoebe Waller-Bridge smoking in a deck chair in Chateau Marmont, still in her Monique Lhuillier gown, satisfied, tired, and with her Emmys glistening around her went duly viral. Her messy, foul-mouthed, slutty character had reaped her all this success, and fuck if we weren't happy for her. Unlikeable female characters seemed to finally be breaking through the self-imposed ceiling of likeability and cashing in.

A *Gawker* article from 2010 called shows focused on women going through emotional or mental crises "'ladies with problems' shows," referring to series like *The Good Wife* or *Nurse Jackie*, which had both begun their runs the previous year and revolved around the oft-problematic coping mechanisms their protagonists found to deal with their lives, careers, and families. The conversation around the rise of the female antiheroine didn't reach the mainstream until the late 2010s. Most of the essays that concerned themselves with this seemingly novel surge of unlikeable female characters seemed to make out that there had been no such thing before.

Lies.

The 2010s did not invent unlikeable, unruly women. There were *plenty* before. But we did, finally, develop the language to understand and articulate what social tensions these characters were tapping into, and we had the access to platforms to voice this. With the diminishing barriers between stars, critics, and audiences, we started to hash out those conversations and look back at the culture that had shaped our thinking.

So how did we get there?

THE FIRST GOLDEN AGE OF THE UNLIKEABLE FEMALE CHARACTER

The early days of Hollywood were dominated by women. It might be surprising to hear this now, after years of dismal statistics about the representation and well-being of women in the screen industries, but initially a good number of early Hollywood screenwriters, editors, and directors were female. Women wrote almost half of the outlines of all the scripts produced in early Hollywood. In the 1910s, at Universal Studios alone, eleven female directors made 170 movies, and women comprised 83 percent of the moviegoing audience. It should be noted that these numbers paint a rosy picture, a "manless Eden" as one writer would describe it, but these positions of creative power were still held mostly by white women.

Alice Guy-Blaché, already a successful producer and director in her native France, moved to the United States and built one of the very first film studios, where she is purported to have shot over 1,000 films (of which only a handful remain); Lois Weber learned from Guy-Blaché and became the highest-paid director in Hollywood; Frances Marion went from semisuccessful actress to extremely successful screenwriter, becoming the highest-paid scribe in Hollywood and penning over 300 films; Dorothy Arzner, who directed films way into the 1940s, started off as a typist and worked her way up to director, becoming one of the very few female directors working within the studio system at the time; Mary Pickford, one of the biggest stars of the 1910s and 1920s, founded her own studio, cofounded the Academy of Motion Picture Arts and Sciences, and then cofounded and ran United Artists. There was a desire among performers to choose and control the material they were working with, how they were presented to the public, and how much money they were making from it. When the stars were dissatisfied with the roles that were written for them, they wrote the scripts themselves (or hired other women to do it), directed, and even started production companies. The movie supply chain was controlled by women. In the *Guardian*, silent film expert Pamela Hutchinson quotes an article from 1915: "In the theatres, in the studios and even in the exchanges where film productions are marketed and released to exhibitors, the fair sex is represented as in no other calling." On the screen, women's star power held significantly greater importance than that of their male counterparts. "Most of the films of the twenties were romances and melodramas dominated by a single star, billed above the title, and the women stars outnumbered their male counterparts," writes film critic and historian Mary Haskell in her seminal book *From Reverence to Rape.*

Hollywood was being forged, with women right in the thick of it producing stories and attracting crowds to this new, exciting place called the cinema. Film stars were goddesses of the silver screen, and the newly formed industry was just figuring out how to use them. Clara Bow, an early silent film star who made a film called *It,* became the first "it girl."[2] The blond Jean Harlow was the first bombshell of the screen. Joan Crawford was a star created by and for the public (literally, her name came from a magazine competition), and her public persona evolved as she aged to satisfy her public.

While female movie stars were magnets for audiences and their cash, female sexuality was, since the beginning of the movies, a sticking point. Silent Hollywood stars like Pola Negri and Theda Bara embodied the vamp persona that was alluring, dangerous, and always presented as female. They were sexually dominating, their sexuality overpowering and even ("vamp" being short for "vampire") deadly. A short film from 1913 called *The Vampire* literally features a woman dancing on top of a man in a frenzied state. The film has since been lost, but the association remains. From the very start of the screen, femininity was seen as a weapon that some women knew how to wield, and those women were dangerous.

---

2   A term as nebulous as "unlikeable" itself, it's a catchall, media-friendly definition that is still used today to refer to young women, usually film or pop stars, who embody the moment. What Clara Bow was for the 1920s, Zendaya is for the 2020s.

As the movies started to speak, female characters found their voice, losing a whole roster of actresses whose vocals did not serve this new kind of talking picture and discovering a totally different breed of velvety accents to titillate audiences.[3] Hollywood imported actresses like Greta Garbo and Marlene Dietrich and explicitly capitalized on their sexuality, their European je ne sais quoi, their every move flirting with queerness and implying that they were more hedonistic than their American counterparts. Hollywood made their natural beauty otherworldly with strategic lighting and leveraged the acceptable exoticism of their lightly accented speech. They blurred the line between genders and appealed to both men and women: Dietrich dressed in a tuxedo and kisses a woman in *Morocco* (1930), causing a bisexual frenzy; Garbo, in the titular role as Swedish monarch in *Queen Christina* (1933), wore in male clothes and is obviously in love with her handmaiden. Both actresses' screen personas skirted around their sexual availability and inclinations. Haskell writes of Garbo as being the "perfect metaphor for the Hollywood film, the high priestess at the holy communion of American romance where sex is converted into love, body into spirit, and transitory experience into an ultimate and permanent grace." To be blunt, Garbo and Dietrich fucked. And because they were foreign imports, it was fine.

Things would start to change and become policed in 1933.

---

3   This is parodied to perfection in the classic musical *Singin' in the Rain* (1952), where a silent film actress has the perfect look for the screen but a squeaky voice that simply does not mesh with films, so they have to hire an unknown to dub her. Shenanigans, musical numbers, and romance ensue, of course.

But before then, Hollywood gave us extraordinary female characters that smirked in the face of conventions. Joan Crawford first made a name for herself playing ambitious flappers who worked their way up the social ladder, one man at a time. Mae West, who I'll talk about more in depth later on, wrote and starred in movies in which sex was dripping from every single line of dialogue. Her first big break came in 1926 with a Broadway show she wrote, directed, and starred in called, no joke, *Sex*. She ended up spending time in jail because of it, but her plays continued to garner attention and commercial success, eventually leading her to the movies. It's no surprise, then, that West and her work would be the focus of a lot of the censorship that swept through Hollywood in the early thirties. Sexy times would come to an end in 1934, when the Production Code began being meticulously enforced by the Motion Picture Producers and Distributors of America (MPPDA), a department led by politician and censor czar William Hays and set up largely to cover up sexual or criminal scandals of early movie stars. Before 1934, the Code had been a series of guidelines that were barely enforced and were tacitly tolerated by the film studios in order to avoid any real repercussions or government censorship on their productions. The Code, a literal list of all the big no-nos of cinema, was predictably obsessed with sexual purity, traditional values, and marriage, and deeply informed by racism and misogyny. The rules stipulated the subjects that could not, under any circumstance, appear onscreen, including profanity, sexual perversion, and ridiculing of the clergy.[4] The

---

4   My personal favorite being the banning of "scenes of actual childbirth—in fact or in silhouette."

Code existed to enforce a very limited idea of morality whereby any character who dared to transgress any heteronormative ideas around gender, sexuality, family, and morality could only be shown onscreen as a cautionary tale. Adhering to the Code, and being given a stamp of approval by its enforcing body, became a legal necessity for any film released after July 1, 1934. This Code required that "the villain had to die or, if the hero or heroine had erred, their contrition and conversion had to be triumphantly shown." In broad terms, what the Code would set into place was the demonization and punishment of anyone who deviated from what the (heavily Catholic) Code deemed to be "decent."

Of course, writers and filmmakers would find ways to include subtext in their work, but the damaging legacy of this Code cannot be overstated. Even beyond film scholarship, it doesn't take much to see how the banning of any display of nonheterosexual love or attraction had a ripple effect that persists to this day, when we still have headlines that praise film studios for "introducing their first gay character."[5] Consider why we are still having debates about whether it's okay for a female character to show sexual agency onscreen, whether it sets a bad example, whether talk of lubrication is too dirty for public consumption (but cum jokes are A-okay[6]). In 1933, a Czech film showed a woman having an orgasm and created a roaring controversy, angering everyone from Hitler to the

---

5   Even in 2021, *Forbes* mockingly summarized it: "It's a familiar milestone for the company, as Disney has pioneered their 'first' gay character at least 7 times, give or take."

6   Even on a film poster. Remember *There's Something about Mary* (1998)?

Pope. That woman was the actress-inventor Hedy Kiesler, who later changed her name to Hedy Lamarr when she moved to Hollywood.[7]

After the wild days of gorgeous and flawed women of pre-Code Hollywood, in 1934 one of the first truly unredeemable villainesses of Hollywood was portrayed by a young Bette Davis, not yet a star but a striving young actress that the studios didn't quite know what to do with. She played the scheming Cockney waitress Mildred in *Of Human Bondage* (1934), a woman who emotionally tortures a hapless artist and uses his infatuation with her whenever she needs something. At the end, Mildred dies from consumption, destitute, punished with poverty, disease, and death for being such a mean bitch. Davis had campaigned hard to get the role, despite it being a character so wretched that other actresses stayed away for fear playing her would damage their reputations—but it turned Davis into a star and established the seeds of a reputation for playing barbed roles. Later that decade, *Gone With The Wind* (1939) was released to much acclaim and box office success, with Scarlett O'Hara (Vivien Leigh), a self-centered and vain Southern belle, at the heart of the historical epic; she was selfish and petty but also determined and didn't defer to men. She became an equally reviled and revered character, a problematic fave in a film riddled with problems, from the glamorizing of the antebellum South to its instrumental role in creating the "mammy" stereotype of Black women whose existence was built around serving and protecting young white women like Scarlett. The films of the 1930s,

---

7   Lamarr was a pioneer in more ways than one: she was the first woman to cum onscreen and she gave us the blueprint for what would become Wi-Fi technology.

even after the Code came into play, were the first golden age of the unlikeable female character.

SHE MUST BE PUNISHED

With the Code being enforced, Hollywood films entered an era of symbolism and subtext. The forties and fifties would birth the femme fatale trope, an untrustworthy woman who used her beauty to seduce, trick, and even murder men for money. The femme fatale is synonymous with film noir, a term devised by French film critics to amalgamate the postwar thrillers of the 1940s and 1950s that centered morally complex detectives, devious women, and dangerous criminals. These films were visually moody, as morally ambiguous as the times that spawned them. They were tragedies masquerading as potboilers, and in their darkest of hearts were questions about goodness and morality, these notions having been put through the ringer during World War II. The femme fatale is the embodiment of many anxieties of the time around women entering the workforce after WWII drafted men into the war effort. These characters would be immensely sensual, mysterious, and alluring. They often posed as distressed or put-upon to attract the help of the man they were targeting, weaponizing their femininity. The idea of a devious woman who uses her beauty for nefarious, greedy, or murderous purposes is one that has been traced back to early myths: the sirens of *The Odyssey* would lure sailors to their death; in the Ancient Babylonian *The Epic Of Gilgamesh*, the goddess Ishtar declares war on the hero Gilgamesh because he rejects her; Morgan le Fay, in the Celtic legend of *King Arthur*, schemes against Arthur after being rejected by Lancelot. The femme fatale would use the slightest hint of sex, beauty, and allure to weave a web around her mark, happily discarding them when she got what she wanted. They were flammable creatures, and anyone who got too close would inevitably get burnt. And because of their wretchedness, they were always punished.

Brigid O'Shaughnessy (Mary Astor) tricks private detective Sam Spade (Humphrey Bogart) into an international conspiracy in order to get her hands on a big stack of cash in *The Maltese Falcon* (1941). She goes to jail. Phyllis Dietrichson (Barbara Stanwyck) seduces an insurance salesman and convinces him to kill her husband so she can claim the insurance money in *Double Indemnity* (1944). She gets killed. Another character, Cora (Lana Turner) manipulates her lover into killing her husband in *The Postman Always Rings Twice*. Although they are in love and about to get away with it, she gets killed. In *Mildred Pierce* (1945), we see a rare example of one woman being the downfall of another. The greedy, vain Veda (Ann Blyth) kills a man and tries to have her mother, the titular Mildred (Joan Crawford), who had grown a successful restaurant business, take the fall for her. The plan doesn't work and she goes to jail. In a rare example of a color film noir, *Leave Her to Heaven*, Ellen Berent (Gene Tierney) is a socialite so spiteful that she seduces a man into marriage, drowns his brother, forces a miscarriage, and dies by suicide in order to frame him and another woman for her murder. She dies. The femme fatale storylines would always punish the woman with disrepute, jail, or even death. It wouldn't be until the 1980s that her descendants would be able to get away with murder (and actually end up sleeping with some of the men they were using).

But Hollywood demanded a formula that would be replicated across this genre, and actresses playing these roles would be identified with these types of characters. The femme fatale was always coded as a warning sign to other women: this is how you're not supposed to behave, and this is the punishment you'll endure if you cross the line. It visually coded female sexuality as something fearsome—at best contained, and at worst punished.

The most interesting female characters of the 1950s were closer aligned to the Crazy Woman archetype than the femme fatale. These characters were less extreme in terms of their actions, but psychologically rich, dense with wants, and often consumed by their own desires. Although their punishment was not as extreme, they were rarely allowed happy endings. They could live, but they'd have to be miserable. *All about Eve* (1950) gave us two of the most exquisitely written female characters of the screen, both complicated and in constant tension with one another: the aging theater actress Margo Channing (Bette Davis) and the up-and-coming Eve Harrington (Anne Baxter), who poses as a starstruck fan to ingratiate herself into theater society and eventually take over Margo's role. The same year, *Sunset Boulevard* (1950) pulled back the curtain on the toll that the glamorous life of a Hollywood star can take on a person with Norma Desmond (Gloria Swanson), a washed-up silent screen star whose grip on reality comes completely undone by the final frame of the film. These women didn't want a man; they wanted success and recognition. Their punishment was loneliness or insanity, or both. These women were driven mad by wanting too much and, pointedly, by aging. They had passed their shelf life of social and sexual relevance, so they must either fit inside their designated box or be driven mad. Interestingly, only a few decades later a new genre would rise, alternately called "hagsploitation" or "psycho biddy," which would give a second wind to the lagging careers of some of classic Hollywood's greatest actresses in genre films of varying quality that all had the same premise: old women are scary.[8]

Continuing the tradition of pathologizing horniness, there were characters who, despite the so far well-enforced Production Code, were telegraphed as deeply sexual beings whose desires overwhelmed them and often led them astray. *The Night of the Hunter* (1955) saw a widowed mother so horny for Robert Mitchum's psychopathic, serial killer preacher that her judgment was completely impaired as to his clearly murderous intentions. *A Streetcar Named Desire* (1951), though mostly remembered for Marlon Brando's breakout performance (and erotic mumbling), has the emotionally frail Blanche DuBois (Vivien Leigh) pushed into a nervous breakdown by Brando's Stanley Kowalski, his nagging psychological taunts, and sexual assault on her. Another Tennessee Williams adaptation, *Cat on a Hot Tin Roof* (1958), sees Maggie "the Cat" Pollitt (Elizabeth Taylor), who desperately wants to sleep with her drunken,

---

8   The best one of these, and the film that kick-started this peculiar subgenre, was *Whatever Happened to Baby Jane?* (1960), starring Joan Crawford and Bette Davis as two ageing sibling actresses.

impotent husband Brick (Paul Newman), clawing at herself with want.

As the fifties came to a close, the Production Code was lapsing. Films that hadn't had the seal of approval of the censor's office, like *Some Like It Hot* (1959), were released and making huge box office money. It became apparent that audience attitudes were changing and that the strong hold the Code had had on film studios had weakened. By the 1960s, the enforcement of the Code was abandoned and the moral rulebook that had dominated Hollywood films for decades was transformed into a rating system, enforced by the Motion Picture Association of America (MPAA), which still operates to this day. As the hippie approach to life, love, and culture swept the United States, independent filmmaking was on the rise too, as an alternative to Hollywood formulas. Meanwhile, the studios were struggling to make films that connected with young audiences. By the end of the decade, the studio system that had dominated Hollywood since its creation was crumbling, the B movie business experienced a boom, and independent filmmakers prioritized authentic stories, true-to-life characters, and bold new filmmaking styles over inflated budgets or big-name stars.

It was the beginning of the New Hollywood, an informal movement of sorts that is used to describe the group of filmmakers that rose up around the same time with independent productions: Martin Scorsese, Dennis Hopper, Warren Beatty, George Lucas, and Francis Ford Coppola all made their name with raw, angry films anchored by frustrated antiheroes. These films didn't really care much for their female characters. They were often paragons of virtue, objects of desire, or helpless victims, there to be saved to redeem the morally compromised protagonist.

Outside of the movie theaters, women were protesting. The 1970s saw the women's liberation movement gain major social traction. Over 50,000 women went on strike, marching down Fifth Avenue in New York City in an effort to show a united front. On the screens, the woman's film of the 1950s, a whole genre of its own that centered on the interior lives of women, often featuring a pursuit of romance or the tribulations of a relationship, became the madwoman's film in the late 1960s and 1970s. In *Who's Afraid of Virginia Woolf?* (1966), megastars Elizabeth Taylor and Richard Burton scream at each other for a whole night and throughout the entire film, spitting out the years of resentments they both carry. *Diary of a Mad Housewife* (1970) is all about the simmering interior life of Tina (Carrie Snodgress), a frustrated housewife to a husband who routinely belittles her, who is mocked even by her group therapy participants. Barbra Streisand, then one of the biggest Hollywood stars, starred in *Up the Sandbox* (1972) as Margaret, an extremely bored young mother and housewife who indulges in extreme fantasies to get away from the daily grind of her life. John Cassavetes, who had risen to prominence both as an actor and as a pioneering independent filmmaker, wrote and directed *A Woman under the Influence* (1974), wherein Mabel (Gena Rowlands), a heavy-drinking housewife, is institutionalized by her husband after exhibiting erratic behavior. In her book *Backlash*, Susan Faludi talks about these films as portraits not of female madness but of the crumbling of an old-fashioned institution: "Marriage, not the woman, is the patient under analysis in women's films of the seventies, and the dialogue probes the economic and social inequalities of traditional wedlock." The Hollywood formula was coming undone, as were the female leads in these films. While the fallen women of the previous decades were still clinging to the illusion of respectable womanhood, driving themselves insane trying to live up to it, the madwomen of the seventies were showing a raw vulnerability.

The cultural reaction to the peace-loving, change-driven hippy culture of the sixties and the protest-heavy disillusionment with the government and the mainstream of the seventies was brutal in the 1980s. Hollywood had found its new set of glossy, big-budget formulas, and the new leading men were buff, greedy, and vain. "Hollywood in the 1980s," writes Faludi, "was simply not very welcoming to movie projects that portrayed independent women as healthy, lusty people without punishing them for their pleasure." This era was marked by films about teen girls and working women, as well as a return to the punishing stories of fallen women from the 1940s. John Hughes created a canon of teen movies, most of them starring his muse and frequent collaborator Molly Ringwald in a variety of teen girl stereotypes, from the popular mean girl in *The Breakfast Club* (1985) to the sensitive-but-tough Andie in *Pretty in Pink* (1986). *Heathers* (1988) is a timeless high school fantasy about a smart, popular teen girl, Veronica (Winona Ryder), who gets involved in a murder spree perpetrated by her walking-red-flag boyfriend J. D. (Christian Slater). In *9 to 5* (1980), a passion project of Jane Fonda, a trio of put-upon secretaries (played by Fonda, Lily Tomlin, and Dolly Parton) conspire to murder their abusive boss. While *9 to 5* was a message-driven comedy, toward the end of the decade the working woman, with her power suits, shoulder pads, and big hair, was turned into a villain. In *Working Girl* (1988), she's played to campy effect by Sigourney Weaver as a boss who undermines and steals the ideas of her female assistant. *Baby Boom* (1987) sees a successful businesswoman struggle to balance a baby and a career, opting ultimately to abandon the corporate ladder. In *Fatal Attraction* (1987), Glenn Close plays a successful book editor who goes "crazy" after a casual affair with a married man (more on her later). The overall message, whether comedy or thriller, was that the pliable, docile, family-focused woman was the cultural preference, and the ambitious woman would be driven mad, or out of business, if she got too big for her heels.

THE SECOND GOLDEN AGE OF THE UNLIKEABLE FEMALE CHARACTER

The following decade, the 1990s, was a unique coalescence of youth culture, new technologies, and the opening of borders, which meant that global cinema was creating stunning, innovative work, new filmmaking stars were being elevated in the industry, and independent and mainstream blockbusters were finding their audiences. Among other fantastic things happening in cinema, it was a moment when feminist characters onscreen went mainstream, with audiences responding to complicated and complete women with agency and rich interior lives.

And so, the nineties were the second golden age of unlikeable women. It was the high point of the erotic thriller, wherein sex and death were intertwined (usually in the form of a gorgeous and dangerous woman). It was the era of the neo-femme fatale, now with a much more explicit sexuality. Catherine Tramell (Sharon Stone) was the bisexual writer who may or may not also be a murderer in the box office smash *Basic Instinct* (1992). Bridget Gregory (Linda Fioretino) is the greedy, ice-cold femme fatale who goes on the run with a big stack of cash in *The Last Seduction* (1994). Madonna played a woman who gets sued for being so good at sex that the men she sleeps with literally die of pleasure in *Body of Evidence* (1994). Contrary to the femme fatales of the 1940s and 1950s, though, these characters usually got away with it. In the nineties, the wholesome, randy teens of John Hughes's eighties films turned dark in a mash-up of genres, the neo-noir-meets-teen-drama (what film critic Gabrielle Moss called the "teen girl murder films") of movies like *Poison Ivy* (1992), *The Crush* (1993), and *Wild Things* (1998), with conniving teenage girls at their center. The works of Shakespeare and Jane Austen saw a revival as they were adapted into teen girl-friendly movies; Emma turned into *Clueless* (1995) and *The Taming of the Shrew* became *10 Things I Hate about You* (1999).

Thanks to the boom of indie filmmaking in the nineties, we had a wide range of heroic female characters, both on television (medical doctor and FBI special agent Dana Scully in *The X-Files*; the formidable warrior Xena on a path of redemption in *Xena: Warrior Princess*; Buffy the cheerleader chosen to fight vampires and other ghouls in *Buffy the Vampire Slayer*) and on the big screen (the rookie FBI agent Clarice Starling, who manages to connect with suave serial killer Hannibal Lecter in *The Silence of the Lambs*). Hit TV shows focused on successful professionals with messy love lives (*Ally McBeal, Sex and the City, Girlfriends*), and while the eighties glorified shoulder pad ambition and bitchiness, the nineties was an era of much anger and despondency, with studio films seeing women face sexism in the workplace, especially in institutions like the military (*G. I. Jane*) and the police force (*Blue Steel, The Silence of the Lambs*). The films that became cultural phenomena centered on female anger, like the best-friends-on-the-run *Thelma and Louise* (1991) or the group of put-upon friends who decide to rob a bank in *Set It Off* (1996).

Part of the independent filmmaking boom of this decade was in radically feminist filmmaking. Although a lot of these titles did not become cultural mainstays in the way that *Reservoir Dogs* (1992) or *Desperado* (1995) did, they pushed the boundaries of the sort of women films were being made about. In a loose movement, new queer filmmakers broke apart archetypes like the housewife, with Julianne Moore going slow into an apoc-alyptic level of hypochondria in *Safe* (1995) and frustrated, deadpan teenage nihilism in *The Doom Generation* (1995). Queer women (*Go Fish, Bound*) and queer Black women (*The Watermelon Woman*) were making films that were formally auda-cious and firsts in many ways, creating a new filmic language that would tell stories that had never been prioritized on the big screen before. There was a generalized dissatisfaction with the glossy, fluffed-up wealth worship that fed into the stories we saw onscreen. This was an era of extreme creativity in filmmaking around the globe, with new forms being created by new voices who had grown up with a form of canonless cinephilia, and sto-ries being told with the bare minimum of equipment resonating with a new generation of viewers who suddenly had the possibility of seeing themselves onscreen.

The nineties, as we know, was a decade that lasted well into the new millennium.[9] In the early 2000s, film got glossy and television went in the opposite direction. The rise of reality TV created strange mash-ups of real people and personas, the "famous for being famous" era dominated by Paris Hilton, who we now know intentionally created a bimbo persona to appeal to a wider audience, including talking in a high-pitched voice an octave above her own and leaning into the dumb blond archetype we're all too familiar with since Jean Harlow and Marilyn Monroe (*i-D* cheekily crowned her "the greatest performance artist of our time"). It wouldn't be fair to call Paris Hilton an actress, but she certainly put on a performance, which in turn influenced the slick, girly girl style of female heroines we got in noughties cinema, including the subversive bimbo-with-brains Elle Woods (Reese Witherspoon) in *Legally Blonde* (2001).

The noughties were the first decade when film culture was overtaken by intellectual property (IP) behemoths—franchises like *The Lord of the Rings, Harry Potter, Pirates of the Caribbean,* and the *Star Wars* prequels dominated the box office. In the first decade of the twenty-first century, women in the public eye were put on a pedestal, and pop culture made a business out of tearing them down. The noughties were a battleground for actresses whose offscreen identities blended with *or* contradicted their onscreen roles, with new millennium bombshells like Megan Fox being equated to Sluts, former child star Lindsay Lohan mocked

---

9   It is a truth universally acknowledged that the nineties is a decade that lasted
     fifteen years. Don't come at me with the math, just look at the fashion.

and ogled as a very public Trainwreck, and way before we started to reconcile just how ingrained this internalized misogyny really was, we relished any coverage of Britney Spears's mental health troubles. Pop culture at this time loved to relish, profit from, and mock female entertainers for sport—but it had a real problem with any unlikeable women onscreen. Being messy, it seems, was only profitable if it was off-screen.

It's tricky to look back at that decade in film culture because so much of it seems be a swirl composed of the last breaths of nineties culture and the nascent stages of the dominating form of filmmaking of the 2010s onward, that is, superhero franchises and IP-based filmmaking. The romantic comedy—which experienced a cultural and qualitative heyday in the nineties, with stars like Julia Roberts and Meg Ryan dominating the genre before passing off the baton to Sandra Bullock, Jennifer Aniston, Drew Barrymore, and Jennifer Lopez—favored a successful, clumsy, but lovable protagonist, very much the "girly girl" with girly professions and girly concerns.

On the other hand, the female action lead became a staple of big-budget productions, with video game adaptations of *Lara Croft: Tomb Raider* (2001) and *Resident Evil* (2003), as well as the gravity- and logic-defying remake of *Charlie's Angels* (2000). The former two established the hitherto arthouse favorite Angelina Jolie and the former model Milla Jovovich as action stars. This millennial brand of badassery was in stark contrast with the other character staple of this decade: the manic pixie dream girl. Perhaps in direct contradiction to the buxom videogame vibe of the action heroine and the midtier rom-com protagonist, the quirky female lead was intended to be feminine but not girly, an adorable oddball, a side character elevated to main character status. The trope was identified and the term coined by writer Nathan Rubin in his 2007 *AV Club* essay about the film *Elizabethtown* and Kirsten Dunst's character in particular, pointing out a type of female character who existed "solely in the fevered imaginations of sensitive writer-directors to teach broodingly soulful young men to embrace life and its infinite mysteries and adventures." That is, she was a pop culture creation that was hot and devoted to the male protagonist, devoid of any interiority. The manic pixie dream girl became, much to Rubin's chagrin, a trope that would dominate "alternative" noughties culture. Instead of latching onto the inherent misogyny that Rubin was pointing out, it became an aesthetic. It was bangs and ukuleles and vintage dresses, scrapbooking and focusing on "feeling totally unique even if it's just for one second," to quote Natalie Portman's character in *Garden State* (2004). Actress and singer Zooey Deschanel became the poster girl for that trope through her roles in *500 Days of Summer* (2009), her band She & Him, and the TV series *New Girl* (2011–2018). The manic pixie dream girl was *designed* to be a pliable, likeable throwback to polite, docile femininity presented in new, quirky packaging.

THE QUESTION OF LIKEABILITY

This question of likeability continues to persist. Why, after decades of exquisite performances, critical acclaim, and analysis, does likeability still matter when it comes to female characters? Surely we should be beyond this. We love messy, complicated, even problematic women, don't we?

and lives of difficult men, we react differently to women. "An unlikable man is inscrutably interesting, dark, or tormented but ultimately compelling even when he might behave in distasteful ways," Roxane Gay writes, but when women dare to be unlikeable (emphasis on the dare), it becomes a conversation, a challenge, a how-dare-she situation directed at the characters, the author, and the performer. We wouldn't want them to be our friends, co-workers, bosses, or partners, would we? Likeability equals money. That's the unwritten law that's dominated filmmaking since, well, the birth of Hollywood. Critics and audiences alike trip all over themselves in analyzing the cool manipulation of Michael Corleone in *The Godfather*, the charming psychopathy of Alex DeLarge in *A Clockwork Orange*, the status-obsessed serial killer Patrick Bateman in *American Psycho*. But when Rosamund Pike played Amy Dunne, the manipulative protagonist of *Gone Girl*, her violent and daring performance was met with shock, fear, and a countless stream of think pieces.

It's a flawed formula that's rooted in bias—and the history of pop culture has shown us who's *allowed* to be perceived as difficult, unruly, or unlikeable and get away with it. With the sheer absence of unlikeable women of color until quite recently, being unlikeable is still mostly the territory of cis, skinny, conventionally attractive white women. The anger or wit of Black women has been routinely transformed into comic relief or used to feed the damaging stereotype of the Angry Black Woman. Their agency and sexuality has more often than not been weaponized against them with the more noxious stereotype of the Jezebel, rendering the depiction of Black women's

"Unlikeable" is code. It's code for "fair game." If a wor
is unlikeable, she is stepping out of bounds. Which make
fair game to decimate her socially, emotionally, or physic
Likeability gives us permission to annihilate women who d
bend to its rules. At the worst, our reaction to unlikeable fen
characters is one of disgust, rejection, and even violence. A
best, it's empathy and understanding.

Likeability onscreen is a tightrope that writers, direct
producers, and (mostly) actors must walk on. It's also a cat
all term that is used to describe all those female characters v
transgress as much as *one* rule of polite femininity. Throu
what is commissioned, produced, released, or published i
how it's received (both at the time and much later), we can
a reading of how our definition of "acceptable" womanhood
evolved. If you're expecting an audience to go on a journey, y
have to give them a reason. And generally speaking, people
accustomed to judging women for the same bad behavior
traits that they accept in men. Hence why the phrase "unlikea
female characters" has become a catchall that refers to any a
all female characters, heroines, or sidekicks that dare to not g
a damn what other people think about them.

The entertainment industry is built on monetizing pe
ple's desire to watch other people. As with many things in t
entertainment industry, likeability is actually code for marke
ability. The real question beneath "Is she likeable enough?"
"Can we sell her to people?" We measure this with money ar
viewership. Box office, audience numbers, and press covera
are the industry's markers of success. While we're comfor
able being fascinated by the dark, twisted, complicated min

sexuality a double-edged sword: the screen paints them as sensual, attractive, and alluring while at the same time nurturing the racist idea that Black women are oversexed. While we're tracing the evolution of unlikeable women, there were scant roles available to Black women and women of color in Hollywood at the best of times, let alone meaty roles that we could deem unlikeable. They've had to walk an even thinner tightrope.

THE RENAISSANCE OF THE ANTIHEROINE

The unlikeable female character is the antithesis of the strong female character. The strong female lead is perfect—and perfectly boring. It is a gilded cage used not just by films themselves but by the industry who tried to capitalize on the rise of pop culture feminism. The love for this trope, which underpinned mainstream pop feminism, is almost gone now. The strong female character is another reflection of a ridiculous binary of good and bad, empowering or disempowered, that erases all nuance and shades of gray. Women are complicated, and we want our characters to reflect that, to be allowed space to breathe. Guide books on how to be a "good" woman belong in the bin, along with the repressive, overidealized versions of womanhood that have been fed to us for decades through our screens, our books, and our music.

We are currently living in a renaissance of unlikeable female characters. A third golden age, if you will. They have taken over our culture and storytelling and created a new canon of fictional and real-life stars. We obsess over glamorous psychopaths like

Villanelle (*Killing Eve*) and Amy Dunne (*Gone Girl*). We have ambitious, ruthless business women like Olivia Pope (*Scandal*), Selina Meyer (*Veep*), Quinn King and Rachel Goldberg (*UnREAL*), Deborah Vance and Ava Daniels (*Hacks*), Shiv Roy (*Succession*), and Annalise Keating (*How to Get Away with Murder*). We laugh along with Trainwrecks like Rebecca Bunch (*Crazy Ex-Girlfriend*) and messy romantics like Fleabag and Rob Gordon (*High Fidelity*). Unhinged characters like Harley Quinn get their own standalone franchises (*Birds of Prey*) and gain layers beyond stereotypes (*Orange Is the New Black*). We can relate to messy, childlike women like Ilana and Abbi (*Broad City*) and Nora (*Awkwafina Is Nora from Queens*). These are now our protagonists and mainstream mainstays.

While the industry has worried about whether they can make money from them, unlikeable female characters have revolutionized pop culture. They have opened the door to the gamut of human experiences. They are always too much in one way or another: too horny, too ambitious, too loud, too smart, too drunk, too messy, too crazy, too sad. Seeing them onscreen opens up the possibility of women being more than just the #strongfemalecharacter. They can be flawed, malicious, self-serving, ruthless, hapless characters—but ultimately unlikeable female characters are liberating, because they are not meant to be seen as morality lessons within their stories. They are not perfect, perhaps they are not even good, and they don't need to be—because the expectation for all women to be good, to be strong, to be nice is an oppressive one. They're not supposed to be aspirational. These characters are valuable beyond their likeability. Once characters are allowed to let go of the pressure to be nice, to conform to an impossible, made-up ideal of how a woman should look and behave, they are allowed to be messy, complicated, angry, vulnerable, and human. And we are allowed to see ourselves in them.

"I have this terminal condition called bitchiness."

LINDA FIORENTINO, ACTRESS

"The people who call you a driving female will come along for the ride. If they weigh you down, you will fight them off. It is then that you are called a bitch."

BETTE DAVIS, ACTRESS

The Bitch

Have you ever been called a bitch? Have you ever called yourself or a friend a bitch? I've lost count of the number of times I've heard this word thrown at me, and the amount of times I've used it, too. Whether this word has been duly reclaimed or not is up for debate, but the power it holds is not.

There is something awe inspiring about a truly coldhearted woman onscreen. It's the contradiction of desires that makes her so appealing and reviled, simultaneously. She's everything you've been told not to be—but presented in the gorgeous wrapping you've been told you should aspire to. Women, we're told, are—not should be, but are—naturally warm, giving, kind, and understanding. What should we make, then, of the beautiful aberration that is a cold, blackhearted bitch?

I remember exactly the moment I fell in awe with Linda Fiorentino: she waltzes into a small-town bar full of plaid shirts, all sharp angles in her black-and-white skirt suit, and barks at the bartender for a Manhattan ("Who's a girl got to suck around here to get a drink?"). Heads turn, and the patrons are visibly taken aback by her. "City trash," one guy calls her, but his friend is instantly smitten. She's rude and dismissive and instantly commands the room. The guy's attempts at charming her are truly pitiful, and only when he tells her that he is "hung like a horse" does she look up. And she demands to see the merchandise, right there in the bar. This is Bridget Gregory, and she is, in her own words, "a coldhearted bitch."

Played by Fiorentino in the 1994 erotic thriller *The Last Seduction*, Bridget is confident, sexually greedy, unrepentant, and cruel, a perfect throwback to the femme fatale of the 1940s—but with an X-rated tongue. There is no room for virtue here; watching Bridget is watching a woman unleashed. She knows exactly who she is, what she wants, and how to manipulate people to get it. "You're my designated fuck," she tells the hapless guy from the bar (his name is Mike, by the way, not that she cares). Bridget likes messing with people's heads, and she's good at it. She's a master manipulator. She doesn't fall in love. She just gets what she wants—be that sex, money, or a Manhattan.

Before I'd ever been called a bitch, or had ever heard of a femme fatale, I knew Fiorentino was playing someone more complex than a simple villain, more charming than a killjoy, more active than a sassy side character. She was not going to be defeated in the end like all the greedy, bloated Disney villainesses. She's got very little time to waste on anyone that's not serving her needs. The Bitch is entirely self-aware and self-serving—and watching Bridget strut into that small-town bar, even now, I struggle to understand why that is a bad thing. And why do we love watching Bitches but cannot deal with them getting away with it?

THE DEVIL HAS THE BEST LINES

Fiorentino's performance is chilly and cool, giving us absolutely no entry point into pitying Bridget. She's never out of sorts, always composed, always in control—a manic pixie dream girl written by a sadist. Most shockingly, she enjoys all the drama that is unfolding around her and because of her. Fiorentino, dressed in the film in strict black skirts and white shirts, eschews the ultrafemininity of her femme fatale predecessors and instead imbues Bridget with the pitiless audacity of someone who knows they're the smartest person in the room.

Linda Fiorentino is not a household name, her career having stopped abruptly after starting off in a charmed way with a leading role in 1985's *Vision Quest*. She enjoyed continuous work but wasn't propelled into magazine cover stardom. Her roles leading up to *The Last Seduction* were mostly secondary but memorable (she played the icy Manhattan artist in Martin Scorsese's *After Hours*). Her last significant role was in Kevin Smith's Catholic satire *Dogma* in 1999, and after a few smaller thrillers in 2000, she essentially disappeared from the screens, becoming a photographer. Bridget Gregory was her second leading role, and the first one for which romance was not a defining part of her character.

At the time of casting, most actresses director John Dahl approached had balked at the character of Bridget, considering her too despicable to play (there are echoes of Bette Davis

fighting to play the villainous Mildred here). "But Linda saw
the potential in the part and recognized it as something that she
could have a lot of fun with," he said to the *New York Times* in
1994. The reception was uniformly positive, most reviews being
both smitten with and scared of Bridget. "Only in the insect
or animal worlds are there comparable models for feminine
behavior. And the female praying mantis is nicer to her mates
than Bridget is to the men in this movie," wrote Janet Maslin in
the *New York Times*. "Fiorentino is superb as the femme fatale
whose sexy, murderous antics range from the delightful to the
deranged," wrote critic Mark Kermode for *Sight & Sound*. Kim
Newman described her as "a hard-as-nails New York bitch" in
Empire magazine. "The problem is not that they don't write
good roles for women anymore; it's that they only write roles for
good women," wrote Richard Schickel in *Time* magazine.

There was a shared delight in watching Bridget mock, use,
and discard men and be unashamedly greedy. It's still thrilling to
watch today, still feels outrageous. Fiorentino has always brought
that caustic, don't-look-me-in-the-eye energy to her roles. With
Bridget, you never know whether she wants to fuck you or
run you over with a car. In 1994, when the film was released,[1]
Fiorentino mentioned to the *New York Times*: "Barbara Stanwyck
would have gotten it if she were alive."

This offhanded quote traces a direct line of the Bitch archetype and the actresses who played her. This type of character
has always been shocking, not so much unlikeable as immoral,
but she has always had agency and been the driving force of

---

1   It was first shown on cable television instead of receiving a theatrical release,
    which made it ineligible for the Academy Awards, still a sore topic in my house.

the narrative. She is self-serving and willful and ruthless in the pursuit of her own agenda. She is confident, proud, and in control, calculating, and not above harming others in the pursuit of her own goals. The Bitch plays with our expectations and, very often, she gets what she wants because of this. Surely, this would be an attractive proposition for actresses. Doesn't, as they say, "the Devil have the best lines"?

PRE-CODE BITCHES

The Bitch really burst on the scene in 1930s Hollywood, before the Production Code took away all the fun. In *Baby Face*, directed by Alfred E. Green in 1933, Barbara Stanwyck plays Lily, a young woman who knowingly and cynically exploits her beauty and youth to pursue money, power, and material possessions, being obsessed with climbing the social ladder. At first, she is an unhappy young woman, basically being prostituted by her dirtbag father in his canteen populated by equally dirtbag men. Her main allies are Chico, her maid, played by African American actress Theresa Harris, and Adolf Cragg, a cobbler who sees her intelligence through her belligerent unhappiness and puts her onto the writing of Nietzsche. In a scene that was cut from the film's original release and only restored to its uncut, immoral original in 2014 (it was believed to be lost until 2004), Adolf gives her a pep talk that would fit right in at a girlboss rally: "A woman young, beautiful like you, can get anything she wants in the world, because she has power over men. But you must use men, not let them use you. You must be a master, not a slave." He instills in her the idea that she can wield power over her situation in life. He tells her, point-blank to "be strong, defiant. Use men to get the things you want." After this moment, Lily's entire demeanor, approach to life, even her voice, changes. She moves to the big city and, quite literally, sleeps her way to the top of a big bank. For Lily, sex is a shortcut to power.

The film's tagline promoted its salacious nature: "She had it and made it pay." The film was so controversial at the time that this scene was heavily edited (lest female audiences get any ideas) and was instrumental in propelling the Production Code into action. *Baby Face* was sending the wrong message: that women could harness their femininity to get what they want; that they could fuck their way to the top and get to *stay* there too.

The reaction to the film was intense. Joseph Breen, who was heading up the Production Code office at the time, demanded cuts. Darryl Zanuck (one of the last great studio tycoons and uncredited author of the screenplay, who Stanwyck worked very closely with on developing the story and the character) protested but was overpowered. He resigned from his position. The Production Code insisted on punishing Lily, because no bitch should get away with having the last laugh, right? In the original conclusion of *Baby Face*, Lily keeps her money and keeps her man. The censors forced the studio to reshoot the ending, wherein Lily gives away her hard-earned cash to her love interest so he can bail out his company, and they return to her hometown. In the censored version, Lily is back where she started. The lesson is clear: ambition and money are not meant for women. Despite the studio acquiescing to the censors and cutting the offending scenes (or altering them—the Nietzsche scene was overdubbed to avoid any direct allusion to sex work),

Baby Face was pulled from cinemas almost immediately after it was released, even with cuts.

Watching the restored, uncut version of *Baby Face* today, it remains striking. It doesn't fit into a neat box of empowering narratives around women, and it wrestles with being a text about a woman's self-determination and a cautionary tale of how mercenary working-class women can be. It's impossible, and unfair to separate the film from its context. "It's the Pre-Code movies about women that are the most remarkable now," wrote David Denby for the *New Yorker* in 2016, "in part because their sexual attitudes don't fit into any obvious political or moral pattern." Alongside *Baby Face*, 1933 also saw the release of *Female*, where a female executive climbs up the corporate ladder while taking several lovers, and *Red-Headed Woman* was released the previous year and starred Jean Harlow as a self-serving blond who uses sex (and a bit of murder) to advance her social position." It's worth noting that although these films are directed by men (Alfred E. Green, Michael Curtiz, Jack Conway), the screenplays were written or cowritten by women (Kathryn Scola cowrote both *Female* and *Baby Face*, Mae West wrote *I'm No Angel*, Anita Loos—of *Gentlemen Prefer Blondes* fame—wrote *Red-Headed Woman*). This is a constant: with film history dominated by male directors, the majority of the films are directed by men but often are based on books or screenplays authored by women.

While her role in *Baby Face* was controversial, Barbara Stanwyck was not. She was known for being kind and open to everyone on set, famously knowing the names of all the cast, crew, and their children.

Bette Davis, then just another contract player, campaigned hard for the role of the scheming Cockney waitress Mildred in *Of Human Bondage*. She wanted to play the first great villainess of cinema, and after six months of relentlessly badgering studio head Jack Warner, she got it. Mildred is a waitress who becomes reluctantly involved with a mild-mannered, clubfooted artist. She is openly disdainful of him from the start but still accepts his advances and eventual proposal but brutally leaves him, in one scene screaming at him: "I never cared for you, not once! I was always makin' a fool of ya! Ya bored me stiff; I hated ya! It made me sick when I had to let ya kiss me."

I try to imagine what it must've been like to go to a cinema in 1934 and see Mildred, screaming at the screen, furious with disgust, wanting to hurt—to really hurt—someone. The film caused a furor, the audience applauding when Mildred got a verbal dressing down, roaring with applause when the film ended. Mildred was dead and Bette Davis became a star.

MOTHER GODDAM

Every single trope, every single unlikeable, antagonistic, or unruly female character owes a debt of gratitude to Bette Davis. With a career spanning six decades, Davis became known for playing difficult women onscreen and cultivated a legendarily prickly offscreen persona. Trained as a stage actress, after moving to Hollywood she worked consistently, never quite breaking through and being constantly reminded that she was not (sigh) hot enough. The Hollywood machine (which at that time controlled and designed every aspect of a new star, from their face to their look, persona, backstory, love life, and even name) tried to mold her into a cute blond ingenue, but that was never going to stick. Bette even dyed her hair back to her natural color after they tried to make her go platinum blond. The studio didn't notice until one year later. At that time, performers were contracted to a studio, who would assign them roles based on their appearance, profitability, or the type of role that audiences expected from them. Davis also knew what type of roles were meatier and was completely unafraid to de-glam herself for a performance, which might be the de facto way to an Oscar nomination now but was the polar opposite to success when Davis was coming up. This dedication to the role would become a trademark of hers: she shaved her eyebrows and hairline to play Queen Elizabeth I (*The Private Lives of Elizabeth and Essex*), wore fake eyelashes and narrowed her mouth to make herself look older (*The Little Foxes*), wore fake eyebrows and padding for the first half of *Now, Voyager*, and years later, did her own grotesque makeup to play former child star Baby Jane in *Whatever Happened to Baby Jane?*

The acclaim she got for her performance as Mildred allowed Bette to continue playing unsympathetic roles that would challenge audiences. She was obsessed with the craft of acting and played actresses in some of her greatest onscreen roles: the washed-up, bitter alcoholic actress in *The Star*[2]; a legendary stage actress, quietly having her role usurped by a scheming, social-climbing fan in *All About Eve*; and the deranged titular character from *Whatever Happened to Baby Jane?*, a grand guignol about

---

2   This character was allegedly based on the woman to whom Davis would be compared to her entire career, Joan Crawford.

sisterly envy and aging that paired her with Joan Crawford, created the legend of an infamous feud between the two actresses,
and reignited both of their careers in one fell swoop. Every role
had to be a new challenge, which meant there was simply no way
of typecasting Bette Davis, and while audiences hated her characters, they loved Bette.

In each of these roles, the femininity of the character—
whether it was a tool or being questioned—was a key entry
point into the role. While Hollywood didn't quite know what
to do with her, Davis's fearlessness in portraying so many shades
of womanhood made her adept at portraying women who were,
in their most basic interpretation, deliciously bitchy but fundamentally trying to navigate a life intent on reducing them to the
status of "woman" and little more.

WOMANHOOD AS WEAPON

The Bitch is acutely aware of her status as a woman and where
she stands in the social landscape. She understands the limitations and implications of her womanhood and the inherently
unfair rules of a patriarchal society—and she plays the game
to get what she wants. These women know they live in a world
designed for men. They're not trying to change the system,
they're just trying to play it to their advantage. The Bitch weaponizes traditional notions of femininity and is able to use
men's desires against them. There is no room for collective
thinking in her—she's never pursuing a greater good or the
betterment of her situation for other women—it's all entirely
self-serving.

This self-interest can take the form of greed or pride. In Milos Forman's 1988 adaptation of *Dangerous Liaisons*, the Marquise de Merteuil, played gorgeously by Glenn Close, is fully aware of the rules of power and high society—and how they play out differently for men and women. From the very first moment we meet her, she is admiring herself and displaying great self-control and self-satisfaction, saying all the right things and fooling everyone around her. She revels in her power over men and the stupidity of others.

The Marquise holds a high status in eighteenth-century French court and often convenes (that is, gossips over tea) with her fuckboy best friend, the Vicomte de Valmont (played by John Malkovich, exuding a sex appeal that is, frankly, unacceptable). They enjoy each other's company as smart people who enjoy playing with others, performing the court's pleasantries while verbally disemboweling everyone behind their backs. When she's rebuffed by a lover, the Marquise's pride is hurt, and she enlists Valmont to run a scheme that will ruin the reputations of two young women as a means to get back at her ex. She wants to take revenge—not because he has hurt her feelings but because he has hurt her pride. She's not gaining anything here, except the pleasure of seeing someone else's ruin.

In a delicious scene of intellectual back-and-forth seeped in sexual tension, Valmont inquires about her manipulation tactics: "Women are obliged to be far more skillful than men," she says. "You can ruin our reputation and our life with a few well-chosen words. So of course I had to invent not only myself but ways of escape no one has ever thought of before. And I've succeeded because I've always known I was born to dominate your sex and avenge my own."

Marquise de Merteuil is a virtuoso of deceit. Her control extends to her body, how she presents herself, and her voice. She has invented herself, skillfully, quietly, in full view of others. She listened and learned, playing a game that she has rigged in her favor. Reviewing the film upon its release in 1988, the *New York Times'* Vincent Canby described the sheer pleasure she takes in toying with people: "The Marquise de Merteuil seems always about to burst, not because of any engineering failure but in anticipation of some delightful new viciousness, a plot of such subtlety that only she can appreciate it. She keeps control of herself and simply smiles." Although the Marquise's machinations are motivated by the rejection of a lover, it's pride, not heartbreak, that she's avenging. Glenn Close plays the role with unblinking coldness, coming alive only when she's scheming with Valmont or when she sees one of their schemes play out just as she planned. Watching Close play her is like watching a python wrap itself around its prey, waiting until the right moment to squeeze the breath out of it. It's electrifying and erotic. The shift is almost imperceptible until it's right there on the screen, aflame in Valmont's face. When Valmont challenges her, pinning her against the wall and demanding sex, she reminds him: "I'm better at this than you are." The Marquise never marries ("despite a bewildering amount of offers," she says, flexing) because she cannot tolerate being ordered around by a man. It's the only time she raises her voice. To paraphrase *Dirty Dancing*: nobody puts the Marquise in the corner. "Haven't you had enough of bullying women," she asks Valmont, before shifting to a baby-sweet voice to reject him once more. In a single word, in a single close-up, looking straight into the camera, the Marquise declares, "War."

Let's circle back to Bridget Gregory, the blunt, chain-smoking, suit-wearing con artist with a viper tongue and no time to waste. Linda Fiorentino portrays her with an abandon that shows no interest in redeeming her. Reviews at the time noted her sexiness, framing her lack of niceties as humorous and a modern take on the femme fatale. In a blog post, critic Jason Cuthbert describes Bridget as such: "If she were able to stoop any lower in the ethical department, she would need a ladder to reach Hell." While there is nothing redeemable or likeable about Bridget, she's watchable like only true movie stars are watchable. Fiorentino's performance is all rough edges, straight-talking, blunt to the point of rudeness, and unfaltering. Bridget is ruthless in the pursuit of her own agenda and has no time or patience for politeness. She and her husband Clay (played by the ultimate character actor specializing in schmucks, Bill Pullman) steal a substantial amount of money from a drug deal. But just as they're celebrating, Clay makes the mistake of slapping Bridget. In the film, she is barely shaken by it. She promptly runs away and, following the advice of her trusty and shady lawyer, bides her time in a nothing town on her way to Chicago.

Like the Marquise de Merteuil and Bridget Gregory, the Bitch is an expert at playing with people's expectations of her, and of women in general, to her advantage. However, there is also a tra-dition of punishing onscreen bitches in order to show that their behavior is inappropriate at best and immoral at worst. Bridget is one of the rare examples of an unlikeable, unrepentant female character that gets away scot-free after conning and manipulating her way out of every sticky situation.

Meanwhile, the Marquise, despite how good she is at playing high society's game, must be punished. Her deception is revealed to everyone through the disclosure of her letters to Valmont. She is booed by everyone at the opera. Even at this moment, the mask doesn't slip. Never in public. Never for others to see. Her machinations, her bitchiness, have been revealed. She takes in all the boos, then silently and softly turns around to leave, stumbling briefly. In the last shot of the film, the camera slowly zooms in on the Marquise's face. It is quiet; there's no music, no booing. It's only the Marquise and her reflection, her poise intact but shaken, taking off her mask literally and figuratively. Her jewels come off, then her makeup. Her eyes are downcast, and her face fades into black. While she is alive, the Marquise has been socially annihilated, and she knows it.

Twenty years later, Close would play the high-powered, icy lawyer Patty Hewes in the series *Damages*. "I realized that her power came from keeping people off bounds. The only time that she shows her true feelings was in private. She would never let her power go by being emotional—unless it was calculated," Close broke the character down for *Vanity Fair*. She could've said the same thing about the Marquise. Glenn Close, a virtuoso performer who had some of her best roles in the 1980s, imbues her characters with a humanity that exists in between the lines she's given. In Glenn's hands, the villains are never just villains, the bitchiness never just for bitchiness's sake.

At the end of *The Last Seduction*, Bridget kills her husband

Clay by emptying a pepper spray bottle down his throat and convinces her boy toy Mike to enact a consensual-non-consensual scene where he pretends to rape her to satisfy a fantasy. She records this, goading him into a fake confession of murdering Clay, and uses this tape to get him arrested. Bridget gets away with literal murder, keeps the money, and drives off wearing a black power suit in a shiny limousine.

ENTER ALEXIS CARRINGTON

We could not talk about onscreen bitchiness, and its camp legacy, without mentioning Dame Joan Collins. This is the one name that will come up in every single conversation about bitches onscreen, something that Collins herself has cultivated—albeit reluctantly—as part of her persona. In her role as Alexis Carrington Colby in *Dynasty* (1981), she embodied an over-the-top, fabulously cruel, flighty character to be feared and never messed with. In her own words: "Steely but with panache." Alexis, introduced in the second season of the soap opera, turned *Dynasty* into a watercooler show, a ratings juggernaut, and gave Collins, who'd been acting since 1954, her first and only Golden Globe Award. Throughout her portrayal of the shoulder-padded antagonist, from 1981 to 1991, she schemes against her ex-husband, undermines his new marriage, and exerts fierce control over her children. Alexis is ruthless, conniving, and manipulative and was often described by critics as a "superbitch" and "the quintessential character you love to hate." It turned Collins—aged forty-eight when she was cast—into a global star, and despite being somewhat uncomfortable with the title, she embraced it, playing into interviews on talk shows and appearing on an episode of *Lifestyles of the Rich and Famous* that could've easily been outtakes from *Dynasty*.[3]

Collins, who before the soap opera was a working actress but never quite a star, had started to find it difficult to find work. Her career had begun in the twilight years of the studio era, and she was whisked from RADA (the Royal Academy of Dramatic Art) in London into supporting roles in Hollywood. When that dried up, she engineered her own return to the big screen—and got her first true box office smash—with the disco soft-core films *The Stud* (1978) followed up by *The Bitch* (1979), which follow the exploits of greedy, hyperhorny Fontaine Khaled as she uses men for money and/or sex.

GREED IS NOT FOR GIRLS

It's very difficult for us to accept self-interest in women. It's deeply tied to the notion of surviving and prospering in a man's world. Because of this, the Bitch is often presented as a morality lesson. An ambitious woman is a greedy woman, and an ambitious woman is any woman who wants more than what she's been doled out by the men around her. She must be punished for her greed and willfulness.

---

3   Interesting to note that Collins and Nolan Miller (the costume designer for *Dynasty*) had the same frame of reference when designing the look of Alexis: Joan Crawford. Alexis herself was a key inspiration for the character of Cookie Lyon, played by Academy Award–nominated actress Taraji P. Henson, in Lee Daniels's *Empire*, a high-camp show centered on the politics and schemes of a Black family in the music industry. The Bitch canon is all interconnected.

In women, ambition and greed are interchangeable and equally dirty words. Writer Julianna Baggott writes about female ambition as "suspicious," "selfish," and "ugly." If a woman is ambitious, she's "going against society's virtuous goal for her: motherhood." If she's a mother and ambitious, then she must be sacrificing her children's well-being to serve herself. That bitch.

These characters are just as seeped in their own very specific frames of references as the word itself is. We're terrified and in awe. We know we shouldn't like them, and that's how they're presented to us, but we also sort of want to be them. Which is the same reaction the word "bitch" provokes. It's brash, emerging from a misogynistic history, but it's impossible to ignore.

So she must be made into an example, or transformed into a virtuous woman—or pit against one, so we can truly appreciate the extent of her villainy. A type of capitalist villainy, of course, that is venerated in male characters, like Gordon Gekko's "Greed is good" speech in *Wall Street* or Jordan Belfort's con man antics in *The Wolf of Wall Street*. The greedy bastards of cinema become poster boys for masculine enterprise. Ambitious women, though, are usually pitted against each other or shown to be unhappy in some aspect of their life. While being sold the notion of "having it all"—career, romance, health, family—the movies also tell us to "settle down."

There is a long-running tradition in cinema of punishing female ambition. Or at the very least, of taking it down a peg. In the 1988 workplace comedy *Working Girl*, we see two types of ambitious business women. Our likeable, modest protagonist Tess (Melanie Griffith) has big business aspirations and is genuinely excited about working for another woman, the tough-as-nails Katherine

(Sigourney Weaver). You know she means business by the size of her shoulder pads and her fake warmth, but Katherine has no interest in helping anyone other than herself. She steals Tess's idea and passes it off as her own. In a male-dominated movie, this would be a passing betrayal; in *Working Girl*, it's the central moral conundrum. How could a woman possibly do this to another woman, Tess asks herself. So she turns to the men for help— specifically the client that Katherine had passed her idea on to, Jack (Harrison Ford), who likes her instantly because of her fem- ininity ("You're the first woman I've seen at one of these things that dresses like a woman, not like a woman thinks a man would dress if he was a woman"). Because this is a romantic comedy, they wind up smitten with one another, and it's with Jack's help that Tess exposes her boss's deceitful ways. She humiliates her in an executive meeting room, letting the men speak for her, con- firming that it was indeed her idea and not Katherine's. In return, Tess gets a chance to climb up the corporate ladder and secure her very own secretary. She's not welcomed to the boys' execu- tive level, but she did help them, so they let her stay. Ambitious women are cool, if they're ambitious in the right way.

The millennial version of this tale is *The Devil Wears Prada* (2006), a surprisingly dark take on toxic workplace culture in which recent graduate and aspiring journalist Andy (Anne Hathaway) gets a job working as an assistant to the powerful fashion maga- zine editor Miranda Priestley (Meryl Streep). Andy is dismissive of this industry, openly scoffing in meetings and rolling her eyes at Miranda's other, ubereager assistant Emily (Emily Blunt). Andy thinks she's too good for this place, but she's also not very good at her job. Meryl Streep, until then not known for her comedic roles as much as for her dramas,[4] plays Miranda with a total detachment. Video essay channel Be Kind Rewind calls *The Devil Wears Prada* the moment when "Meryl became *Meryl*." Miranda never needs to raise her voice, she needs only to wave her hand or purse her lips to command the room or address an order. Famously and very evidently based on Vogue's creative chief Anna Wintour, she is a workaholic with an icy cold demeanor, and while the movie gives us many opportunities to revel in her power, it also presents Miranda, ultimately, as pitiful. In a domestic scene that Andy interrupts, we see Miranda arguing with her husband. Her New York City brownstone might be enviable, her wardrobe exquisite, and her influence on her industry unparalleled—but that's not enough for her to keep her marriage. In a scene that's meant to show Miranda's vulnerabilities, but which really defangs her, she laments her success: "Dragon lady. Career obsessed. Snow queen drives away another Mr. Priestley." Ambition is renamed "career obsession" for women only. Andy just looks on, seeing the same potential future for herself. Miranda Priestley, the film tells us, for all her power, is still to be pitied because she failed as a woman.

In Gus Van Sant's 1995 film *To Die For*, Nicole Kidman plays the narcissistic striver Suzanne Stone, who is determined to become a famous broadcaster. Suzanne lives in a small town and marries a perfectly middle-of-the-road nice guy, Larry (Matt Dillon), essentially to keep herself financially stable while she pursues her broadcasting ambitions. Larry is the kind of guy who's happy if he gets to have a beer at the end of the day, a barbecue on the weekends, and a wife who looks good serving him that beer.

---

4   Disrespectful toward *Death Becomes Her*.

When Larry starts getting a bit too comfortable and asks her to
take time away from her network ambitions to help out at his family's eatery, she decides to get rid of him and seduces a gang of local
teenagers to murder him. The film is structured as a mockumen-
tary, forefronting the dark comedy, but Nicole Kidman's central
performance is chilling in the way she turns her seductiveness on
and off depending on what she's trying to get. Roger Ebert wrote:

> Her clothes, her makeup, her hair, her speech, her manner,
> even the way she carries herself (as if aware of the eyes of
> millions) are all brought to a perfect pitch. Her Suzanne is
> so utterly absorbed in being herself that there is an eerie
> conviction, even in the comedy. She plays Suzanne as the
> kind of woman who pities us—because we aren't her, and
> you know what? We never will be.

The real bitch in both these films isn't the boss from hell,
it's capitalism, and the idea that women must compete against
one another if they ever dream of succeeding. These scenes are
betrayals. I want to see my bitches prevail. Perhaps this is why the
Bitch is so watchable, because she lets us live out our most ambitious fantasies. Fantasies of busy, glamorous lives, of movie professions that seem out of reach—and that are always presented as
a choice: you either want the glamorous career, or you want to be
happy. You can't have both.

MONEY DICK POWER

It's on TV that female ambition has been allowed to thrive,

with characters that are doctors like Christina Yang (*Gray's Anatomy*), lawyers like Patty Hewes (*Damages*) and Diane Lockhart (*The Good Fight*), high-powered consultants like Olivia Pope (*Scandal*), or TV producers like Quinn King and Rachel Goldberg (*UnREAL*). The extended timeframe of television allows these characters to become three-dimensional beings, with their ambition explored in its many thorny angles. Most of the pop culture images of successful women we see show us their ambition as the source of their failings elsewhere.

On *UnREAL*, ambition is the defining and most troublesome trait of both its leads: seasoned reality TV executive producer Quinn King (Constance Zimmer) and her ambivalent mentee, producer Rachel Goldberg (Shiri Appleby). The series is anchored by their push-and-pull rivalry, friendship, and codependency. When the series starts, Rachel is returning to work on the set of *Everlasting*, the fictional dating show from which she was fired after suffering a breakdown caused by severe burnout. Quinn brings her back, lording over her with this favor in the same breath as she commends Rachel on her almost savant-like producing abilities. In this world, producing is in part equal to manipulation, getting the contestants to go to extremes that will make compelling television. While Rachel has a self-hating element to her, she also leans into her prowess, sometimes blurring the lines between her personal relationships and the narratives she pushes through onto the show itself. On more than one occasion, she's dubbed a monster by those around her, an accusation that barely gets a reaction out of her. Appleby's performance is one of ambivalence: Rachel is always aware of the threads she's pulling and the reactions they'll get, but she's also desperate for a genuine connection—and desperately aware of how slippery the notion of honesty is in her world. The first shot of the series is Rachel lying on her back in a limousine surrounded by several of the show's gorgeous contestants, wearing a "This Is What a Feminist Looks Like" T-shirt as she fabricates enthusiasm for the program she so clearly detests. Zimmer, on the other hand, is playing hard into the foul-mouthed, macho bravado that was so popular in shows like *Entourage*. She walks and talks like a bro ("I am SO HARD right now!") while simultaneously rallying against the bro-ey network executives and male rights activist showrunner[5] for limiting her professionally because she's a woman. Even the show is aware of how contradictorily cringe these displays of power are, with the supporting characters often side-eyeing Quinn's giddy outbursts of faux-chismo.

The show was devised by a former producer on *The Bachelor*, Sarah Gertrude Shapiro, loosely based on her own experiences and frustrations as an aspiring female filmmaker. Cocreated with TV veteran Marti Noxon (who had worked on *Buffy the Vampire Slayer* and *Mad Men*), Shapiro has crafted two characters that have feminist intention behind them but are sadistic and unlikeable by design.

The balance of power between Quinn and Rachel fluctuates, but one thing remains constant: their cutthroat ambition and the crippling chokehold it has on them. At the start of the second season, in a bonding moment, they get matching tattoos that say "MONEY, DICK, POWER." Those are their priorities, and in that particular order. Somehow, they use these tattoos as

---

5   Who also happens to be her long-time lover. This show gets complicated with the interoffice relationships.

reminders of their loyalty to one another, a loyalty that rarely lasts an entire episode. They blackmail and backstab each other constantly, and yet somehow it's always a surprise to them.

UnREAL is challenging but also feeds into the women-pitted-against-women narrative so present in films like *Working Girl* and *The Devil Wears Prada*. Both Quinn and Rachel are decidedly good at their jobs and very clear in their purpose, with very little pretense of social change (especially Quinn, who has no interest in changing the status quo, no matter how much it's oppressed her, unless it directly benefits her). They have been undermined by the men around them but are making no effort to change the landscape for the women who come after them. We see this pattern of feminist sadism repeated several times, with Quinn and Rachel and with Rachel and the production assistant, Madison.

Much like *Scandal*, the show dedicates plenty of time to the personal lives of its characters. After all, their work is their lives and the majority of their personal entanglements take place at work. Like the films that came before it that inevitably showed ambitious or professionally accomplished women as sad and desperate and with empty personal lives, *UnREAL* falls into a similar trap. Both Quinn and Rachel are shown as pathologically messy at best and undeserving of love at worst. *UnREAL's* biggest, boldest swerve, though, is that it refuses to judge them. The sliminess of their world is entirely devoid of charm, yet while the male characters around them crumble at the slightest affront to their egos, Quinn and Rachel wrangle their way out of almost any situation. Their ambition is callous but so is their talent. At least they're honest about it.

GASLIGHT, GATEKEEP, GIRLBOSS

Female ambition has never been more de rigueur than it was in the period between 2014 and 2017, when the term "girlboss" rose to brief pop culture prominence as a millennial take on girl power rhetoric, packaged, merchandised, and hashtagged in chalky pink and neon before being spit out shortly after as white feminism's attempt to make bare-faced capitalism seem like social activism. While the real-life phenomena is rooted in powerful business women's aspirational rhetoric that's only slightly more complex than "You can do it, bestie; be your bossy self," the girlboss era started and ended with the same story: Sophia Amoruso's memoir #Girlboss and the Netflix series based on said memoir. Amoruso's rise to power and fortune was chronicled in her memoir, which single-handedly popularized the term "girlboss" and also became the foundation of her second business, the Girlboss media empire (a website, newsletter, podcast, and series of events eventually made up the platform). Nasty Gal (the first business she set up), as she'd recount many times over in interviews, started as an eBay clothing store when Amoruso was just twenty-two. A mere decade later, she'd be on the cover of Forbes as one of the richest self-made women in America.

The Netflix series based on her memoir, produced by Charlize Theron and Kay Cannon, starred Britt Robertson as a fictionalized version of Amoruso, styling her journey to business success from "dumpster-diving anarchist to a punky CEO" around the same time as Nasty Gal was being sued by four former employees who alleged they were fired before—or because—they went on maternity leave. The show might have survived the bad real-life press if it understood what made the story of female ambition appealing. Julia Raeside tore the show a new one in the *Guardian* by singling out its faux feminist appeal covering up its lack of character building: "The same vapid, non-specific, something-to-do-with-feminism-in-hot pants fluff but with added narcissism and less of a sense of humor." The fictional Sophia Amoruso is so confident of the inevitability of her own success that there's no room for any growth, vulnerability, or even unlikeability. She keeps telling the audience that she's fabulous without actually *doing* anything fabulous. She's a cardboard cutout, hindered by the show's need to be an advertisement for the very real company whose name it shares. #*Girlboss* was an attempt to commercialize the unlikeable female character without paying any attention to actual character development through storytelling.

Ambitious women need not always be successful—or even particularly talented—either. Just look at Shiv Roy, the evolution of the Bitch into a new, deliciously entertaining arena: the female flop. In *Succession*, Shiv (Sarah Snook) is the only daughter of media mogul Logan Roy, and at the beginning of the series appears to be disinterested in the succession war that's going on between her father and her brothers. She believes herself to be the smartest of the siblings and, at first, we're led to believe that too. Partly because when we meet Shiv, she has built a life outside of being a Roy. She works as a political strategist and media pundit, and she's cocky and cutthroat but still has some semblance of a moral compass (emphasis on "semblance"). Shiv is never presented to us as a good person (everyone on *Succession* is objectively a terrible human being; it's a sliding scale of awfulness), but compared to her brothers (the screwy Kendall, knucklehead bon vivant Roman, and deluded aspiring politico Connor), she seemed, at first, the most level-headed of the Roy clan. However, Shiv is just as much of a flop as her brothers. Smart enough to see her own mistakes, but not smart enough to avoid making them, her job throughout the first season is, ironically, to manage the likeability of a female political candidate. ("I guess she comes off as a kind of a bitch. But, like, you must get that a lot.") She does, eventually, get embroiled in the internal battle for the big girl CEO job, and it's never quite clear if it's out of her own ambition, out of spite, or because it's inevitable as a Roy kid. Does she actually want the job? Or does she just want to prove to the men that she's better than them? Does she want it because she can't really hack it anywhere else?

While the first season sold Shiv to us as the most liberal and progressive thinking of the Roy clan, perhaps untouched by their moral murkiness, she shows herself to actually be just as corrupt when she helps cover up decades of shady dealings and rampant sexual abuse at Waystar Royco, tapping into the exact same language of victim blaming that is synonymous with wider rape culture. When needed, Shiv performs a welcoming, under-standing version of herself: she approaches the whistleblower cautiously, takes her shoes off, complains about her father (Shiv Roy, she's just like us!). The character in itself is a take on the girlboss narrative that had been sold to us only a few years prior. Shiv's femaleness both hinders and aids her. Despite being born and raised in an environment of rampant greed, wealth, and power, Shiv is still expected to put other (men's) interests ahead of her own. When she is offered the CEO seat, her husband Tom (Matthew MacFadyen) is stunned—not because of the offer but because she didn't fight for it to be redirected to him ("I thought it was something we wanted for me"). She wants to escape being defined by it, to be more than "the only daughter," but she keeps getting reminded by her brothers that she'll always be an outsider to the boy's club ("It's only your teats that give you value," Kendall spits at her. "All the men got together at the men club and we decided, sweetheart, everything's fine").

As she fully enters the corporate rat race, confident that she is going to be the successor, the punishment for her ambition takes on an egregious, nasty taste. At no point are we meant to like Shiv, but I can't help but recognize the particular flavor of the microaggressions directed her way. Even her father's (relative, very relative) patience with his fucked-up sons is significantly more than he has for her. On the surface, and on the surface only, she is getting all the things she wants. She is anointed the smartest child by her father. She gets a fancy-sounding job, president of domestic operations. She gets to ride the private jets and, on occasion, even has her father's ear. Yet she is mocked for being overeager and chastised by Logan for being annoying ("Stop buzzing in my fucking ear!" he yells at her). Shiv's abasement at the hands of her father, her brothers, and other Waystar executives cannot be separated from her femaleness. Her elder brother Connor, a man who's never held a job yet fancies himself a political intellectual, compares her new position at their father's company to her bossing the siblings around as children. Logan tells his assistant to "give her a medal" when she makes a company-saving deal. Roman refuses to explain the details of a big deal to her, sniping that he'll "check in with Dad whether to loop her in or not." In the most humiliating moment for Shiv, in her first public (and globally broadcast) appearance as the new, understanding face of Waystar, Kendall blasts Nirvana's "Rape Me" on speakers. The song keeps blaring until Shiv and her carefully planned corporate speech are completely drowned out. Back in her corner office with the impressive view and the boxes of brand-new tech still on the floor, she knows no one will forget this particular moment. She's done before she even started— and spits in her notebook in quiet, disgusted frustration.

In the vein of *Working Girl*, once disempowered, Shiv turns against the other women of Waystar: when Roman accidentally sends a dick pic to his father instead of his obsessive sexual interest Gerri (J. Smith-Cameron), now the interim CEO of the company, it's Gerri's job that's on the line even though it's Roman's transgression. Shiv springs into action, angling the opportunity to become the favorite child once more—even if it means throwing Gerri under the bus with her faux feminist pretense of eliminating sexual harassment. ("If you can't deal with your own sexual harassment...it's not a good look.") It's a clever devolution of the Bitch: she appears to have the drive, self-confidence, and agency, but she fails at everything she sets out to do. Shiv's downfall becomes her own hubris and lack of self-awareness, her desperate need to be the smartest person in the room, which makes her overlook everyone else's interests.

The most important thing about the Bitch is agency. These characters are not passive participants in the story but rather initiators of the action. They plot, they scheme, they make the moves and are drivers of the story—whether we know from the beginning or not. Bridget Gregory is in the driver's seat of *The Last Seduction* from the start. Marquise de Merteuil is the puppet master of everything that's going on in *Dangerous Liaisons*. It's because they want things for themselves and they are driven by their ambitions that they propel the plot forward. But Shiv, fascinating as she is, doesn't have as much agency as she thinks she has. There's hardly anything aspirational about Shiv Roy,[6] and the show wickedly plays with the notion that because she is a woman—the only woman—in this milieu, she must be admired.

In any other show, at any other time, Shiv would've been a character in the vein of Alexis Carrington or Theresa, a powersuit-wearing shark. The layered, caustic writing of the show and Sarah Snook's performance—the devastating detail of each smirk, each wince, each eye roll—elevate Shiv Roy into one of the most fascinating antiheroines of recent pop culture by letting us spend so much time next to her and by allowing her to be a failure, a Bitch in her flop era. Her ambition is not her downfall, her arrogance is. Shiv, just like her brothers, craves power so much that she doesn't actually wield the power she already has. Her betrayal at the end of season three, at the hands of her own mother and husband, was telegraphed way in advance for us. If she were smarter, she would've seen it coming, but she never considered Tom capable of such a move. The shock of the final shot of the finale, a close-up of Shiv's face, is doubly shocking not because of the betrayal she has suffered but because her image of herself is finally pierced. The only one of the Roy siblings left to bear the humiliating knowledge of Tom's betrayal and her own debasement at the hands of someone she considered beneath her, Shiv, perhaps, finally understands that she is not that great.

---

6 Except her backless turtleneck from season two.

PLAYING THE BITCH

The importance of the actor cast to play the Bitch is paramount, not least because it can define an actress's offscreen persona. These bitchy roles are juicy parts for great actresses to really showcase their talents because, to paraphrase *The BITCH Manifesto*, the bitch dominates the story. As film writer Virginie Sélavy said in a talk she gave at the British Film Institute, "She will not be confined to a side character." It's understandable why this is so appealing to actresses. This can be a double-edged sword, as audiences still have a hard time reconciling the fact that an actress playing an unlikeable character is not necessarily a terrible person herself. It might be that onscreen and offscreen just get confused by audiences—and this is not something that happens that much to male leads. *Cruel Intentions* (1999), the nineties teen adaptation of *Dangerous Liaisons*, transforms the Marquise de Merteuil into Kathryn Merteuil. Actress Sarah Michelle Gellar, going against her good girl image (Buffy Summers being mean and talking about anal sex? Shocking to behold), revels in the bile of this teenage, hyperprivileged hell-raiser. Gellar is the saving grace of this otherwise highly questionable adaptation that tries to make Valmont the main character of the story.

The Last Seduction was a hit on home entertainment. In an interview with film critic Roger Ebert in 1995, Linda Fiorentino joked:

> I've gone on a few dates since *The Last Seduction* came out and I could see the disappointment in the eyes of men who thought I was going to be a hot date and teach them all this weird stuff. And then they find out I'm just

a normal person, you know, and I don't have leanings toward strange sexual behavior and it's like a disappointment crosses their faces.

In this interview, Ebert pointedly describes her as "likable and warm," but Fiorentino, despite receiving accolades for her performance, was branded as "difficult" fairly swiftly and didn't have any more leading roles after *The Last Seduction*, disappearing completely from the film industry in the late nineties. It was reported that, despite the ending of *Men in Black* implying that there was a future for her character, actor Tommy Lee Jones only agreed to return for the sequel if Fiorentino was not part of the cast.

Unlikeable characters fuck with the audience. They're constantly asking us: Do you like me? Do you fear me? Do you want to be me? Do you want to get rid of me? These roles, when embodied by women, play on the star persona and screen charisma of the actress more than with male performers. It's not surprising that many actresses refuse to play unlikeable, or unredeemable, characters—even if successful, it might be damaging to their careers. There is an industry-wide awareness of how strangely difficult it is for audiences to separate the woman from the character. Other actresses, of course, seek these types of characters out (Davis, Stanwyck, Fiorentino). They are meatier roles. And this is why the Bitch is inextricably linked with the power of the performer who embodies her.

Because it's always a question of power. Despite talent, beauty, and success, actresses have to consciously tiptoe around the old-fashioned expectations of likeability both onscreen and off. There is spitting distance between being a bitch onscreen and being branded "difficult" offscreen. As critic Kristen Lopez writes, "When it comes to an actress's stardom, success is never attributed to the individual, but failure is." Whereas we afford the luxury of "innocent until proven guilty to men," especially powerful ones, once a woman is accused of being a bitch—that's it. Fiorentino, like many other actresses before and after her, was branded "difficult" and that was that. She's never spoken publicly about what really happened or why she stopped acting, whether the roles dried up or there were industry politics involved. The label of "difficult woman" is notoriously, painfully obtuse. But once it's there, it's almost impossible to unpick. Lopez continues: "The 'bitch' persona started to take hold, situating her as an actress men would have to break down or chip away at."

The intense push-and-pull reaction of audiences to bitchy characters onscreen is that they make us react. They inspire both feelings of attraction and rejection. We both want to be them and we despise them. Author Laurie Penny, in her 2017 book of essays *Bitch Doctrine*, writes: "We're taught, as women—especially as women—that before anything else, we must make ourselves agreeable. We must shrink ourselves to fit the room, and shave down the ideas to fit the times." The Bitch does the exact opposite. She *explodes* from the screen. When we see Bridget Gregory rudely demand a Manhattan, or Miranda Priestley demolish a designer's new collection with a single side-eye, we want to scream at the screen, "God, what a bitch." And then we laugh. We want to keep watching. Lena Headey (who played Cersei Lannister in *Game of Thrones* from 2011 until 2019) has spoken about the bile poured on her by fans of the show. Talking to *Time* magazine in 2017, she explained about how this reaction changed as the seasons of *Game of Thrones* progressed: "I get people saying what a great performance, and that's obviously a very nice thing to hear. But it's changed a little bit, because at the beginning, people were like [in American accent] 'Oh my God, you're such a bitch!'"

WHO GETS TO BE A BITCH

There's been something that has permeated the examples I've brought to the forefront so far: these women that play the Bitch, most of them are young and all of them are white. Most of the time, they are also rich (or aspire to be). It's worth noting how dangerously close the notion of Bitch strays to the pervasive, racist stereotypes of the Angry Black Woman or the Dragon Lady. Anne Helen Petersen writes: "The prevalence of straight white women serves to highlight an ugly truth: that the difference between cute, acceptable unruliness and unruliness that results in ire is often as simple as the color of a woman's skin, who she prefers to sleep with, and her proximity to traditional femininity." Petersen is not talking strictly about film and TV here, but the same notion applies.

That's been the case with cinema, a space where, for a long time, the closest a Black woman was allowed to get to being a bitch onscreen was Dorothy Dandridge's interpretation of Carmen in the 1955 musical *Carmen Jones*. Based on the Georges Bizet opera, the film was notable at the time for being the first large-scale Hollywood musical with an all-Black cast, led by Dandridge and Harry Belafonte as her love interest, a handsome and naive Army officer. Carmen is a seducer, and enjoys destroying a man's life and future marriage because she is bored. Which makes her a fantastic character, and Dandridge goes all in with her performance, spikey and seductive. But spoiler alert for a story from 1875: she is killed at the end for her transgressions.

It would be on television, though, and not the big screen, that a Black woman would be first allowed to be as nasty as her white counterpart and benefit from it. Circling back to *Dynasty*, alongside Alexis, her archnemesis Dominique Deveraux and the actress who plays her, Diahann Carroll, are incredibly important. In a filmed interview from 1984, Carroll declared in no uncertain terms: "I want to be the first Black bitch on television." Carroll called her manager and got them to "get the word around and call Aaron Spelling" to ensure her casting.

Dominique first appears in season five—mysterious, elegant, wealthy, ruthless—as the show's main villainess. Carroll pitched to the *Dynasty* producers:

> I think the most important thing for us to remember is to write for a white male, and you'll have it. We'll have the character. Don't try to write for what you think I am, write for a white man who wants to be wealthy and powerful. And that's the way we found Dominique Deveraux.

In an interview at the time, Carroll said: "I've never played a role quite this unlikeable. And I like that. I like that very much because I think very often, particularly minorities, it's almost required of them that they are nice people, and I don't want to play a nice person." Before Dominique, there were very few

Black actresses allowed to play characters who would fit in this archetype of the Bitch.

Eartha Kitt's take on Catwoman was one, a character who continues to be one of the most influential comic book villainesses, a recurring foe (and often romantic interest) of Batman. Kitt would be the first but not last Black woman to play her, in the series' third and final series in 1967.[7] It was deliberate casting on the part of the show's producers (they called it "a very provocative idea"), and despite only portraying the character for one season, Kitt's artistic choices can be felt in every subsequent iteration of the character. The purring intonation, the flirty elongation of her words, the swagger with which she carried herself into every scene. Hers was a Catwoman who enjoyed being bad and who was more interested in amassing jewels, cat-themed paraphernalia, and power than she was in seducing Batman.[8]

Cookie Lyon on *Empire*, Annalise Keating on *How to Get Away with Murder,* and Olivia Pope on *Scandal* have marked an evolution, each a complicated protagonist with equal amounts of admirable and unlikeable traits. Cookie (Taraji P. Henson)— whose over-the-top antics and power player costuming owe much to the styling of Alexis, Dominique, and a dash of Joan Crawford—is a devoted wife and mother who did time in prison in order to protect her husband Lucious. *Empire* begins with Cookie's release from prison and determination to get the money and, most importantly, credit that she has earned and paid for.

---

7   Halle Berry followed in the ill-fated *Catwoman* (2004), and Zoe Kravitz voiced her briefly in *Lego Batman* (2017) and then took on the role in *The Batman* (2022).

8   The ugly truth of this shift away from the sexual tension between Catwoman and Batman was due to the taboo of interracial romances. The ban on interracial marriage was struck down only in 1967, the same year as Kitt's casting as Catwoman.

Cookie is outrageous in her ferocity but never falls into stereo-types. Instead, she explodes them ("You step between me, my artists, or my family again, you won't even hear the knock on the door"). She's competitive and commanding but has the talent-spotting and producing skills to back up her bravado. The soap opera stylings of *Empire* favor her OTT (over-the-top) outbursts, and there's many a scene of Cookie walloping her ex-husband, his girlfriend, or their grown sons; there are catfights and trash talk scenes aplenty, but Cookie's volatility is underpinned by a fierce defense of her family and their, and her own, legacy.

Olivia Pope (Kerry Washington), the media fixer and crisis manager at the center of Shonda Rhimes's *Scandal* is, at her best, an endlessly watchable moral conundrum. She is always immac-ulately dressed; lives a bougie, high-end lifestyle; owns her own business; and has a team devoted to her. She operates at the high-est levels of power, holding her own with people who make up the very system that is designed against people like her (as her villainous father constantly reminds her, she has to be "twice as good as them to get half as much"). Olivia's professional instincts are flawless and highly in demand, but the work itself is murky business. Her moral compass is constantly being negotiated—within herself and with us. This dance around what is good and what is necessary is symbolized throughout the show with a lit-eral and metaphorical "white hat." Kerry Washington plays Olivia with an unblinking ferocity that pivots the show from being a political thriller to a saucy soap opera from one scene to the next. She is in many ways the *opposite* of an unlikeable charac-ter: she is so likeable that we forgive her her moral transgressions, whether they be lying, cheating, manipulating, or even murder.

It's never quite clear where Olivia's self-preservation ends and her villainy begins. The stakes throughout *Scandal* become comically high—the show evolves from a crisis-of-the-week format to include political subterfuge, murders, secret spy organizations, and a long-standing affair between Olivia and the president of the United States—but it never lets us off the hook with this main question: Is Olivia Pope a good person doing bad things, or is she a villain who has convinced herself she's a good person?

In *How to Get Away with Murder*, another Shonda Rhimes creation, Annalise Keating, played by the formidable actress Viola Davis, exists in the same universe as but on a completely different moral playground from Olivia. Annalise, a successful defense attorney and university professor, elicits the same kind of dogged adoration from her team as Olivia does from her "gladiators." Yet, while Olivia's messiness is covered in layers of cashmere, there's a rawness and self-loathing to Annalise. While Olivia's murkiness and power grow as the seasons of *Scandal* progress, Annalise is broken down to the very raw parts of herself, her imbalances seemingly excused by a history of mental illness, her ambition treated not as a weapon but almost as a curse. "Who I am is a fifty-three-year-old woman from Memphis, Tennessee, named Anna Mae Harkness. I'm ambitious, Black, bisexual, angry, sad, strong, sensitive, scared, fierce, talented, exhausted," she declares herself when put on (literal) trial.

Annalise starts off as high powered, in control, and unwavering in her judgment of others, but as her backstory is revealed, the show seems to revel more in the damage she has incurred so that her unlikeable qualities become—again—excused by formative trauma. In a crossover episode in *Scandal*'s seventh season, Annalise and Olivia Pope meet and work together. Olivia calls Annalise a "hot mess" and Annalise fires back at Olivia for being a "bougie ass." Both characters are differently hued explorations of the Strong Black Woman stereotype, and how liked they are because of or in spite of their messiness is what sets them apart. "You judged me immediately, just like a white man in a boardroom, because my hips are too wide and hue too dark," snaps Annalise at Olivia as they sit in a hair salon. "Your skin tone and measurements are not why people don't like you. It's you. You, Annalise Keating, are a bully who insults people and then wonders why they won't help you." Olivia Pope chose likeability, while Annalise Keating chose self-awareness.

I hesitate to call these characters Bitches because they have elevated and complicated the archetype. They have gone beyond the campiness of Collins and Lange. Cookie, Annalise, and Olivia are ruthless, self-assured, and relentless—but they are not cruel. Television, with years of material and space to breathe and a renewed respect from the industry and the audience, lets its characters grow and develop and expand—but these characters sometimes play on the campiness of the performative bitchiness we know from previous incarnations to produce something a bit more sinister, like the icy political maneuvering of Claire Underwood (*House of Cards*). To quote the Guerilla Girls, "The 'bitch' is a stereotype in transition."

THE B WORD

The word "bitch," which I've been using so sparingly over this chapter so far, is one of the oldest words in the English language.

If you've made it this far, it may not be offensive, but chances are it's still an uncomfortable word to hear or read. I'm not ignorant of this tension. I have my own relationship with the word, as I imagine most women do. While I may be comfortable using it, individual reclamations do not make up for the cultural history of the word and how it's been used. Film writer Pamela Hutchinson wrote for *Tortoise Media*: "There's no denying the word has power, but that power has not yet been tamed."[9]

In 1968, writer and activist Jo Freeman published *The BITCH Manifesto*, a feminist pamphlet in which she defined characteristics that were considered negative in women but natural and assertive when displayed by men. She wrote:

> A Bitch takes shit from no one. You may not like her, but you cannot ignore her... [Bitches] have loud voices and often use them. Bitches are not pretty... Bitches seek their identity strictly thru themselves and what they do. They are subjects, not objects... Often they do dominate other people when roles are not available to them which more creatively sublimate their energies and utilise their capabilities. More often they are accused of domineering when doing what would be considered natural by a man.

At one point, I found this definition empowering. Now you

---

9   Full disclosure: Hutchinson's essay on the cultural history of the word was in response to my own program of films at the British Film Institute in June 2019 and an event I programmed where writers and thinkers debated whether it was possible or even appropriate to use this word in a public sphere. Even though we stood on different sides of the argument, the considered tone in the essay was, I think, the best outcome of that debate.

can't scroll through Instagram for more than twenty seconds without stumbling upon a motivational post about being a "bad bitch," friends calling each other "bitch" affectionately, and unending "basic bitch" memes. The word is no longer banned on TV (my mind instantly goes to *Ted Lasso*, where the thirteen-year-old niece of Rebecca Welton calls her a "boss-ass bitch" as the ultimate seal of teenage approval and admiration), which it was until relatively recently (Britney's "Work Bitch" video was not allowed to be screened in the United Kingdom before 10:00 p.m. in 2013).

The word "bitch" may have lost some of its bite, but it's not lost its power. In all honesty, I'm not sure where I stand on the word myself, even though I use it sparingly with close female friends. I use it as an exclamation point, as a token of affection, to refer to myself. I've also been called a bitch without the endearment, and when armed with a different intent, it feels like a gut punch. It's a word seeping with intention, and depending on who's saying it, and in what context, it can morph from a term of empowerment to a heinous insult.

The origins of the word lie in the Old English "bicche," referring to a female dog, and its earliest use as an insult was to refer to a promiscuous woman (the insult "son of a bitch" makes sense with this in mind). The term started being used as a gendered insult in the eighteenth century—when new terms had to be found for actual bitches, meaning female dogs. The generalization of the word has always been tied to culture and politics. There was a dramatic rise in the use of the word after some women got the right to vote in 1920 (the use of the word in newspapers and American literature doubled between 1915 and 1930). There was another cultural spike in the 1970s with second-wave feminism and in music: Jo Freeman released her *The BITCH Manifesto* in 1968; Miles Davis named his 1970 jazz album *Bitches Brew*; the Rolling Stones put out the song "Bitch" in 1971; the same year, David Bowie released "Queen Bitch"; and in 1974 Elton John put out "The Bitch Is Back." In 1979, popular author Jackie Collins published her seventh novel, *The Bitch* (with the tagline "She's a woman who always gets what she wants"), which got adapted into a film that same year starring, who else, Collins's sister Joan.

The "bitch" moniker went from referring to promiscuous women to referring to ruthless women via its first attempted reclamation by feminists and turned violent in the 1980s, fitting in with the backlash to feminism that Susan Faludi wrote about, and in the late eighties and early nineties, the "bitch" became a battleground in music and politics. Third-wave feminists tried to reclaim the word using music as a battleground, with female rappers at the forefront: in 1993 Queen Latifah rapped against the word in her anthem for gender equality, "U.N.I.T.Y."; that same year, Salt-N-Pepa referred to bitches as successful women being criticized for their success in "Big Shot"; Lil' Kim crowned herself the "Queen Bitch" in 1996; rapper Trina released the single "Da Baddest Bitch" in 1999, redefining the bitch as a woman in control of her sexuality and of her life; and Missy Elliott reclaimed the insult in her 1999 track "She's a Bitch." Outside of rap, "All Women Are Bitches" was released by the all-female band Fifth Column in 1994; Meredith Brooks had a pop hit with her single "Bitch" in 1997; and in 1996 Madonna declared, "I'm tough, ambitious, and I know exactly what I want. If that makes me a bitch, OK." Since the 2010s, the expression "resting bitch face" (or RBF) has permeated pop culture, becoming a widely used term understood to denote a woman's blank facial expression.[10] The stupidity of this concept has been much parodied, but it is yet another microweapon to use against women on a daily basis. If you're not smiling, you're not amenable. If you're not projecting a welcoming presence, you must "fix your face." When a word is historically rooted in discomfort with women gaining any power, it's going to need a bit more than a catchy tune to untangle all the hate it carries. The nineties turned the word "bitch" into a girl power brand. Alison Yarrow writes about it in her study of nineties media culture: "'Bitch' and its villainous corollaries became a bad-girl identity to sell—a sly marketing tool."

After months of rewriting this chapter, I still don't know where I land. I've said it plenty and embraced it on many occasions—and then that reclamation has been punctured by the reminder that not everybody is onboard with it. Not everyone is thinking of Britney's "You better work, bitch" when they say it. Not everybody who's called me a bitch was thinking of Jo Freeman's manifesto. No matter the reclamation, it's still a one-word punch. I know what men mean when they've called me a bitch.

And yet, it's not the songs I think about, it's not pop anthems that I think about. I think about the confidence of Bridget Gregory—not trying to be inspirational, not trying to sell me empowerment on a T-shirt, not trying to teach me a lesson, but

---

10   In 2015, there was a study conducted by researchers from Noldus Information Technology that determined that RBF was a "real thing" that expressed contempt even when in a neutral resting mode. Science.

simply taking on the misogynistic violence of the word and turning it around. Because she's a Bitch and she wins. She's not ignorant of the misogyny implicit in the word, but she's not letting it
touch her. She's impervious.

"*The weird thing about hanging out with Regina is that I could hate her, and still wanted her to like me.*"

CADY HERON, *MEAN GIRLS*

"*God forbid I exude confidence or enjoy sex. Do you think I relish the fact that I have to act like Mary Sunshine 24/7 so I can be considered a lady?*"

KATHRYN MERTEUIL, *CRUEL INTENTIONS*

"**Grace:** *You're a terrible person.*
Chanel Oberlin: *Maybe. But I'm rich and I'm pretty, so it doesn't really matter.*"

CHANEL OBERLIN, *SCREAM QUEENS*

The Mean Girl

In high school, appearances are everything. So even the illusion of power is enough to cause permanent psychological damage. A teenage girl who knows how to wield her power, even if her kingdom is barely more than the halls of a high school, is terrifying. So when the most popular girl in school tells you your skirt is "adorable," that's a ray of social sunshine. And if you overhear her, a second later, say, "That is the ugliest f-ing skirt I've ever seen," well, that might be silly, but it stays. We've all had a Regina George in our lives, and since 2004, she's become the default Mean Girl, a trope that has been present in teen cinema so much that she is ubiquitous in the genre.

Try to think of a single high school movie without a mean girl. I'll wait.

It's impossible. Often, they are the standout characters of their respective teen movies because they are provocative, rude, and fearsome. Teen movies—next to horror—make for one of the subgenres where female villains thrive. It's only within the highly structured world of high school that we can explore the extremes of human emotion, backstabbing, and seemingly immense stakes, all while not actually risking all that much. The Mean Girl looms large in this genre as an amplification of a teenage bully, or antagonist, or frenemy that we've all had in our lives. She gets her strength from creating a culture of fear, and the specter of our own personal mean girls can live on for years after we've left the high school hallways. Unlike horror films, where the stakes are your life, in high school the most important thing of all is your reputation. The barometer of reputation might have changed from having good hair to your number of Instagram or TikTok followers, but the principles of popularity remain the same. Everyone's been a teenager, so it's a genre that's constantly being recycled, with an endless audience.

A BLOND DICTATOR

We first see Regina George being carried onto a field atop the shoulders of men, like teen royalty. The queen bee of *Mean Girls* (2004) is presented to us through her reputation and through rumors before we ever hear her speak.

"She has two Fendi purses and a silver Lexus," says one girl.

"I hear her hair's insured for $10,000," says another.

"I hear she does car commercials. In Japan."

"Her favorite movie is *Varsity Blues.*"

"One time, she met John Stamos on a plane. And he told her she was pretty."

And the kicker: "One time, she punched me in the face. It was awesome."

The story of *Mean Girls* is Cady's education in the microcosm of high school society. Although Cady is the protagonist (and Lindsay Lohan was at the peak of her career as a teen star at that point), Regina George is the most memorable—and memeable—character from *Mean Girls*. This was Rachel McAdams's (now an Academy Award–nominated actress) breakout role. At this point in her career, the Canadian-born actress's biggest gig had been playing the teenage girl that Roy Schneider body swaps with in *The Hot Chick* (2002). She was a fresh face onto which we could project all the real-life mean girls we'd known.

"Evil takes a human form in Regina George," says Janis (Lizzy Caplan), the art goth and former childhood friend of Regina who is still seething about being iced out by her years ago. "Don't be fooled, because she may seem like your typical selfish, back-stabbing, slut-faced ho-bag. But in reality, she is so much more than that." Janis is talking to Cady, a new student at their high school who's just moved to Chicago from Africa[1] and who is essentially a social virgin, never having been enrolled in a school before. As Regina is royally deposited on the lawn, she laps up the attention in slow motion to the tune of Missy Elliott's "Pass that Dutch." The image that she has created and that perpetuates itself.

Regina is—literally—elevated to a regal status. Like a monarch (or a blond dictator), she is feared and revered. It's exactly how we elevate our high school mean girls, granting them a quasidemonic level of meanness, imbuing them with a desire to

---

1   *Mean Girls*, while brilliant in many ways, also has a lot of problematic elements, namely its casual racism, which doesn't end with its conflating the African continent with a country.

hurt other kids so intense that we are prone to forget that they are kids themselves.

I've had Reginas in my life too. Girls that age have been attuned to psychological warfare like no one else. When I was fourteen or so, having recently changed schools due to relentless bullying, I was targeted by two older girls almost instantly. They would sit either side of me at lunch and order me to not listen while they spoke. They'd test whether I was really listening by whispering insults into my ear. If I reacted, I'd be caught. If I didn't, they'd still do it the next day. Mean Girls know how to set a psychological bear trap.

We don't need to dig too deep to understand why the Mean Girl is one of the most popular unlikeable female character tropes. She's pretty to look at, quotable, and, to quote Damian (Daniel Franzese), "always looks fierce." Nobody likes a bully, but it becomes difficult when the bully also embodies all the aspirational qualities that teenage girls are meant to strive for. The Mean Girl is always beautiful, always popular, always smart. So why, then, is she so damn mean?

PLUG IT UP

As with most good things, the Mean Girl started crystallizing as a trope in the first golden age of slasher horror films in the 1970s and in the related golden age of 1980s teen movies. In 1976's *Carrie*, Brian De Palm's adaptation of Stephen King's debut novel, the titular character is a shy, socially inept teenage girl who's being bullied by her hyperreligious mother as well as the teen girls at school. One of them, Chris Hargensen (Nancy

Allen), is so committed to making Carrie suffer that she literally talks about the girl while giving her boyfriend a blowjob.
"I hate Carrie White," she says, both her boyfriend's penis and
Carrie's name in her mouth. She plots with another girl to make
Carrie prom queen so they can dump a bucket of pig's blood on
her. They succeed, and Carrie is humiliated. Unfortunately for
the Mean Girls, the distress of this situation makes Carrie lose
control of her burgeoning telekinetic powers and she annihilates
everyone at the prom.

In the 1980s, writer-director John Hughes dominated the
teen genre with films like *Sixteen Candles* (1984), *The Breakfast
Club* (1985), *Weird Science* (1985), *Pretty in Pink* (1986), *Ferris
Bueller's Day Off* (1986), and *Some Kind of Wonderful* (1987).
Hughes's preoccupations were mostly with teenage boys—
more specifically, how nerdy teenage boys could get the girl,
or any girl—except for one exception: any film starring Molly
Ringwald, his collaborator and muse, who starred as the popular, mean-adjacent girl in *The Breakfast Club* and was the lead
in *Sixteen Candles* and *Pretty in Pink*, in the latter of which her
character, Andie, was the target of Mean Girls for the social sin of
being poor. Hughes's films were rewritings of high school experiences as fantasies, ones in which the nerds were the protagonists
and got to hook up with the cute girls. Sometimes even the cute
girls (especially Ringwald's characters) read as gender-swapped
variations on the nerd. Hughes wrote honestly and earnestly,
with problematic warts and all, about the experience of being an
awkward teenager. But he couldn't write mean.

Before *Mean Girls*, there was *Heathers*. A film designed to
be timeless, it was released in 1989 but could've just as easily

been made in the 2000s, having a level of bile and casual girl-on-girl misogyny that would become so identifiable with the noughties. *Heathers* was written by Daniel Waters (brother of *Mean Girls* director Mark Waters) as an attempt to make "a Stanley Kubrick teen film."[2] Both Waters and the film's director, Michael Lehmann, were relative newcomers to filmmaking, and this was their first film. They were not deliberately trying to make a cult classic (no one who intends to manages to), but they did. Despite being a box office bomb at the time of its original theatrical release, *Heathers* feels timeless. Although the shoulder pads and the cast (Winona Ryder, Shannen Doherty) might give it away, the dialogue is purposely not placeable in any particular era. "How very" is how they describe something cool. Someone who's complaining too much is being "a pillow-case." And who hasn't exclaimed, "Fuck me gently with a chain-saw, do I look like Mother Theresa?" when frustrated with a colleague?

Heathers is the first teen film to be truly concerned with the inner lives of mean girls. The title comes from the quartet of color-coordinated teens who are at the top of the high school food chain. There's Heather Chandler (Kim Walker), always in red; Heather Duke (Shannen Doherty), always in green; Heather McNamara (Lisanne Falk) in yellow; and the newest addition, Veronica (Winona Ryder), who wears blue. Veronica is smart, which allows her to see the power structures of their high school. So she decides to trade up:

---

2   He even sent the screenplay to Kubrick with the hopes he would direct it
    (Kubrick never replied).

My parents wanted to move me into high school out of the sixth grade, but we decided to chuck the idea because I'd have trouble making friends, blah, blah, blah. Now blah, blah, blah is all I ever do. I use my grand IQ to decide what color lip gloss to wear in the morning and how to hit three keggers before curfew.

She ghosts her childhood bestie in order to fit in with the Heathers, even though she doesn't even like them. None of them actually like one another, especially not Heather Chandler, the de facto leader.

While all high school experiences are inherently dramatic because they are being experienced for the very first time, *Heathers* takes it up an operatic notch by adding murder to the mix. Heather Chandler is accidentally-on-purpose poisoned by Veronica and her new manic pixie psycho boyfriend JD (Christian Slater), a new transplant to the school who wears a duster coat and equals her in his contempt for high school society. Heather Chandler's death shifts the movie into a new dimension. Teenagers aren't *supposed* to die in teen movies. They're definitely not supposed to murder each other, no matter how mean their behavior is (or how much we've all fantasized about getting back at our bullies). JD and Veronica frame Heather's murder as a suicide, which goes down so well that they begin a rampage, offing teenagers who annoy them. They lure two homophobic jocks to their death and frame their murders as a gay lovers' suicide pact. "Suicide gave Heather depth, Kurt a soul, and Ram a brain," muses Veronica in her dramatic diary entries. JD's outsider appeal is camouflaging a propensity for violence because, as Naomi Fry writes in the *New Yorker*, "he feels that first, his mom, and later, his girlfriend, didn't love him enough."

While Veronica is busy murdering with JD,[3] there is a power vacuum developing among the Heathers. There must always be a Mean Girl, the rudest and bitchiest among the group. Heather Duke, trading in her green colors for red, edges her way into the power seat, becoming even meaner than her predecessor. She has taken Heather Chandler's red scrunchie, the symbolic crown of their high school, for herself. When Veronica confronts her about it, asking, "Why are you such a megabitch?" Heather simply replies: "Because I can be."

Heather Chandler casts a dark shadow over the entire high school, though she is eliminated pretty early on in the film. She is all the things that we expect from a Mean Girl: pretty, rich, white, thin, blond, and relentlessly cruel. There's almost no humanity to her, except for one scene in which she is forced into a sex act she's clearly not comfortable with. In the next scene, we see Heather looking at herself in the mirror. Disgusted, she spits at her own reflection. Heather Chandler isn't just mean, she's angry, but she'll never allow anyone to see that. The Mean Girl's power is in maintaining appearances; a very specific appearance at that. For the film's thirtieth anniversary rerelease, I wrote about how, behind all the quippy quotes and mayhem, it's about how easy it is for us to ignore real teenage pain unless it is shown in excruciating, exaggerated form. The enduring power

---

3   It should be noted that it's mostly J. D. who does the murdering, and Veronica assists him, naively believing his claims that they're only going to give the kids they're targeting a scare. Red flag.

of *Heathers*, the source of its timelessness, is not the fashion or the colors: it's the fear. Even watching it as an adult, I'm kind of scared of the Heathers.[4]

Veronica knows she's better off being one of the Heathers than being one of their targets, even if being one of them makes her miserable. True to its operatic tone, *Heathers* ends with a literal bang: a huge bomb that is meant for the entire school, but which ends up only killing JD thanks to Veronica's interference—the film being a painful precursor to the sort of high school shootings that have become an all too normal fixture on the news. She is free. She takes away the red scrunchie and declares, much like burly men at the end of Westerns would, with a mix of solemnity and glee, "There's a new sheriff in town." And the new sheriff just intends to watch movies on prom night.

While Hughes's movies were fantasies, the high school of *Heathers* is a battlefield. At the end of the film, covered in soot, blood, and scratches, Veronica lights a cigarette, content for the very first time in the film. She's hardened and vindicated by her experiences. After all this, Veronica doesn't give a flying fuck about her reputation anymore—and that is true liberation for a teenage girl. *Heathers* is brutal, but its ending is somewhat optimistic, with Veronica releasing herself—and, it's implied, the rest of the high school—from the clutches of the Heathers' reign of teen terror. We'll never know what happened next, but I like to think that Veronica used her grand IQ for something more fulfilling than picking out lip gloss.

---

4   When I met Lisanne Falk, who played Heather McNamara, the yellow Heather, and the film's director, Michael Lehmann, for a Q&A I was hosting with them, I had trace amounts of fear. They were both lovely though.

SOCIOPATHS IN HEELS

While *Heathers* was ahead of its time, in the 1990s and the 2000s the teen genre fully took form, mining classic literature for stories and reinventing them for a teen palate. Jane Austen's *Emma* became *Clueless* (1995), wherein valley girl and argyle-print enthusiast Cher Horowitz meddles in her friends' lives. Shakespeare's *The Taming of the Shrew* was transformed into the alt-teen girl classic *10 Things I Hate About You* (1999) with Julia Stiles, and *Othello* became the very somber *O* (2001), with Mekhi Phifer as Othello, now a high school basketball player, Josh Hartnett as the jealous Iago, and Julia Stiles (again) as Desdemona. *Twelfth Night* got turned into *She's the Man* (2006), with Amanda Bynes passing herself off as a boy to infiltrate her high school's soccer team. And Baz Luhrmann's *Romeo + Juliet* (1996) used the Bard's words verbatim but placed the action among nineties LA criminal gangs, with baby-faced Leonardo DiCaprio's Romeo reimagined as a suit-wearing, softboi dream-boat who falls madly in love with Claire Danes's Juliet, the quirky princess daughter of the rival gangleader.

The horror space was once again reignited by teenagers with *Scream* (1996), a metaslasher that both delivered on and made fun of the genre; *I Know What You Did Last Summer* (1998) continued the slasher craze; *Disturbing Behavior* (1998) and *The Faculty* (1999) both reinvented *Invasion of the Body Snatchers* for a fresh audience with fresh faces; there were multiple sequels and remakes of classic teen horror properties, like *Carrie 2: The Rage* (1992), *H20: Halloween* (1998), and *The Craft* (1996), which combined mean girl dynamics with witchcraft, becoming a staple of Friday night cinema trips and sleepovers for several generations (show me anyone who hasn't tried the "light as a feather, stiff as a board" routine). These movies made money, and they were *fun*, bringing teenagers back into the cinema, who enjoyed seeing themselves onscreen being slashed and diced by one masked killer or another.

On TV, some of the biggest shows of the nineties and the noughties were focused on teens, including *Buffy the Vampire Slayer* (1998–2003), *Dawson's Creek* (1998–2003), and *Beverly Hills, 90210* (1990–2000). There was a generation of teenage stars who populated these movies and series; tall, clean-shaven young men who felt things very intensely, and straight-haired girls with doe eyes and feisty personalities. The appeal of the nineties star caste system was that it let us know exactly what to expect from Freddie Prinze Jr. (politely boring but reliable small-town boy), Ryan Phillippe (fuckboi with anger issues), Skeet Ulrich (probable psychopath with great hair), or Josh Hartnett (tall bad boy with abandonment issues) and created types of aspirational womanhood with their young female stars: Reese Witherspoon (virginal good girl), Katie Holmes and Jennifer Love Hewitt (obnoxiously gorgeous girls next door), Tara Reid (cool girl with a potty mouth), and Sarah Michelle Gellar (opinionated, petite badass).

In 1999, *Les Liaisons dangereuses* was turned into *Cruel Intentions*, the teenage thriller about high school politics and aggressive horniness. Any subtlety in the Pierre Choderlos de Laclos novel is erased in favor of campy and explicit dialogue between uberprivileged teenagers.[5] The premise is essentially

5   I'm not complaining, but it is what it is.

the same: bored, rich teenagers play with the lives, emotions, and virginities of others. The film turns the flirting socialites into stepsiblings, adding a little incestuous spice into the mix. Sebastian Valmont (Ryan Phillippe) is bored of having sex and humiliating every girl in the Upper East Side's social elite, and Kathryn (Sarah Michelle Gellar) makes a wager with him to get back at her ex-boyfriend, offering up herself as the prize. Sebastian is to bed the virginal Cecile (Selma Blair), and if he succeeds, he gets to bed Kathryn too.

Kathryn is a "predator in brown lip liner" played by the then beloved star of *Buffy the Vampire Slayer* Sarah Michelle Gellar, who goes against her established star persona and trades her wholesome image as the (literal) savior of the world for that of an Upper East Side manipulatrix who keeps her cocaine in a crucifix necklace. The *New York Times* called her "a snide, potty-mouthed brat." Kathryn, like all Mean Girls, is extremely intelligent—and extremely frustrated. She understands the limitations and expectations of her gender. In an icy monologue, she complains about having to pretend to be the "Marcia fucking Brady of the Upper East Side"; having to hide her true nature makes Kathryn even meaner ("It's okay for guys like you and Court to fuck everyone, but when I do it I get dumped for innocent little twits like Cecile. God forbid I exude confidence and enjoy sex. Do you think I relish the fact that I have to act like Mary Sunshine 24/7 so I can be considered a lady?").

In her opulent house, she wears two faces: the Catholic schoolgirl who is a model student and president of the student union and the manipulative, coke-addicted, bored, Mean Girl who enjoys toying with everyone around her, including

Sebastian. Kathryn is punished at the end when Cecile distributes copies of Sebastian's diary to the entire school, exposing her. The film was a commercial success (grossing $13 million in its opening weekend), and it was a bold choice for Gellar to play a villainous character, considering her star was rising as a vampire-hunting valley girl on television. But like all Mean Girls, she must be punished, and not rehabilitated.

That same year, another dark fairytale of high school politics came out in cinemas. *Jawbreaker* (1999) started off with a teen girl, Liz, being accidentally murdered by her group of friends in a birthday prank gone wrong. Egged on by their Mean Girl leader, Courtney Shayne (Rose McGowan), they stage a supposed crime scene to make it look like Liz had been assaulted and killed by an unsavory partner. Courtney is remorseless, even callous about her friend's death. ("I killed Liz. I killed the teen dream. Deal with it.") When she realizes a mousy student called Fern (Judy Greer) has overheard (and, unbeknownst to her, recorded) her accidental confession, Courtney remakes Fern into a slicker, prettier, more popular version of herself, renaming her Vylette ("You're the shadow, we're the sun"). When Vylette, who's learned too well how to be a Mean Girl, out-bitches Courtney, she tears her down without a second thought, revealing to the entire school that Vylette is just Fern. *Jawbreaker* purposefully doesn't give us any explanation as to why Courtney is quite so spiteful, which in itself is subversive. Speaking to *Refinery29* on the film's twentieth anniversary, McGowan called her "punk-meets-sociopath-meets-Bette-Davis-meets-hell-on-wheels" and relished the fact that there is no explanation for her meanness. "Courtney is angry, dark, and ruthless simply because it is," she said.

Just like Kathryn in *Cruel Intentions*, Courtney gets her come-uppance in the form of public humiliation. When she's crowned prom queen, her cover-up of Liz's death is revealed, and she's booed off stage by a disgusted crowd of students. In agonizing slow motion, Courtney falls apart. The camera stays still on her contorting face as she moves through the prom crowd hurling insults and corsages at her. She's reduced to a friendless, disheveled mess and photographed at her most humiliated. In *Cruel Intentions*, once Kathryn is exposed she has to endure her school looking at her, at the real her, feeling the disgust in their eyes, her carefully built reputation falling apart before her. Kathryn's eyes well up with tears, but we're not supposed to care. The Mean Girl's worst nightmare is to be exposed like this, to be hated by the peers she once ruled over. The films that feature these Mean Girls take pleasure in delivering their comeuppance, usually employing slow motion to really drill down how much we should enjoy the undoing of these teenage girls.

While she must be desirable, the Mean Girl must remain unattainable—so she has to police her sexuality. She might be promiscuous, or sexually savvy, but no one should ever know, lest it diminish her acceptability in high school society. It's her secret power that she uses to continue exerting control over others: in *Jawbreaker*, Courtney makes her boyfriend give a blowjob to a Popsicle, exerting her dominance over him. In *Cruel Intentions*, Kathryn uses sex to lure Sebastian into doing her bidding, literally rubbing herself against him ("I hate it when things don't go my way—it makes me so horny") and offering herself up as a prize. In a more explicit way than her adult predecessor, Kathryn is overtly sexual but keeps that as a secret, knowing that enjoying sex will brand her negatively. *Cruel Intentions*, while featuring comically titillating scenes (think of the slow-motion French-kissing lesson between Gellar and Selma Blair), is as sex negative as the decade it was conceived in. While Sebastian—who has a very limited grasp on the idea of consent and starts off the film with an act of early-internet revenge porn—is so bored he barely considers the women he's having sex with as people, the only female character whose sexuality is not played for laughs or as a damning personality trait is Cecile, who only loses her virginity to Sebastian after they fall in love with each other.

The Mean Girl is a constant staple of the teen movie, and for the most part she's not been allowed to evolve that much. She's the foil to the protagonist, she's a bully, she's vain, and she's in love with the power her social status affords her. Every film needs to end by putting her in her place one way or another—with the protagonist taking away her boyfriend through a public humiliation or, in the blackest of comedies or horror scenarios, with her grizzly death. Her preoccupation is never to get more power—there's never any ambitions post-high school for her—it's always about the preservation of power. The Mean Girl exists only in our collective memory of high school, which explains her ubiquity in teen pop culture and the larger-than-life power she's given onscreen, which merits her larger-than-life punishment.

In these films, the Mean Girl is mostly preoccupied with her looks, her boyfriend, and her social status (which is derived from the former two). The fact that all these films include a transformation of a good girl into a Mean Girl supplements the performative nature of girlhood. Heather Duke becomes the new Heather Chandler in *Heathers*; Vylette tries to become the new Courtney in *Jawbreaker*; Cady becomes the new Regina in *Mean Girls*. In these films, teenage girls are taught that they can only yield power by zeroing in on a provocative yet inaccessible sexuality that is tailor made for men, and by channeling all their bile into belittling other women. The Mean Girl is always a source of fear and at the top of the high school social hierarchy. If we consider high school to be the training ground for adult society, then the Mean Girl is a bitch in training, but one who must keep the edges of her personality in check for the (mostly male) authority figures.

On rare occasion, the Mean Girl is allowed to be redeemed (unless she is fully murdered). On *Buffy the Vampire Slayer*, Cordelia Chase (Charisma Carpenter) was the high school antagonist to Buffy, annoyed that she'd spurned being in her queen bee clique in favor of the less cool Willow and Xander. In a town overflowing with supernatural creatures, Cordelia is still the meanest one of them. While Buffy has the super-strength of the Slayer, Cordelia has a mean streak that will quiet even demons ("See, in the end Buffy is just the runner-up. I'm the queen. You get me mad, what do you think I'm gonna do to you?"). Her character evolution took her from classic Mean Girl to someone entirely different, resolute, and generous. She begins as a mirror image of Buffy Summers (Sarah Michelle Gellar), who has all the ingredients to be a Mean Girl but has been forced to grow up much more quickly due to the responsibility of being the Slayer. Throughout the three seasons of *Buffy the Vampire Slayer* in which she appears, Cordelia goes from presenting herself as a ditzy, superficial queen bee (the self-described "nastiest girl in Sunnydale history") to a full-fledged member of the Scooby Gang. Cordelia's journey involves realizing that she's allowed to have a full spectrum of emotions, including the painful ones ("You think I'm never lonely because I'm so cute and popular?"), and that despite her Sunnydale status, she is not untouchable.

EVERYONE IS A MEAN GIRL

While it took Cordelia several seasons and two different shows to evolve from a Mean Girl into a rich, empathetic character, Regina George marks the perfect evolution of a Mean Girl from villain into main character in a single film. *Mean Girls* is the first movie in which every single character is mean—Regina, Cady, Janis, and almost every background character—but also gets a chance to redeem themselves. There is not just one "bad apple" in *Mean Girls*; the film recognizes that the entire system is broken.

At the end of the film, although it's Cady who's punished socially and not Regina (though she does get run over by a bus), the whole high school popularity contest is called into question. Cady redeems herself by breaking up, literally and symbolically, the prize that they had all been fighting for: the prom queen crown. I'm sorry, the Spring Fling queen crown. She divides the plastic crown among the girls she's hurt, as well as among other girls from the school. Her point: that it's all pointless anyway, so why should we demonize each other over nothing. The social hierarchy of their high school is torn down, and Regina finds a new niche and a healthier way to express her aggression in sports ("...because the jock girls weren't afraid of her"). Cady and she exchange a knowing nod, and they're both happier outside of the oppressive, reductive role of the Mean Girl.

Mean Girls crystalized all the appeal of watching high school sadism from afar and captured the public consciousness in a way that has persisted throughout the years. Regina thrives on control, and that control comes from manipulation and bullying. Tina Fey, who spearheaded the project, basing it on the 2002 self-help book *Queen Bees and Wannabes*, which explores the psychology of teen girl cliques and the patterns of relational aggression that exist between girls, recalled that she

> revisited high school behaviors of my own—futile, poisonous, bitter behaviors that served no purpose. That thing of someone saying, "You're really pretty" and then, when the other person thanks them, saying, "Oh, so you agree? You think you're pretty?" That happened in my school. That was a bear trap.

In April 2014, celebrating the film's ten-year anniversary, the *New York Times* reported that Tumblr "users have created more than 10,000 posts and 477,000 notes related to the film" that month alone. October 3 has become known as Mean Girls Day (after one scene in which Cady's crush, Aaron Samuels, asks her what day it was: "On October 3rd he asked me what day it was"). Lacey Chabert, who plays Regina's second-in-command, Gretchen, has said that she has "fetch" tweeted at her at least a hundred times a day. "So you agree," taken from a moment of pure girly manipulation in the film, has become a meme used to critique political hypocrisy. Ariana Grande's music video for "thank u, next" starts off as a direct homage to *Mean Girls*, including a cameo by Aaron Samuels himself ("Ariana Grande said my hair looked sexy pushed back").

The Mean Girl is cruel and, with the exception of Cordelia (and until Regina came along), had always been presented as irredeemable. She's evil, rotten to the core, and if allowed to progress, she'll surely end up hurting more people. She's rarely allowed an inner life and is usually painted as such a black-and-white villain that we are meant to relish her pain. Perhaps burdened by my own inability to escape the real-life Mean Girls of my life, I always saw them as sadistic creatures. Growing older, and rewatching these films, there are always hints at a brewing frustration that had nowhere to go.

MISERABLE SUPERBITCHES

In *Heathers*, although we only see a glimpse of that frustration, when Heather Chandler is aghast at seeing that Veronica does not go through with the sex acts that the frat boy was trying to force on her—while Heather did and visibly regrets it. She lashes out at Veronica out of anger at herself. In *Cruel Intentions*, Kathryn is frustrated by having to maintain appearances and not having the freedom of her half brother Sebastian to be anything but sweet and compliant. In *Sex Education*, the Netflix show created by Laurie Nunn, the Mean Girl evolves into a full-fledged character. In fact, two full-fledged characters.

Maeve Wiley (Emma Mackey) is introduced in a very similar way to Regina George and Courtney Shayne. We hear the rumors about her before we hear her speak:

"I heard Maeve Wiley bit Simon on the scrote and now it's all wonky. Like a discount avocado."

"I heard she sucked off twelve guys in ten minutes for a dare."

"She's basically a nympho."

Even Otis (Asa Butterfield), who will spend the next three seasons quietly pining for Maeve as they become friends, says, "She's not popular; she's scary." We see her in full war mode (remember, high school is a battlefield). Maeve is a Mean Girl with a different kind of power: she's not popular; she's *feared*.

Ruby Matthews (Mimi Keene), meanwhile, falls in the more traditional category of the Mean Girl. She's pretty, is well liked, has an entourage who she treats like shit, and loudly passes judgment on everyone who walks by her as a hobby. Similar to the Plastics in *Mean Girls*, her clique has a name: the Untouchables. She remains firmly in the Mean Girl mold for most of the first two seasons, until slowly more details about her are given, revealing that her rich girl pretensions are a cover-up for a much humbler upbringing.

At the end of the second season of *Sex Education*, after a forgettable first sexual encounter with Otis, we start to see more of Ruby. The show's expansive net of characters allows even the meanest of the Mean Girls of Moordale to have layers. We learn that she doesn't come from a wealthy background, despite her obsession with expensive clothes. She's embarrassed about her home, and it's a major step for her to bring Otis to her house. Her father has recently been diagnosed with multiple sclerosis, so she is a caregiver. None of these are bad things: they are life experiences that give Ruby depth; they make her human, while traditionally the Mean Girl has been anything but.

Ruby and Maeve are two sides of the same Mean Girl coin. They are deeply afraid of people hurting or judging them, especially their peers, and see the adult responsibilities they've had to take on as negatives impacts on their character. Ruby rolls joints for her dad because his illness won't let him. Maeve parents herself—and her half sister, and occasionally her mother, who is struggling with addiction issues. They have had to make hard choices, and the easier path for them is to establish an untouchable reputation, either through fear or popularity—one that will let them navigate high school with the least amount of hassle and finger-pointing.

Their sexuality is a big part of that, as it always is with fictional Mean Girls and with real-life teenage girls everywhere. Maeve is slut shamed on the regular, while Ruby has tight control over who she's seen with. She begins a sexual relationship with Otis in the third season, keeping a tight lid on it because he is not "good enough" to be known to be sleeping with her. The highly crafted persona of Ruby the Mean Girl starts falling away as she reveals more of herself to Otis—and to us. She is tender, caring, and so very afraid of not being worthy. Her self-confidence is all for show and is attached to the markers of popularity: beauty, expensive-looking clothes, and her clique. Once she starts dating Otis publicly, she invites him into her home (which she is visibly embarrassed about) and declares her love for him. The series shows her twirling her fingers around the phone cord as she readies to tell him, "I love you," her face full of sweet excitement and anticipation at her feelings being reciprocated. Otis only responds with, "That's nice." It's a devastating moment, when a Mean Girl is allowed to be vulnerable.

Maeve, meanwhile, has her own will-they-won't-they romantic entanglement with Otis, which forms the backbone of the first three seasons. She is a deeply untrusting person, expecting everyone to let her down because, well, everyone has so far. She's also wildly smart and passionate about literature, especially female authors. Maeve is not actually aggressive at all, but she is an asshole in a way that all teenagers are assholes when they don't know how to react to an awkward or difficult situation. In an episode in the first season, in which a picture of Ruby's vulva is leaked to the entire school, Maeve is adamant about finding the culprit, correctly realizing that it must've come from another girl (because "emotional blackmail, demanding an apology: this is some girl shit"), not because of loyalty or friendship with Ruby, but because she is familiar with how easily shame sticks to a girl. It's the idea of "girl world" from Mean Girls all over again, and girls will use sex as a weapon against each other. Maeve recalls how she got her nickname, "Cock Biter":

Do you know how long I've been called Cock Biter? Four years. People I've never met call me Cock Biter to my face. I bit Simon Furthassle's scrote. I had sex with four guys at the same time. I fucked my second cousin. I'll give you a hand job for a fiver if you like. Do you know how it started? Simon tried to kiss me at Claire Tyler's fourteenth birthday. I said no. So he told everyone I'd given him a blow job and bitten his dick, and that was it. This kind of thing sticks.

Sex Education takes its time to uncover Maeve's character, and it never makes her into a charity case: it makes her vulnerable so we understand—but don't excuse—her meanness. The camera stays on Maeve's face after others around her leave, and that's when we see the real her. She almost says something sweet but then, backing down, falls into the performance of Mean Girl.

Maeve's and Ruby's meanness is treated as a relatable defense mechanism, an awkward and aggressive cover-up for their vulnerability. The show doesn't let them off the hook, though. They are, after all, really unkind to people around them, even and especially people they care about. They are never, however, presented as inhuman. The more we discover about their lives off campus, the more their behavior makes sense. The show lets them breathe and grow as characters who are full-fledged, with unlikeable qualities but qualities that are human. *Sex Education,* which *Esquire* described as being "the life and times of about a dozen high schoolers who really, really like to fuck," succeeds in recycling and building on the familiar high school tropes, including the Mean Girl.

While we had to read these layers of depth into even the most beloved of teen movies, like *Mean Girls* or *Heathers, Sex Education* makes the inner lives of its Mean Girls explicit. All the markers of meanness are still there, but the program shows the humanity beneath the meanness and breaks down the performance of being a girl trying to get through adolescence, mean or not. What this reveals is the internal battle that happens within every Mean Girl. On the one hand, there's all the privileges that youth and beauty affords them. On the other, there's the pressure of both bending to a power structure not designed for them (Mean Girls, after all, are disposable: they are not part of the high school economy in the same way that high school jocks are) and holding themselves to an impossible standard.

Looking back at several decades of the most memorable and

acid-tongued Mean Girls in pop culture, it all comes back to the early stages of slut shaming. The Mean Girl is always overly sexualized—but her actual sexuality is neutered in favor of a sexless sex appeal. The Mean Girl is designed to be fuckable, but not to actually fuck. Whether she does or doesn't, she will be punished. At worst, her own sexual agency is completely ignored or removed from her. I'm haunted by Heather Chandler being forced into oral sex and angrily lashing out at Veronica because she had refused to do the same. It's a short moment, but it's the one instance when we realize that Heather had no idea she could actually say no. So, although she is the Big Bad of every high school movie—and of many, very real high school experiences, including my own—there's nowhere for the Mean Girl to go but down. The way she is ultimately punished reinforces this idea that once a teenage girl transgresses the limits of her power, the most important thing about her—her *reputation*—will be irreparably damaged.

The larger-than-life figure of the Mean Girl on our screens taps into the muscle memory of our teenage insecurities, learned during a time when we were being fed vastly different narratives around our own sexuality depending on how we were socialized. The narrative around girls' virginity—and its sanctity—is everywhere: in horror movies, a virgin's blood is both a powerful tool and a delicacy; in teen movies, a virginal girl is unimpeachable and automatically deserving of respect; a sexually active teenage girl is de facto a Slut. Even Janis Ian from *Mean Girls* happily slut shames Regina. It's the go-to insult for the Mean Girl. She might be cruel, but what's worse is that she's *loose*. The quest to lose one's virginity is fodder for many teen comedies centered on boys—but it is treated as a life-or-death matter for a girl, a decision that everyone in their lives feels entitled to have a say in and that seems to have less to do with the act of sex itself and more to do with a girl's reputation. The discovery that a popular girl is a sexually active girl is equated by these films to her social demise—and a public one at that (remember the predilection for slow motion?). On shows like *Sex Education*, these social dynamics are explored at length and through multiple perspectives, male, female, and nonbinary, from straight and queer characters' points of view, and from the perspective of able-bodied and disabled characters. Exploring this interiority, and the push-and-pull pressure of being sexy but not too sexy, we see how quickly slut shaming can stick to a girl and the emotional baggage it leaves behind.

Growing up as a girl, there are contradictory rulebooks: you want to be as cool, as pretty, and as powerful as the Mean Girl (or at least enough to be on her good side), but you also don't want to step outside the bounds of what's sexually acceptable before you even understand your sexuality. I have distinct memories of girl assemblies that felt like UN negotiations: How and when is it appropriate to "lose it"? How long, how many dates, who with, what prerequisites do they needed to fulfill? The pressure, we're told, is life defining—and it's compounded by the self-fulfilling prophecy of pop culture narratives reinforced by our peers. But their biggest win is making us think that the teenage girl, mean or not, is a static being.

"Anger is reserved as a moral property of boys and men."

SORAYA CHEMALY, AUTHOR AND ACTIVIST

"What would the world look like if girls were taught they were volcanoes? What if instead of breaking their wildness like a rancher tames a bronco, we taught girls the importance and power of being dangerous? What if we told girls to erupt! What keeps girls from knowing their power?"

MONA ELTAHAWY, AUTHOR (@MONAELTAHAWY)

"There is little more threatening to the social order than a woman who's angry. The only thing scarier is a woman who's angry about something. The only thing scarier than that is a woman who's right."

JESS ZIMMERMAN, AUTHOR OF *WOMEN AND OTHER MONSTERS: BUILDING A NEW MYTHOLOGY*

The Angry Woman

Cinema has historically rewarded performances of angry men.

Jack Nicholson spit-yelling with fury in *A Few Good Men* (1992)? You get an Oscar nomination. Al Pacino's raspy outbursts in…every movie he's been in since 1992? Nomination, Oscar, nomination. When Leonard DiCaprio's screaming his face off in *The Great Gatsby* (2013), the vein on his forehead popping, breaking a cocktail glass? His entire face turns red and quivers with rage. He's doing so much work, we must applaud it! In *Pulp Fiction* (1994), Samuel L. Jackson's delivery of "Say 'what' one more time. I dare you, I double dare you, motherfucker!" has become a favorite moment in the cinephile and film bro canon. As Jules, he is torturing a man and recites a passage from the Bible that's all about "righteous fury." One of the most famed monologues delivered in screen history is that of Peter Finch's unhinged broadcaster Howard Beale in *Network* (1976). At this point in the film, Beale is to be unceremoniously fired from his newscaster job after decades of working for the same news division. He bursts into an angry tirade live on air, and this anger resonates with the executives and audience alike. His call to action is for people watching him to express their anger, stick their head out of their window, and scream: "I'm mad as hell and I'm not going to take it anymore!" What follows is a cacophony of voices, heads popping out from windows, screaming the mantra of anger into the city. The whole scene lasts just under four minutes, and it's four minutes of glorious fury.[1]

The quick-to-anger space-emo Kylo Ren (Adam Driver) in the newest entries into the Star Wars universe spawned a million memes, compilation videos ("Kylo Ren having anger issues for 1 minute and 22 seconds" has 1.4 million views on YouTube), and a hilarious *Saturday Night Live* skit in which Kylo is an undercover boss that "accidentally" kills any employee that bad-mouths him. Charlie Barber (Adam Driver again) punching a wall during an argument with his ex-wife Nicole (Scarlett Johansson) in *Marriage Story* (2019) has given birth to countless meme variations. Meanwhile, the most prolific Angry Woman memes are of Taylor Armstrong from *The Real Housewives of Beverly Hills* yelling at a cat and Bernadine Harris (Angela Bassett) walking away from a fire, a scene taken from *Waiting to Exhale* (1995)— a scene of triumph, judging by its meme legacy, taking away the painful context of Bernadine's complete betrayal at the hands of her husband of eleven years.

---

1   This monologue has become such an actor's staple, an exercise in fury, that it got Anya Taylor-Joy the role of Furiosa (in Spanish, "furiosa" is literally the feminized version of "angry"), and it was used by Agathe Rouselle in rehearsals to play the role of Alexia in the Palme D'Or–winning film *Titane*.

More recently, in 2019, *Joker* became a sensation as an origin story of sorts for one of Batman's most infamous foes. In the Todd Phillips film, the Joker is presented as an angry loner named Arthur Fleck (Joaquin Phoenix), forgotten by the system and dealing with severe mental health issues that are woefully unattended to by an overwhelmed medical system. This leaves him angry at everyone, individuals who have wronged him and a system that has ignored him, so he lashes out, killing an anchorman live on television and inadvertently kick-starting a radical movement of people just as angry as he is. *Joker* was knowingly trying to tap into the disillusionment and resentment felt by the protagonists of the early efforts of Martin Scorsese, like *Taxi Driver* (1976) and *The King of Comedy* (1982), but with the added value of a broad appeal superhero film. "The thing that this movie is really about is white male rage, white male rage, white male rage," *Saturday Night Live* staffer Melissa Villaseñor sang in a Weekend Update sketch about both *Joker* and, ironically, *The Irishman* (2019). The reactions to the film—which included both overwhelming critical support for Phoenix's performance and an aggressively defensive fandom—are a very recent example of the differences in how we talk about angry men versus how we talk about angry women. Angry women onscreen still scare us. Angry men do not.

In 2015, a study about jury deliberation bias conducted at Arizona State University found that "when men expressed their opinion with anger, participants rated them as more credible, which made them less confident in their own opinion. But when women expressed identical arguments and anger, they were perceived as more emotional, which made participants more confident in their own opinion." The same can be said in the context of movies. Cinema loves angry men but it doesn't quite know what to do with angry women. Cinema's angry men become icons, fan favorites, award winners, and thirst traps. Meanwhile, angry women are often severed from their anger, becoming either triumphant, one-note memes or messy reminders that angry women will never win unless they channel it into something productive. The screen loves those angry men who are righteous in their rage as well as those who just have short tempers. But we've got a real problem with allowing women to express that same range of emotion. We're told there is something uncouth, unseemly, unladylike, or ugly about a woman enraged.

Angry women onscreen are either cute anomalies (*Kick-Ass*), sexy assassins (*La Femme Nikita*), or righteous avengers (*Revenge*). These characters are always the exception instead of embodying a widespread, near universal feeling amongst women: simmering rage. Mostly their stories have been focused on the individual character. She's never angry on behalf of other women, and there has definitely been little room for intersectional anger; it's always a single bad apple or a traumatic event (usually a form of sexual assault) that has pushed a character to an emotional extreme. There needs to be an explanation; otherwise, it's just "her problem." Despite this, it's the female rage films that strike a cultural chord.

OFF THE CLIFF

In a 1991 road trip movie, two friends, Thelma (Geena Davis) and Louise (Susan Sarandon), both stuck in unhappy relationships, just want to go on a lil' getaway, have a nice time, get drunk, have a dance, see some sights. But a near rape forces them to go on the run. Louise saves her friend from the assault, but something dark within her is triggered by the sight (it is implied that Louise herself was assaulted in the past), and she shoots the man dead. The women are so convinced that the system would never believe them that they see no option but to go on the run. The men they encounter on the road are unapologetic, even when they have a gun pointed at them. Louise is ready to let Thelma's almost-rapist go, but he persists: "Suck my dick," he tells her. When a catcalling truck driver pulls over, they demand an apology with the same gun pointed at him. "Fuck that!" he says, and gloats about calling them "beavers." They shoot up his truck, and still he's at it ("You bitches from hell!"). Even the hot hitchhiker (Brad Pitt) Thelma spends a night with, and who steals their money, forcing them to rob a bank, does not apologize even as he's being hat slapped by the detective investigating Thelma and Louise. With police on their tail, they make a decision. "Everything we got to lose is gone anyway," says Thelma. They drive over the cliff, holding hands. Freeze-frame and fade to black.

Thelma & Louise struck an odd nerve when it was released. Although relatively tame by comparison to films released in the same year, like *The Silence of the Lambs* or *Cape Fear*, people accused it of promoting violence, of being "man-hating propaganda," of reducing men to "pathetic stereotypes of testosterone-crazed behavior." Thelma and Louise, who just wanted a break, were accused of being bad role models for women—the worst possible sin a fictional woman can commit. When something like *Network* or *Joker* comes around, male anger is rarely just about the one individual; it becomes an example of a universal truth, a commentary on wider injustice or an unfair system. These angry men are misunderstood prophets, truth tellers, a bit unhinged but ultimately right in their message. But when it's a woman's anger, they are seen to be bad apples at best and bad examples at worst.

Thelma & Louise's screenwriter, Callie Khouri, was angry at the "passive" role of women in movies when she wrote the screenplay: "They were never driving the story because they were never driving the car." She added that audiences "don't really want to see women operating outside the boundaries that are prescribed for them, misbehaving and enjoying themselves." I'd add to that they really didn't want to see angry women misbehaving.

Thirty years on after its original release, which was a box office and critical success despite the controversy, the film was elevated to canonical status. We often forget the darkness in *Thelma & Louise*, how trapped these women are that they decide that driving off a cliff is a better option than facing the authorities. There is an understanding between them—and the audience—that the system is just not built for them. Even in the case of the one good man cop who seems to empathize with them, there is no guarantee he'll protect them. It doesn't matter if their killing was justified or not; they're bound to be punished. If anything, it makes them even angrier, but at least they get to enjoy their outlaw lives for a minute. Louise doesn't shoot a man because he tried to rape her friend—she shoots him because she's angry, about Thelma's near assault, about her own assault, about the audacity of this man who doesn't care, not even a little, not even when there's a gun in his face. Louise knows that somehow they'd find a reason to blame it on them. After all, Thelma had been dancing with this guy all night. "We don't live in that kind of world, Thelma!"

Trauma begets violence in the Angry Woman. In all these films, the women die at the end or are bound to their anger in some way. Although they are radically different films, both stylistically and thematically, *Thelma & Louise* and *Promising Young Woman* (2020) share the same angry heart and hit a similar raw nerve.

SHE'S PRETTY WHEN SHE'S ANGRY

Picture this.

A woman, dressed in a slutty nurses' outfit, white knee-high stockings, ad a multicolored wig stands in front of a man tied to a bed. Her makeup is a grotesquerie of sexiness, extreme lashes, and thick red lips, pandering to the blind drunk, overgrown frat boys that are the attendees of this party. She ties the man to the bed and says her name is "Nina." That's not her name, but it gets a reaction from him, as expected. This is not a sex scene; it's a confrontation. Her name is Cassie, and Nina is the name of her best friend, who was raped by the man who is now tied to the bed. Devastated by the incident, Nina died by suicide. And now, years later, Cassie wants him to make a confession.

"I want you to tell me what you did," she demands.

"I didn't do anything; we were kids."

"If I hear that one more time." She tries to laugh it off.

"Maybe she regretted it after… I don't know."

"Oh yeah, she regretted it."

He's struggling, upset, denying any wrongdoing. She is simmering.

"I didn't do anything!" he pleads. Unconvincingly. We already know he's guilty. She knows it too.

"Wrong!"

This last one, it's a scream, her voice rising abruptly. This is the only time Cassie screams in the film, her anger overflowing. When you're angry, there is always a breaking point. This scene, in the final act of the film, is Cassie's. Played by Academy Award–nominated actress Carey Mulligan, Cassie in *Promising Young Woman* became a divisive symbol for female rage in 2020. And she made everyone extremely uncomfortable, because she required our looking directly into an ugly kernel of anger that is both righteous and self-destructive all at once. *Promising Young Woman*, with all its achievements and all its flaws, made us ask ourselves: How do we feel when confronted with female anger? What does it look like? Does it, or should it, have an acceptable face?

There is, as with everything else, a set of expectations for what female rage should look like. It has to be productive in some way, or at the very least entertaining. In the last decade, there have been few films that have galvanized, irritated, and provoked as intense a wave of anger as *Promising Young Woman*.

Written and directed by Emerald Fennell, who was nominated for three Academy Awards for her work on the film, it has achieved that rare thing for a movie: people can't stop talking about it. In the niche world of film critics and pundits as well as among mainstream audiences, it is extremely unusual for a film to continue generating conversation for as long as *Promising Young Woman* has. Film campaigns are flashy and concentrate mostly on the first week of release, when the publicity aligns reviews, interviews, profiles of the cast, glamorous photo shoots, and funny social media stunts to promote awareness of the film's release. After its buzzy premiere at the 2020 Sundance Film Festival (traditionally a stage for the most interesting new filmmakers and up-and-coming talent), the film languished in COVID-19 release limbo, with its U.S. and U.K. release dates being moved and pushed back for months till it landed on video on demand in the United States in January 2021 and in the United Kingdom on Sky Cinema in April 2021, just a few weeks before the Oscars ceremony.

For a film without a major release, without having even been screened in cinemas, to have galvanized a widespread conversation that had industry people frothing at the teeth with opinions is telling. *Promising Young Woman* is a Trojan horse of a film, not only in its exploration of the insidiousness of rape culture and the permissions we, as a culture, allow men but in how it shows the toxic unruliness of anger through Cassie. For all its flaws, *Promising Young Woman* accidentally sparked a conversation about just how uncomfortable we are with angry women when that anger has no clear target. The reactions to the film were, to be polite, mixed.

In an interview with *Entertainment*, Mulligan said, "We don't see women angry at all. We see lots of muted women." Cassie is muted until that moment when she yells "Wrong!" which comes out not as an outburst but as a detonation. Cassie is the Angry Woman in this film. She is a broken mess of a person, a shadow of herself who mourns the loss of her best friend, Nina. After Nina's suicide, Cassie drops out of med school and lives a shell of an existence. She's paralyzed, incapable of developing meaningful relationships, and managing her anger through revenge against all men. After her shift at the coffee shop is over, Cassie dresses up, pretends to be drunk in a bar, and waits. She allows herself to be picked up by men, and before a sexual assault happens, she "wakes up." Fully sober, fully in control, and to the shock of her would-be assailants. At night, Cassie lures these nice guys into… what exactly?

I love to see anger onscreen. It's an explosive, all-consuming emotion that I've experienced in others and that has engulfed me at times. It's cinematic, bodily, a full-throated feeling. White-hot rage blinds you and makes your blood run hot. It can be exhausting, destructive at its worst, and when controlled, can be turned into a positive. While it's a terrifying emotion to feel, it's exhilarating to watch, so I understand why it's attractive for actors—its scope is limitless, but it requires so much control of the craft to portray it convincingly, to make us feel it without getting burnt. If anger is a gradient, seeing a character go through one shade of rage to another is akin to feeling it yourself without ever being in danger of losing control.

Everyone has experienced it, felt rage at something or someone, at an annoyance or an injustice, at their own foolishness or someone else's maliciousness. Movies just dial it up to eleven. But there seems to be a knee-jerk reaction to seeing female rage onscreen. There seems to be, once more, a correct way for women to be angry—and a whole lot of unacceptable ways.

HELL HATH NO FURY

When men get angry onscreen, they're angry at the system. When women are angry onscreen, they're angry at someone. Women are not allowed to be angry at the system, because that would be a tacit acceptance that we're all participants in the oppressive patriarchal structures that create this pressing, everyday anger. Women onscreen are only allowed to be angry at one person, one wrongdoing. Something they can fix. Something that doesn't antagonize audiences too much. There have been, historically, a few acceptable ways that female rage has been presented to us onscreen.

It's okay if it's a woman scorned by a romantic partner. The saying "Hell hath no fury like a woman scorned" is actually a misquote from William Congreve's play *The Mourning Bride*, which actually reads: "Heaven has no rage like love to hatred turned, Nor hell a fury like a woman scorned." In her 2016 video for "Hold Up," from her album and accompanying visual album *Lemonade*, Beyoncé created an image of rage that fits the full sentiment of this quote. In a mustard-yellow Roberto Cavalli dress and Yves Saint Laurent heels, she skips over to a car owned by (the lyrics imply) a cheating lover and bashes it with a baseball bat while musing if it's better to be seen as jealous or crazy or both. The video ends with Beyoncé blowing a kiss at the camera before smashing it also with her baseball bat. The underlying message of a woman scorned, of course, being that finding and sticking by a romantic partner is the be-all and end-all of a woman's life. If that gets taken away, her rage is justifiable because it's directed at one bad apple—her ex-boyfriend, ex-husband, ex-partner. Mind you, this type of anger is very rarely directed at a partner in a same-sex couple.

In *Waiting to Exhale* (1995), Bernadine (Angela Bassett), having just been unceremoniously dumped by her husband for his white mistress, collects all his belongings, loads them up into his car, and sets it on fire. In his methodically organized walk-in closet, she rips his clothes off the racks, ranting at him, but mostly at herself ("Couldn't have started that damn company without me... I got a master's degree in business and there I was, his secretary, his office manager, and his computer!"). Bernadine has given this marriage, this man, eleven years of her time, her knowledge, her work. She put herself second to him: "I need you to be the fucking background to my foreground!" It's a delicious rage, that of women done wrong by men. Bernadine's husband has used her wits, her MBA, and her work to build a business just for himself. Her investment in him, not just in terms of her time but also her labor—intellectual, emotional, and physical— has left her with nothing. So she burns all of it. This scene, and Bernadine walking away from the flames, has become a digital shorthand for fury.

This display is both clumsy and determined, disconsolate and unhinged. Most importantly, it's private. And as such, it's untethered. There's a shame associated with the physicality of female rage that speaks to how we are socialized to keep at bay emotions that are considered too much or too ugly. In *The Wife* (2017), Joan Castleman (Glenn Close) has quietly written books for her husband, eventually earning him the Nobel Prize in literature. We don't learn this until late in the movie, and with that knowledge her rage is reframed entirely. In a quiet but climactic scene at the table for the Nobel Prize award winners, her husband seems to be on the brink of revealing that he has not, in fact, written the books that have earned him the prize. It was all Joan, all along. Close's expression barely shifts as his speech taunts the possibility of a recognition long denied, but then, of course, it's just platitudes ("She is the inspiration for every decent impulse I've ever had").

In a world where a woman's respectability is directly linked to her ability to stay quiet about her grievances, it becomes understandable that a woman's rage must be icy, kept under wraps, never to be externalized in an ugly way. True female outbursts of unfettered rage and vulnerability, like Bernadine's often happen at home, when women are by themselves. In the film, Bernadine is still wearing her nightgown, with no makeup on, and runs around collecting her philandering husband's items barefoot, sometimes stumbling in her rush. Close-ups of her face show her eyes darting around her husband's closet, trying to pick the most valuable items to burn, the ones that will hurt the most. There's nothing beautiful about this scene,[2] nothing about her fury is meant to be inspiring. It's painful. This desperate, private display of hurt is the one we forget when we see the GIF of Bernadine walking away from the fire she just set, smoking and smoking hot in her nightgown and pearl necklace and unmade face.

A display of anger is also understandable if a woman is protecting her—or any—children. In *Three Billboards Outside Ebbing, Missouri* (2015), Mildred Hayes (Frances McDormand) is willing to burn her entire town to the ground to take revenge for the rape and murder of her daughter and the police's incompetence in the handling of the case. It's a natural extension of

---

2   Except, obviously, the fact that she's played by Angela Bassett.

motherhood. But even when her anger is justified by a specific traumatic event that we get to witness, a woman enraged is terrifying to behold. In *Carrie* (1976), Carrie White (Sissy Spacek), already bullied at school and abused at home, is pushed to massacre her entire high school after a particularly nasty prank. In *Mad Max: Fury Road* (2015), Furiosa (Charlize Theron) takes off with Immortan Joe's wives, not motivated by saving them, but by having had enough of his shit.

Returning to *Promising Young Woman*: Who is Cassie angry at? She didn't, after all, suffer the assault herself. Her anger has calcified until the moment when she yells out, "Wrong!" The film initially leads us to believe that Cassie is avenging her own assault, or recreating it. It takes on a different, sadder, tone when we find out that she's processing the assault, death, and erasure of her friend. Her friendship with Nina is what she's grieving, and there's no name for it, so it's transformed into something amorphous and toxic that's eating Cassie from the inside. When she decides to punish those who protected the rapists and forgot Nina, she goes after everyone, not just the men. She tries to go after the university, which operates with a "We can't ruin a good boy's life over an accusation" policy. She goes after a former friend, who reveals that she has had video evidence of the assault on Nina for years, but had dismissed it as college antics. Fennell spares us from seeing the assault, but she shows us Cassie's expression as she watches the video of her friend's violation. Bearing direct witness to it, reliving Nina's pain with the knowledge of what would come after pushes her to go after Al Monroe (Chris Lowell), the man who had assaulted Nina in college.

There is an entire subgenre for the enacting of female rage

through violence and murder, but it also necessitates the re-creation of trauma. Rape revenge films present female avengers who take back the power that was taken away from them after a sexual assault. In *Ms. 45* (1981), a young woman (Zoë Tamerlis) is brutally raped (twice) and rendered mute by the shock, so she goes on a killing spree, killing any man she sees assaulting women. This is an extraordinarily powerful subgenre, one that is easily dismissed as torturous and misogynistic, but one that holds women's pain at its center. A double whammy, being part of the horror realm and centering women, often has it dismissed, but excellent film analysts Alexandra Heller-Nicholas and B. J. Colangelo have widely articulated how cathartic these films can be.

Promising Young Woman was marketed as one of these films, but it is fundamentally different. It's a film about anger and about vengeance, but it is categorically not a rape revenge film. To quote Colangelo: "Trauma is not the event. Trauma is the response to that event." Cassie's response *is* the trauma. It was curious to witness the backlash to the film *because* there was no killing of men, no violence, no death—except Cassie's. Just like *Thelma and Louise*, Cassie throws herself off the cliff, knowing that it's a sacrifice she's willing to make for her friend. Or perhaps because her anger has consumed her to the point that she sees this response as being the only possibility for her.

But the backlash to Cassie's actions—or lack of expected actions, like bludgeoning a bunch of would-be rapists—interestingly taps into the expectations of how female trauma and female anger are to be performed onscreen. This reaction comes from both our expectations of female anger—the foundations of which have been laid down by decades of pop culture that uses it as a prop and as another way of making messy emotions sexy—and our inability as a culture to allow space for female anger.

When your very existence is subject to constant abuse or questioning, like it is for women of color, queer women, and trans women, anger can become a tool. Whose anger we're allowed to see onscreen (mostly pretty white women like Cassie), and more importantly, whose rage we take seriously as opposed to transforming it into a stereotype, is vitally important when it breeds empathy. A character's anger can make us feel—not just see—the hurt caused. A woman doesn't need to be abused, raped, or subjected to violence to be entitled to feel anger. Microaggressions and pressures build up, and cinema has the ability to show us private, hidden moments when the seams are undone. Even the character of Marmee in Greta Gerwig's *Little Women* (2019), a figure of endless generosity and warmth, confesses to "feeling angry nearly every day." Everyday, barely contained seething makes for powerful, relatable performances.

The Angry Woman onscreen has had to dress up and sell her rage in order for it to be palatable. *Promising Young Woman* centers female rage in a way that is uncomfortable to look at because it's ugly and fundamentally unproductive. So how come this pretty blond woman riled people so much? Because *Promising Young Woman* doesn't try to glamorize anger. It doesn't care about Cassie being a fuckable avenger. It doesn't excuse her inability to process her grief and her rage by making it attractive for us to watch. As well as attractive, there is a demand for female rage to be *useful*. Cassie's revenge was deemed pointless by critics because she doesn't kill men. There is not enough spectacle for us to engage in an escapist fantasy of violence. Instead, it's confronting because it's pointless. Because it reminds us: one woman can't change the patriarchal system, she can't make them care, she can't make them remember—even with all her privileges.

In a four-part podcast diving deep into the themes, release, and reception of *Promising Young Woman* that I produced, the *Independent*'s Clarisse Loughrey pointed out that Cassie's self-sacrifice is the final part of her plan. Her death guarantees that the tape will be shown in court and that Nina's case will be reopened—because the death of a white woman has more currency than the rape of a white woman who's already dead.

With men it is understood that their anger is ever present, and it's a question of keeping it in check. If they slip up, it's rarely their fault, because of just how much effort it must take them to keep that anger in check. We don't want them to be angry, so it's everyone's job to prevent them from detonating, because it is everyone's job to clean up after they do. Even if there is violence, there are rarely consequences for the angry man, at least not long-term ones. The promise of a man is more important than a woman's life.

While women are trained from very early on to acknowledge and accept the possibility (or even the probability) of male rage, it's also ingrained in us that we must never, ever show our own. So we learn to hide in plain sight. Fennell explores this visually in *Promising Young Woman*. It's a high-femme, glossy, pastel-pink, poppy visual language that sits discordantly with the aesthetics of revenge cinema. Revenge, surely, is expected to be bloody; rage is a territory of crimson and fiery colors—not of sing-alongs to Paris Hilton pop tunes or candy-colored wigs. Fennell sets Cassie's determined, funereal march up to the stag house to an orchestral rendition of Britney Spears's "Toxic." The visual language of *Promising Young Woman* can be summed up in what Fennell described in an interview as the "feminine uncanny." The dissonance that exists between the prettiness of the film and the ugliness of Cassie's rage is acidic, leaving the viewer with a sour aftertaste.

There's also the object of the rage. Who is the anger directed at? Depending on the answer, we will be able to justify it or not. Cassie's anger is multifaceted. She's angry at herself; she feels guilty about not having been able to prevent Nina's ordeal or help her enough after it. She's angry at the system that allowed Nina's rape to occur, and at everyone who let it happen, who forgot about it and about her, both in life and in death. She's angry at Al Monroe and his buddies, who just get to move on and live their lives, Nina's pain and Cassie's guilt barely a blip in their stories. And, of course, she's angry at everyone who doesn't make the right choice—not just the clumsy, opportunistic would-be rapists she encounters in nightclubs but also the women from her past she confronts directly—all these people who don't make good choices, even when they're offered to them. It's despairing to watch, as Fennell points out, "her gesturing toward these open doors for people to escape, and they just don't." There are too many reasons, too much rage.

Cassie's trapped by her anger. "It takes over everything else," Fennell told *Vulture*. "Rather than, like, a gunshot wound, it's like an ingrown toenail."[3] It festers. An irresolute, unsteady anger so toxic it would make no sense for Cassie to be able to escape it at the end of the film. There is no room for a morning after in *Promising Young Woman*. While romantic comedies and revenge movies—the two subgenres whose influence is felt most intensely in the film—usually end in a "moment of triumph," Fennell's film sets us up for one and then doesn't deliver it. What would Cassie's moment of triumph look like? What does any Angry Woman's moment of triumph look like? Cinema tradition has shown us that the Angry Woman must always lose. She must either die, be imprisoned, or be punished. Cassie did achieve a sort of retribution for Nina, but she still had to die. Her anger was unsustainable, crippling, and all-consuming. She wasn't even alive, instead persisting in a state of arrested development.

Meanwhile, the most revered white male rage films usually end before we see any consequences of the characters' actions. *Joker* ends pseudotriumphantly, with the protagonist being lauded by a mob of angry people, all wearing clown masks, the city of Gotham set ablaze behind them. Arthur is confused about what he's started but too enamored with the attention to care. White male rage films and shows are a whole subgenre of pop culture. Except it's never called a subgenre when it's about white male rage—it's just called cinema. These scenes are memorable because they are revered. They were recognized by the industry with awards and critical praise, canonized as examples of great acting. Peter Finch and Joaquin Phoenix won Oscars for their roles. Meanwhile, actresses are rewarded for their "bravery"

---

3   https://www.vulture.com/2021/01/promising-young-woman-ending-emerald-fennell-explains.html.

in letting themselves appear angry and, by implication, *ugly* onscreen.

Male anger is threatening—when men finally explode, it's presented as painful for the characters, so we are encouraged by the narrative to empathize with them. Female rage, meanwhile, has been shown as dangerous to the women themselves. "Trauma sparks an anger in women that leads to violence and threatens to consume them," writes Angelica Jade Bastién. So we bottle it.

WHO GETS TO BE ANGRY?

The short answer to this is: skinny white women.

The more complicated answer to this is that pop culture has created and nurtured reductive archetypes for nonwhite characters, who continue to be few and far between. Black women and women of color have not been allowed to embody characters with a full range of emotion and instead have been fitted into convenient character archetypes fueled by racist stereotypes. Black female anger became the Angry Black Woman. Asian women became Dragon Ladies. And Latina women became the Spicy Latina.

Roxane Gay writes, "Black women are often characterized as angry simply for existing, as if anger is woven into our breath and our skin"—and the racist portrayal of Black women as angry by default has been woven into our pop culture for decades. It makes their anger irrational, comical, something not to be taken seriously.

The Angry Black Woman stereotype, also called Sapphire, is

traced back to the character of Sapphire Stevens on *The Amos 'n' Andy Show*, a radio sitcom that had a run as a television show between 1951 and 1953. The show had a predominantly Black cast, and Sapphire, the character played by Ernestine Wade, became the blueprint of a loud, sassy, perpetually mad Black woman. Previously, the only type of roles that Black women were allowed to play onscreen in Hollywood were those of maids, and Sapphire was both a welcome evolution and one that would get perverted over time. In his book *Raised on Radio*, scholar Gerald Nachman calls her the "Black Alice Kramden" (Kramden being the nagging wife on *The Honeymooners*) and admits that although the name became synonymous with a "hectoring female," Sapphire Stevens was the only character capable of bringing down her husband on the show, with most of the comedy being derived from hearing her berate him into submission.

It would be unfair to blame on the actress what a majority white and insidiously racist Hollywood system took from her character, but that's what happened. The fact that out of that character was born the cultural stereotype of the Angry Black Woman tells us that Hollywood took any emotions felt or displayed by a Black woman and automatically interpreted them as anger. Throughout the years, this anger would be presented as either comedic or threatening, but never taken seriously. Looking back on Bernadine's rage in *Waiting to Exhale*, there's an additional lens we must look at that scene through. Bernadine had been performing throughout her entire marriage. She mutters about her own time wasted ("You can't start a catering business this year, why don't you wait a few years"), how her husband used her smarts and her education and her skills to prop himself up while never lifting her up, and most painfully for Bernadine, about how he was using their children to try to assimilate into corporate white culture ("Making my children go to a school with only two other Black children because you don't want them to be improperly influenced"). All that performance, all that effort, all that diminishing of herself, and she still got screwed over. I think again about the privacy of this moment from a film from 1995, how it would play out and feed into the Sapphire stereotype if it were displayed in public, contrasted with the arresting audacity of Beyoncé's rage in "Hold Up," which doesn't hide and even draws attention to itself. They are both playing the role of the fury.

With Latina women, meanwhile, anger became sexualized, a part of their "hot and spicy" personalities. Instead of being seen as a threat, as Black women would be, Latinx women were expected to get angry easily, and that made them attractive, often being compared to food like "spicy tamales." In the 1940s, Mexican actress Lupe Vélez made her name in a series of films called *Mexican Spitfire*,[4] which capitalized on her "fiery temper," prolonging the stereotype. The acclaimed Puerto Rican actress-singer Rita Moreno (an actual EGOT[someone who has won Emmy, Grammy, Oscar, and Tony Awards]) had to, for many years at the start of her career, fit herself into the "sexy smoldering spitfire" type. Even on contemporary mainstream television, Colombian actress Sofía Vergara plays a comedic take on the spitfire on *Modern Family*, as the loud, quick-to-anger wife of an older white man. This racial fetishization also means that real anger, real

---

4   A literal film franchise, which produced eight films released between 1940 and 1943, both named after and creating this stereotype.

disappointment, is treated as a joke. These character stereotypes are the bare minimum of representation and are rooted in racism.

Film has not been kind to these stereotypes. It has leaned into them and amplified them, giving audiences cultural fodder with which to reinforce their biases. The subversion of these is often found in the physicality of female rage. It transforms into steel. In *Kill Bill Vol. 1* (2003), when offended by one of her underlings (who calls her a "Chinese-Jap-American, half-breed bitch") Yakuza chief O-Ren Ishii (Lucy Liu) quickly and quietly chops off his head. She is murderously calm, only raising her voice as a punctuation mark. O-Ren's chokehold on power lies not just in how ruthless a killer she is but also in her icy focus.

Only recently have Black, Asian, and Latina creators been at the helm of stories that center fully realized characters with complicated inner lives, unlikeable traits, and experiences that are informed, but not defined, by their race.

FORMATIVE TRAUMA

These performances of quiet fury have a difficult time achieving the iconic status of some of the more explosive ones. If pop culture has given us these iconic angry men, and rewarded the actors who play them for their contorted faces and spitting fury, where are all the angry women?

They're on TV.

When Liz Feldman was developing the Netflix show *Dead to Me*, which centers on the unlikely friendship that develops between recent widow Jen Harding (Christina Applegate) and Judy Hale (Linda Cardellini), the former having just lost her husband in an unresolved hit-and-run, she got one note back from the studio: Jen was too angry. The friendship that develops between Jen and Judy is based on grief, guilt, and, in Jen's case, a grief tinted with rage and without closure. In an article Feldman penned for the *Hollywood Reporter*, she spoke of this pushback: "There was a genuine fear that it made her unlikable. I, of course, was not surprised by the concern. It echoed my own fears about expressing anger—that people would think I'm a shrill, domineering monster undeserving of love, kindness and employment."

This was in *2019*.

"Why isn't angry likable?" Feldman asked herself in this piece. She writes about being angry about this reaction to her character, which made her lean into it even more. Her response to being called out for being too angry was to become even *more* so. It's the creative's response to being told to "calm down." It makes you even less calm. Is the reason we're so uncomfortable with female rage that it defies the underlying expectation that women should be in control? Whereas self-control is praised in men (and excused when it's lacking), it is assumed to be the default in women. Women should know better, we're told.

In the last ten years, television has explored the layers of female rage through a myriad of genres, from prestige limited series (*Big Little Lies*, *The Morning Show*) and caper dramedies (*Good Girls*, *GLOW*) to superhero stories (*Jessica Jones*) and dystopian dramas (*The Handmaid's Tale*). And while it feels revelatory, it's not particularly new. We are so used to pushing down anger, to sublimating it into productivity, to looking away from rage, that when we see something centering it, it can be too much to bear.

In the second season of Marvel and Netflix's *Jessica Jones*, the central theme is rage as it's felt by four different lead characters: Jessica (Krysten Ritter), who is still full of rage even after killing her assailant; her best friend Trish Walker (Rachael Taylor), who is angry at her own powerlessness in a world that hides away bad men and discards young girls; Jessica's mother, Alisa Jones (Janet McTeer), whose superhuman rage issues are so huge she has to be cuffed to the bed at night; and the high-powered lawyer Jeri Hogarth (Carrie-Anne Moss), who finds all her power and cunning useless when she's diagnosed with ALS (amyotrophic lateral sclerosis). All these women are both propelled and paralyzed by their rage.

In one scene, Jessica helps Trish confront a film director who assaulted her when she was fifteen. While Jessica is angry for her friend, Trish is livid that she cannot stare down the monster from her past herself—which pushes her into taking performance-enhancing drugs, relapsing into addiction, and experimenting on herself. Jessica, though reconnected with a mother she believed to be dead for the majority of her life, is terrified of her monstrous anger, which is barely held in check—and which could be in her future too. And Jeri is allergic to vulnerability; a disease that she cannot control makes her vulnerable to being conned, to losing everything she built. Her rage at her fate makes her even more ruthless. Throughout the season, we see how anger affects these women in differing ways, reshaping them, but not always for the positive.

COLLECTIVE RAGE

It is telling, however, that most of the films and series I've singled out are focused on an individual woman's rage. Female anger is always treated as an individual issue and never a political one. That is, until recently. The protagonists of shows like *Good Girls, I May Destroy You, Dead to Me, Jessica Jones, The Good Fight,* and *The Handmaid's Tale* use their rage not for personal vengeance alone but as propulsive energy, as a catalyst for change that will affect others, not just them.

The contradiction inherent in female anger is that it exists on an almost universal and nearly daily plane, but women are so socialized to keep it down that it is treated like an individual issue. If you're angry, it's a *you* issue—and one that *you* have to work on. Social reliance on women's patience, resilience, and anger management has given us entire cinematic genres that, even in their own most low-budget iterations, are aiming to provide a catharsis for this anger.

Anger is a difficult emotion to tolerate because it's not pretty, and being pretty is the primary expectation of women onscreen. If it's directionless and it reinforces the idea that women are functionally incapable of managing their emotions, if it's directed at one specific person, it's a "her" problem. Anger is often lumped in with the rest of the unpretty emotions, and women who dare to experience it are simply tagged as "emotional." The worst phrase you can hear when angry is "calm down." Much like "unlikeable," it's an innocuous phrase on the surface that has specific connotations for women. It's a way of negating, not diffusing anger.

The comfort these Angry Women provide us, and the turn to entering a shared, collective rage ring in more recent films and shows, is that they're understanding the anger, not denying it. When we're being held accountable for every single action, our own and those of others, for our facial expressions and our bodies, the content of words and the tone of them, for assaults committed against us and our reaction to them, it can be overwhelmingly lonely.

There is comfort to be found in collective rage. A horde of women who are "mad as hell" is a powerful thing, whether they're silent and hooded figures in uniforms or daughters, girlfriends, wives, and mothers. "They should never have given us uniforms if they didn't want us to be an army," as says Offred in the TV adaptation of *The Handmaid's Tale*.

"I will not be judged by you or society. I will wear whatever I want and blow whomever I want as long as I can breathe and kneel."

SAMANTHA JONES, *SEX AND THE CITY*

"The word 'slut' just means 'a lot of people wanna give you orgasms' and ur like 'sure that sounds great.' how is that bad."

LANE MOORE, COMEDIAN AND AUTHOR (@HELLOLANEMOORE)

The Slut

In January 2021, the internet exploded over the news that *Sex and the City* was being rebooted—without Samantha Jones, the show's proud slut. *Sex and the City* ended in 2003. It's not, by any means, the only mainstream show that showed women living a semblance of a sexually liberated lifestyle, but it was the first one that put women's sex lives front and center.

After the announcement, there were rabid responses to Samantha Jones's absence from a reboot of *Sex and the City*, defending her as the soul of the show and the most sex-positive of the characters. That there was no room for the sluttiest character on a show centered on women and sex reminded people of both the cultural impact and the problematic elements of the show. You could argue that the show couldn't even bring back the title *Sex and the City* and get away with it anymore. Granted, the decision to not come back to the show was entirely up to Kim Cattrall, the British-Canadian-American actress who played the character on the show. She was asked, and declined. She was done with the character. But the furious reaction to Samantha's absence is much more interesting than the absence itself. Whatever the behind-the-scenes shenanigans might be, the absence of the show's most sex-positive character changed its very DNA.

The word "slut," much like "bitch," has been weaponized in so many different ways it's not even used to describe promiscuous women anymore. It's used to shame women who have many sexual partners, women who refute someone's advances, women who have been sexually assaulted, women who pursue sex, women who enjoy sex, and women who simply exist as sexual beings. So to trace back how we got to Samantha Jones and her dick puns, as well as her slutty successors in *Girls*, *Broad City*, *Fleabag*, *Daphne*, *Girls Trip*, and *Diary of a Teenage Girl*, we need to think about how women's sexual agency has been presented onscreen. Because when we're talking about film and TV, there's nothing as controversial as a woman's sexual pleasure. So, what space have the Sluts occupied in pop culture? What *exactly* makes the Slut a slut? Or, more specifically, how is sluttiness coded in culture? Is it the number of sexual partners? The way a woman dresses? Or the female body in and of itself? Is it just talking about sex or seeking it out that bothers? Or is it something else, perhaps a woman accepting and acknowledging her desires, her sexuality, and embracing her body? All of the above? None of these sound bad on paper, but the image of a woman enjoying her sexuality for herself still sends us into a panicky frenzy.

WHEN I'M BAD, I'M BETTER

There is hardly a traceable history to slut shaming, as the shaming

of women's sexuality in general and female promiscuity in particular has always been a double standard embedded in our culture.
Second-wave feminism and the advent of the birth control pill in
the 1960s and 1970s did much to relax views on premarital sex,
and since 2011 there has been a concerted attempt on the part
of activists to call out and dismantle slut shaming through organized marches like the SlutWalk, as well as a slow cultural reclamation of the term by comedians, podcast hosts, and writers.

The portrayal of female sexuality has been a source of both
mockery and fear since the inception of the film industry. In
pre-Code Hollywood, for a brief, glorious moment when unfil-
tered creativity and commercial savviness coexisted before the
censors intervened, women in movies enjoyed their sexuality
unapologetically onscreen. Marrying for love, getting rid of toxic
husbands, taking lovers, and making dick jokes.

If you try googling "slutty film characters," you'll get a thousand pages of listicles with variations on titles like "Top 50 Sexiest
Characters," "Characters from Film/TV to Lust After," or "Best
Sexy Outfits from Film/TV." You might get some porn links. It's
all about sexiness, but it isn't about sexual desire or agency, and
most definitely never about the fun of sex. In her book exploring sex, desire, and cinema, *She Found It at the Movies*, film critic
Christina Newland writes: "We see women who are the objects
of desire but rarely do we see actively desirous or promiscuous
woman characters in a film that gives her agency and respect."
She can have sexual agency or respect. But not both.

Since 1933, and even after the collapse of the Production
Code, the films that get the harshest treatment are those that
center female sexuality no matter what the intention. You could

argue the Code was all about sex; specifically, that is was about eliminating any notion of women enjoying sex at all, and especially out of wedlock. No one challenged this more than Mae West, the brash, witty sex symbol of 1930s Hollywood who wrote and starred in films that catered to her sex pun-filled style of humor and paired her with dashing men who she unashamedly lusted after (and usually conquered).

Mae West was a stage and screen superstar who created a persona that worked for her onscreen and off. Arguably the first popular sex-positive Slut of the screen, Mae West made sure her name was synonymous with sex, and the characters she played never really deviated from the Mae West persona.[1] West was the first proud Slut of cinema, but her career got cut short by prudish censorship. In a Mae West picture, there is absolutely no doubt who has the biggest big dick energy onscreen. It's always her.

Before she scandalized the movies, West scandalized the stage. Her first play, in 1927, was simply titled *Sex* and actually wasn't about sex but about lust, and specifically the contradictory dynamics in which male lust is perceived versus female lust. Mae West played the lead role of a sex worker. While the play got eviscerated by critics, it was a commercial success. "People want dirty in plays, so I give 'em dirt," she told the *New Yorker* in 1928. *Sex* ran for eleven months on Broadway before West and her cast were arrested backstage, brought to trial, and got sent to prison for eight days for "obscenity" and "corruption of youth." She also wrote an overtly gay, celebratory play (culminating in

---

1   The biggest personal scandal she encountered was that she had married at age seventeen and never got a divorce. Audiences were outraged that she got married at all, such was the chokehold of the Mae West persona.

a twenty-minute drag ball) called *The Drag*, which never made it to Broadway past a few previews.[2] Her next play was another smutty, successful story starring herself as Diamond Lil, a singer in an 1890s Bowery brothel, essentially a period version of herself. When writing Diamond Lil, she deliberately wanted to attract a more female audience, appealing and scandalous as it was to hear a woman talk the way West did in general, let alone in front of an audience.

Her plays were deemed "too sexy," but they also garnered her bucketloads of publicity, which in turn got the attention of Hollywood; specifically of Paramount Pictures, a studio that was at the time on the brink of bankruptcy. When she went to Hollywood, West was already forty years old. There was interest in her adapting some of her plays (even though the Production Code office had put her plays on a list of banned works that could never be adapted for the screen). She was given a supporting part in *Night after Night* (1932), which she rewrote entirely rather than read dialogue she hated. Paramount and the moviegoing public were sufficiently impressed that they offered to adapt Diamond Lil for the screen. She demanded to write her own script and design her own costumes in exchange for signing exclusively with Paramount.[3] At the studio, she made *She Done Him Wrong* (1933), based on her own play, and *I'm No Angel* (1933) in the same year. In the latter, she'd quip the oft-quoted line "Come up

---

2 It should be noted, though, that despite this play, West's friendships in the dragball scene, and her later status as a queer icon, she became viciously homophobic in her later years.

3 Famously she demanded to earn a dollar more than the head of the studio—and she got it, becoming the highest-paid woman in Hollywood after just one supporting role. The audacity of Mae West remains admirable.

and see me sometime" to newbie actor, future Hollywood icon, and famously handsome man Cary Grant. West looks him up and down, devouring him with her eyes, seconds away from licking her lips like a leering cat. At this point, Grant was not yet a star, just a small-time contract player. But as Karina Longworth put it on her podcast *You Must Remember This*, he was her opposite in every way: "Dark and slim where she was blond and buxom, buttoned up where she was loose." On film, West lusted after him in an ooga-ooga kind of way, and eventually so did the rest of the world. "Anytime you got nothing to do and lots of time to do it, come up," she says to him and just walks away. She just walks away from Cary Grant. Mae West would never beg a man to bed her, but she told the ones she wanted outright that she wanted them.

West and Grant would do another film together the same year, *She Done Him Wrong*, where the tagline was "Her passion… diamonds. Her weakness…men!"[4] "You bad girl," Grant purrs at her. "You'll find out," she purrs right back. This is 1933. Such was its success that there were women-only screenings of the film (much like, ninety years later, there would be women-only screenings of *Magic Mike XXL*), and West became a star almost overnight, having written and starred in two of the top-grossing films of the year. She would become the highest-paid woman in entertainment by 1935. Which also meant that she was targeted by the censors, her work muzzled by the Production Code.

The truly controversial element about West's work is not just the content of her writing or her breathy delivery; it's the

---

4   Should've been the other way round, if you ask me.

fact that she was creating and embodying an image of a sexually voracious woman. She was flesh and blood, peddling a new kind of womanhood, not a fantasy molded in the shape of a woman created by Hollywood producers. Mae West *created* Mae West.

She did so quite literally. West designed her own costumes, preferring corsets and feathers, and wore custom-made shoes that made her appear a little bit taller than her 5 feet. The 9.5-inch double-decker heels gave her a distinctive walk, as notorious as that of John Wayne; a glide more than a walk, giving off the energy of a recently railed woman. She never wore revealing clothes, never appeared naked onscreen, but she always exuded a sexual confidence and self-possession that transcended good looks. Even when she wasn't showing too much skin, everything about Mae West oozed sex—and she capitalized smartly on it. She wasn't a conventional sex symbol, but she was hot. Mae Wes *fucked* and made sure everyone knew it. Her double entendres made sex sound like fun for everyone involved. I think about what it must've been like to be a woman watching Mae West pull Cary Grant, watching her make men blush, cracking jokes that they couldn't provide a comeback to. To watch Mae side-eye a good-looking man is to feel entitled to do the same. There's no tragedy to her man eating; it's always joyous, always fun, always poking at morality's contradictions, always knowing her audience was in on the joke. While there is Mae West the person—a woman, a writer, a performer—there is also Mae West the persona—the side-eye, the wisecracks, the shimmying walk, the platinum-blond hair—one she designed specifically for public consumption. She knew what people wanted of her, and blended her onscreen persona with her star persona. She'd playfully use her famous line, "Come up and see me sometime," at premieres.

The great beauties and stars Clara Bow or Gloria Swanson also played sexually liberated women, but they belonged to the silent era. They were images. Mae West made sex *speak*. She wrote racy, witty dialogue filled with innuendos and come-ons. She is still remembered for her quippy, suggestive wordplay; for her, "essence was not sexual but verbal," writes Mary Haskell in *From Reverence to Rape*. There's always a wink-wink, nudge-nudge element to her jokes, a dialogue with her audience. "She wanted to offer an alternative version of womanhood, in which overt sexual desire wasn't shameful or dirty but an expression of independence," said filmmaker Sally Rosenthal, who directed a PBS documentary about West.

This joyfulness made her a menace. The National Legion of Decency was formed months after the release of *I'm No Angel*, and they cited Mae West as a major reason for the organization's creation, as an agent of chaos who was "corrupting our morals" and "promoting sex mania." Due to this censorship, West's work and appeal was never the same after 1934. Her character ends up married in her next film, *Belle of the Nineties*, which antagonized her audience (Sluts don't get married!) and was a box office disappointment. Her smutty jokes defanged by the censors, her last few movies didn't make money and didn't feel particularly Mae West-y, either. It's not that Mae West got any less dirty, it's that the movies got too puritanical. Since West's appeal was her jubilant smutty personality, it just wasn't the same thing. She made a few more films in the 1940s, but none of them had the same cultural impact or snappy dialogue as her freer work. When the

Slut takes her sexuality into her own hands, she's acknowledged her desires, taking action to satisfy them and having fun doing it. It's the reveling in the fun of sex that annoys people. And it's the active part that irked audiences in 1933 and still does today.

Considering the female sexual icons of early Hollywood, they were always an evocation of sex, but always on other people's terms. Newland writes that "sex is coded into the DNA of the movies." The cameraman that filmed Marilyn Monroe's first screen test famously said she was "sex on a screen," but it would be a mistake to refer to Marilyn as a cultural figure or any of the characters she played as slutty.

Marilyn Monroe, Brigitte Bardot, and Raquel Welch were sex symbols of the screen in the 1950s and 1960s, and their sexiness presumed sexual availability, whether they were playing it as such or not. They were erotic, they held the promise of sex, but were not shown *having* sex. Their screen roles were not slutty in nature, they were not written to have enough agency to be joy-fully promiscuous but rather were prizes for the right man. They were bombshells and bimbos, archetypes of sexual desirability that were designed to be attractive, empty-headed, and easily discarded. Female audiences hated them because the bimbo is not designed to appeal to female viewership. The legacy of the bimbo, a once derogatory term used to put down women who were hot and/or presented themselves as hyperfeminine, has remained the same until very recently, when a TikTok-born movement aligned the bimbo aesthetic with liberal politics and a nonjudgmental attitude that embraced anyone choosing to pres-ent themselves as hyperfeminine. In movies and TV, though, an actress who was a particular brand of hot was by default considered to be unintelligent and slutty. This association often extends to the actress too. In the nineties, model-actresses like Pamela Anderson or Jenny McCarthy were perceived to have a brand of beauty that implied sexual availability without it ever actually being written into the roles they were playing or having anything to do with the women's real lives. So, in actuality, the bimbo is the opposite of the Slut, united only in the way they are collectively shamed by both men and women. The bimbo is judged based on her looks, and the Slut based on her choices.

HORNY ON MAIN

There is a big time jump from Mae West to Madonna, but genuinely, and pitifully, the pop singer exhibits the closest thing to proud pop culture sluttiness since 1933. And if 1933 was Mae West's year, 1992 was Madonna's. In this year alone, she released her *Erotica* album, authored and published the book *SEX*, and starred in the erotic thriller *Body of Evidence*. The previous year, she released her documentary *In Bed with Madonna* (also known as *Truth or Dare*), to this day one of the most fascinatingly constructed documentaries about a pop star.

Madonna's *SEX* is a coffee-table book with black-and-white photographs by Stephen Meisel and art direction by Fabien Baron. Explicit but not pornographic, the photographs mostly feature Madonna in various erotic fantasies, nude or dressed in BDSM (bondage, discipline, sadomasochism, and dominance) attire, posing with both female and male models, with occasional celebrity cameos, including supermodel Naomi Campbell, rapper Vanilla Ice (her boyfriend at the time), and actress Isabella Rossellini. Interspersed are stories and musings, written by Madonna in character as Mistress Dita. The release of the book—itself a hefty item, with an aluminum cover and a wrapping sheet stamped "For Adults" on the back that made it impossible to leaf through without buying—was a publishing milestone. It went on sale simultaneously in the Unites States, the United Kingdom, Japan, Germany, and France and sold 750,000 copies in its first week on sale in the United States. The reviews went from scathing to disinterested, the most gentle of which called the book "boring," the worst calling her the oh-so-familiar "slut" and accusing Madonna of ruining her reputation.

Meanwhile, the erotic thriller *Body of Evidence*, which includes sex scenes with a fully nude Madonna pouring candle wax on Willem Dafoe's chest, got rated NC-17 by the MPAA, which meant it was limited in its distribution and only added to the backlash and Madonna's exposure. *Body of Evidence* is not a great movie, but it holds one unintentionally revolutionary idea: it literally puts Madonna's body and sexuality on trial. In the film, the pop star plays Rebecca Carlson, a woman accused of killing a rich man in order to inherit his money—specifically, she is accused of murdering him by having sex so vigorously that it literally killed him. In the court of law and the universe of *Body of Evidence*, Rebecca is accused of fucking a man to death. No ice pick, just skills. It's a campy premise (at one point during the court trial, the prosecutor yells at her, "Not only is she the defendant, she is the murder weapon itself!"), but one that asks us to consider what exactly we are judging when we see sexually promiscuous women onscreen: their choices or their relationship with their bodies?

Madonna's creative output during this period should be seen as the different branches of one project. It's all an exploration of a woman having sex, thinking about sex, and talking about sex. Similarly to Mae West, Madonna's persona is bigger than any role she could ever play, and her work during this time melded the dominatrix Mistress Dita from the album *Erotica*, Rebecca Carlson from the film, and Madonna the pop star herself. In an interview in 2003, she continues to be asked whether she has any regrets about that era and continues to remain unapologetic: "There was a lot of irony in the *SEX* book and I am poking fun at a lot of things and I am being kind of silly and adolescent and I am being very f- you, if a man can do it, I can do it."

Underneath the controversy surrounding the release of her *SEX* book and *Body of Evidence*, though, Madonna's album *Erotica* was overshadowed. Unlike Mae West, who used language to poke fun at the double standards around sex (and sex work) and profited from people's outrage at a woman publicly discussing sex, Madonna used images. While West became famous because she talked about sex, Madonna already was famous and was derided for talking about sex not because of *what* she was saying as much as because she was a *famous* woman saying it. In 2012, the *Guardian* wrote that the fact "she was penning her own sexual narrative was perhaps the most shocking part of the whole enterprise," which could be said about West too and about Niki Minaj, Cardi B, and Megan Thee Stallion.

FUCK AT YOUR OWN PERIL

Really, what's so bad about being slutty that film has always equated female sexual agency onscreen with danger and death? The prioritization of female pleasure seeking remains controversial. What pop culture has shown us so far is that you can be slutty, but only if it's a phase, only if you're not enjoying yourself too much, and only if you don't get too good at it. Remember: agency *or* respect. But not both.

It's so difficult for us to accept a woman seeking out sexual pleasure or indulging her desires without pathologizing it, explaining it away with a personality disorder, or punishing her for it. In *Looking for Mr. Goodbar* (1977), our lead, Theresa (Diane Keaton), goes out almost nightly, having casual sex with strangers. She ends up being raped and murdered by one of them. Often, Sluts will be mocked or punished because we've been taught that pleasure-seeking women are deviants. When we think about the Slut onscreen, there are two ways this character has traditionally been presented: as comic relief—think Samantha Jones, Meredith on *The Office*, Edna Krabappel on *The Simpsons*—or as pathologically sex crazed—like Theresa in *Looking for Mr. Goodbar*, Rebecca Carlson in *Body of Evidence*, and Catherine Tramell in *Basic Instinct*. The message, however, is always clearly sent: at best, these are not women to be taken seriously; at worst, these women must be feared.

In the late 1980s and 1990s, sex and death became intertwined in their own subgenre: the erotic thriller. Here, the femme fatale got an update. Now they didn't just do the seducing. The new femme fatales actually fucked. Every erotic thriller is about sex and the threat that comes with it. Sex is the entire plot, the text, and the subtext. The formula for the erotic thriller always includes violence—either a murder happens during a sexual encounter or directly because of it, or someone participating in it is potentially a murderer. Every film, from the cheap soft-core titles to the high-budget, starry releases, revolved around sex. For the audience, the appeal was watching sexually explicit content without actually watching pornography.

The first wave of erotic thrillers were remakes of the 1940s titles that had only been able to suggest sexuality. *Double Indemnity* became *Body Heat* (1981), with Kathleen Turner taking on the Barbara Stanwyck role, seducing William Hurt into some sweaty sex, and then getting away with murder. Angelica Jade Bastién writes of Kathleen Turner's Matty Walker as the birth of the modern femme fatale: "She wouldn't just outsmart and outmaneuver the men in her orbit; she could out-fuck and outlive them now, too." *The Postman Always Rings Twice* was also remade, with Jessica Lange and Jack Nicholson in the lead roles as the cheating lovers and sex scenes so incendiary people are still wondering if they were actually messing around onscreen. Erotic thrillers were a playground for dangerous and promiscuous women (sometimes they were one and the same).

In horror films, it's an established rule of the genre that any character who has sex will die before the movie ends. In her influential book *Men, Women and Chainsaws*, academic Carol J. Clover coined the term "the final girl," referring to the woman left alive at the end of a slasher film, usually a virginal and androgynous figure that finds the inner strength to fight off the killer. She's the one that audiences identify with. It's in these horror films, especially the slashers that emerged in the mid-1970s and that have been present ever since, that the rules of the genre were formed. "Don't have sex or you die," resident movie nerd

Randy tells us in *Scream* (1996). It's also the horror genre that would, in recent years, subvert this very rule. In *Jennifer's Body* (2009), Megan Fox plays a slutty high schooler who gets sacrificed to Satan by a middle-of-the-road indie band to achieve success. Because she's not a virgin ("I'm not even a backdoor virgin anymore, thanks to Roman"), the sacrifice backfires and she becomes a succubus, a slutty demon who literally eats boys to stay alive. In the meta-horror-comedy *The Cabin in the Woods* (2011), a group of college students are supernaturally forced into the stereotypical roles of the horror genre (the joker, the stoner, the slut, the virgin). None of them are actually virgins or sluts, but the film knows that it's expected from them: the slut must be killed first, and the virgin must be sacrificed last.

I COULDN'T HELP BUT WONDER

While the erotic thriller shone bright in cinema screens and on the booming VHS market, a show premiered on HBO in 1998 about four women in their thirties talking about relationships, romance, and, of course, sex. *Sex and the City* ran for six seasons (as well as receiving two feature films that shall go unmentioned because they never should have existed in the first place), and as troublesome as many, *many* of its politics were, the cultural impact of the show cannot be underestimated. It has been often ignored in the conversation surrounding the giant shift from film to television as the go-to destination of character-driven, conversation-monopolizing narrative totems. Hardly anyone talks about *Sex and the City* in the same breath as *The Sopranos*. The shows premiered within a year of each other, on the same network, yet gangsters with issues will always make for more serious storytelling than women's friendships and romances. In her seminal *New Yorker* essay on the show, TV critic Emily Nussbaum writes, "Mob shows, cop shows, cowboy shows— those are formulas with gravitas. *Sex and the City*, in contrast, was pigeonholed as a sitcom."

In that piece, Nussbaum argues that the show gave us the "unacknowledged first female anti-hero on television." I'd add that it gave us four. The leading ladies of *Sex and the City* gave us four templates of how women interact with sex, love, and emotions: Carrie (Sarah Jessica Parker), the de facto protagonist, a sex columnist with a remarkably prudish approach to sexuality and a love for drama; Charlotte (Kristin Davis), who believes in monogamy and marriage; Miranda (Cynthia Nixon), a fiercely independent, career-oriented woman who wants a partner who isn't intimidated by her success; and finally, Samantha (Kim Cattrall), a successful public relations executive and the show's de facto Slut. It gave us types to fit into, strong personalities to fit into, and what made them stand out in 1998 was they were single and sexually emancipated.

The thing is, while Samantha herself was unashamedly horny, the show often mocked her. Nobody's sexual or romantic choices came under so much scrutiny as Samantha's. Even a show with "sex" in the title was slut shaming its leading Slut, either by using her retellings of her escapades as the default comic relief (a woman who fucks = comedy!) or by dismissing her as emotionally immature for avoiding monogamous relationships. With the benefit of hindsight, and a more Slut-friendly culture, it is jarring to see the way that *Sex and the City* treated Samantha.

She had the most memorable lines and was sexually adventurous, confident, successful, and completely fulfilled by herself, and yet—and yet—nobody wanted to be "the Samantha" of any friendship group. If you were, as writer and academic Rachel Vorona Cote writes in her book *Too Much*, "You were likely dubbed the 'freaky' one, someone vulnerable to slut-shaming by those intolerant of female desire."

And just like that, a Slut is born.

Throughout *Sex and the City*'s run, Samantha is consistently the character with the most sex scenes and the foulest dialogue (in a study published by Ceros, it was counted that Samantha uttered 210 profanities and had forty sex scenes). People involved in the production of the show called Cattrall "the Lucille Ball of the bedroom" for her gung ho, no-nonsense approach to filming scenes of an explicit nature. Her slutty escapades are often hilarious scrapes, and one of the consistent parts of the show was Samantha recalling her sexual encounters in explicit detail, happily recounting her sex-capades to old and new friends alike over dinner. While the other three leads were in their thirties, Samantha was also the older one of the group (she is forty when the show begins). Her extraordinary confidence was infectious, and throughout the show she overcame her emotional unavailability, always prioritizing her own well-being above anyone's expectations of her. In a show pitched as being about modern women with more preoccupations than just finding a man to settle down with, Samantha is the only character that actually isn't concerned with fitting into the heteronormative path. Samantha's emotional and sexual priority is always herself. No exceptions. In season one, after falling for a man who doesn't sexually satisfy her, she dumps him. Madly in love with hotel magnate Richard in season two, she still dumps him, because despite being in love, their relationship takes a toll on her mental health. At the end of the second film,[5] she leaves her long-term monogamous partner Smith Jerrod because she realizes that, although she is capable of being in an emotionally committed relationship, she's just not happy in one. So she chooses herself. Again, good for her.

SEXY BUT NOT SEXUAL

While Carrie Bradshaw, the show's narrator, protagonist, and a professional sex columnist, calls herself a "sexual anthropologist," she is squeamish, shaming, and openly bi-phobic (in one episode, she dates a bisexual man and cannot get over this fact, declaring that "bisexuality is a layover on the way to Gaytown"). In the group dynamic, Samantha is consistently mocked even by her friends. An entire episode in the fifth season is devoted to Carrie slut shaming Samantha after she catches her in the middle of giving a blow job. When Samantha starts dating a woman, they joke that she "ran out of men" to date. When she sleeps with Charlotte's brother, Charlotte screams at her, "Is your vagina in the New York City guidebooks? Because it should be; it's the hottest spot in town!" When attending a mutual friend's suburban baby shower, the friend whispers to Carrie and Miranda, "She's not still bar-hopping and bed-hopping, is she? It's so sad when that's all you have." Samantha's relationships (especially

---

5   I'm sorry, I had to acknowledge it.

her one relationship with a woman) are not taken seriously, the implication being that, as a promiscuous woman, she is not worthy of a relationship or is incapable of having one. Samantha Jones thrived despite her own show working so hard at making her the butt of the joke. Male characters are called "committed bachelors," from Rhett Butler in *Gone with the Wind* to Mr. Big in *Sex and the City*, but she…she is a *Slut*. Because her priority is her own pleasure, the show consistently reminds us that Samantha—and women like her—shouldn't be allowed to have their cake and fuck it too.

The character's confidence comes just as much from the writing as from Kim Cattrall's performance. Since 1998, and from the very beginning of *Sex and the City*'s run, Samantha owned her sluttiness, waving it proudly like a flag embroidered with all the dicks she'd bagged. She made dirty jokes, she had whatever kind of sex she wanted, with whomever and whenever she wanted, and she at no point made herself or anyone else feel any shame for prioritizing their pleasure. She did not want a relationship, preferring to be independent. By owning and embracing what she wanted, she was the least judgmental, the most supportive, and the most confident of the four protagonists.

Samantha Jones matters. Being the Slut on a hugely successful, mainstream show that became embedded in pop culture made her into the template for pop culture Sluts to follow and for creators to update and add depth to. The idea of a female character proudly embracing her sexuality (dick puns and all) only seemed acceptable if it was a rite of passage, a phase, but not a part of their core personality.

Samantha's promiscuity was coded as a problem, but it didn't make her less than the other characters, who were actively look-ing for a monogamous relationship. While the show, on too many occasions, treated her like a joke, Samantha's confidence and self-awareness never made her the joke of her own narrative. While she started off as a female version of a traditional woman-izer (in the first season of *Sex and the City*, she defines her phi-losophy of relationships as "You can bang your head against the wall and try to find a relationship or you can say screw it and just go out and have sex like a man"), she quickly grew to be one of the most consistently wise and empowering characters on the show. Her sexuality did not dictate her life and did not diminish her ability to love and be loved. Samantha prioritized her plea-sure, and loved herself, her body, and her friends. Is that so bad?

THE WAPPENING

There has been a notable shift in the last decade in the way women talk about their desires and their sexuality, with even the word "horny" being brought back into the public consciousness in recent years. In 2017, journalist Bim Adewunmi and writer Nichole Perkins launched the podcast *Thirst Aid Kit*, in which they discuss celebrities (mostly male actors) they lust after in elaborate detail. It became a sensation, celebrating and articulat-ing female desire in a way that was engaging and entertaining and offered a fresh take on how women experience desire through pop culture. The podcast, initially produced by Buzzfeed before being picked up by *Slate* in 2019, brought the term "thirst" into the mainstream—and it was the start of a female-penned, lust-ier, feelings-centric form of pop culture criticism. *Thirst Aid Kit* touched a nerve because it gave voice to a form of fandom that enjoyed inserting itself into the narrative, verbalizing that desire, and for which a sexual gaze was an active part of watching films. In her 2019 article for the *New York Times*, Tracie Egan Morrissey declared it the year that "women got horny" and reclaimed the once crass term from teenage boys, putting it into the hands of raunchy women who were openly articulating their horniness. And in 2020, we got "WAP." A single song, a slutty anthem, sent the world into a frenzy by describing, in graphic, dripping detail, how much the women singing wanted, enjoyed, and were proficient at sex acts of all flavors.

The Cardi B single, with vocals by rapper Megan Thee Stallion, debuted in August 2020 and quickly became a number-one hit and a watercooler moment in pop culture. With extremely sexually explicit lyrics that celebrated female sexual prowess and appetite, it broke records and shone a light on a double standard that still remains in place. The audacity of "WAP" lies in how much enjoyment Cardi and Megan glean even from sex acts that have always been portrayed as demeaning to women. They write about riding and sitting on faces, giving blowjobs—and doing it well—about the type and size of dick they enjoy, about BDSM, and the tricks they can do in any and all positions. Women can talk about sex, sure, but they're not supposed to show off how much they like having it and how good they are at doing it. Think back to Madonna being put on trial in the court of public opinion (and, fictionally, in a literal court) for being good in bed. While the entire Western visual culture has been shaped around profiting off images of female beauty—around fabricating desirability and selling the possibility, the fantasy, of a lascivious, sexually powerful woman—the same cultural apparatus will cry, "Whore" if a woman actually confirms that she knows she is beautiful, desirable, and sexually capable. Women's sexuality is only offensive when it's women talking about it.

The music video is a dripping—both literally and figuratively—candy-colored, Colin Tilley–directed affair. In just over four minutes, Cardi and Megan set the world ablaze, writhing in lingerie, surrounded by snakes.[6] The video is an ode to lubrication, to sexual prowess, to kinks and orgasms. There's liquid spit on the camera lens as we approach the whorehouse. It is oozing, bathing in sex—specifically sex enjoyed by women. There is not a single man seen in "WAP." It centers pleasure, not domination. Conservative U.S. politicians publicly freaked out over the song. YouTube was flooded with reaction videos to "WAP," including an ill-received mansplaining video by British comedian Russell Brand. The "WAP challenge" became a TikTok dance craze. The lyrics to "WAP" topped the United Kingdom's most googled lyrics of 2020. It was everywhere, it was a bop, and a lot of people were very angry about the entire thing.

The hubbub generated by the unleashing of the song and accompanying video demonstrates that mainstream pop culture will still come under fire when women publicly talk about enjoying their sexuality. And when they dare to imbue their work with sex and make money off their work… Well, we've got some whores in this house.

---

6 The snake as a symbol of woman's temptation is on the nose, but it still works. It's an instant conjuring of phallic and biblical imagery. It worked for Britney Spears's 2001 MTV VMAs performance of "I'm a Slave 4 U" with a snake on her shoulders, it worked for Nikki Minaj's "Anaconda," and it worked for Cardi and Megan.

We cannot separate race and the stereotype of the Jezebel (which stereotypes Black women as promiscuous, seductive, and sexually insatiable) from the backlash to "WAP." The underlying message of the backlash was that people were still shocked by women talking about their sexuality on their own terms because it takes away the power from male creators to sexualize them. Men are not even present in the video and yet they were shocked that two women—two Black women especially—would be singing about exactly what they liked and how they liked it. It was a case of the pot calling the kettle a Slut. While we are extremely used to male coming-of-age tales that center the first romance or the first sexual experience as a key rite of passage for any young man, it's much less common for female characters discovering their sexuality to be the center of a narrative.

THE SLUT IS DEAD, LONG LIVE THE SLUT

When we think about sexually liberated, sex-positive female characters onscreen, promiscuity is no longer the frontier: it's honesty and agency.

We're moving beyond using "slut" as a derogative term and instead centering stories about women taking their sexuality into their own hands. She's acknowledged her desires and she's taking action to satisfy them. It's the action part that irks audiences. Female characters can enjoy sex, but only if they feel guilty afterward, or are punished, or are using sex as a tool, separating their bodies and sex acts from their desires. If they're sexually active and noncommittal, they're either the butt of the joke or broken.

The narratives around women's sexual agency and pleasure

have only recently started heading in a nuanced direction. Happily promiscuous characters are controversial because they pursue pleasure for pleasure's sake, they invite pleasure into their lives without letting it control them. Sluttiness is not a pathology, but slut shaming is now being used as a narrative plot point, not just as a way to judge sexual female characters. The 2010s started a cultural course correction of the savagery directed against young women through a series of films and series that directly questioned why exactly public opinion comes into play on the matter of a woman's sexuality. Narratives around female sexuality and one's agency over it begin so often in teen films, and it's in teen films that the pervasive phenomena of slut shaming is addressed and rebalanced with protagonists who do not buckle at being called sluts but rather pose the question: What makes a Slut exactly?

In *Easy A* (2010), a teen comedy that's a millennial interpretation of *The Scarlet Letter* in the tradition of nineties self-aware teen movies, the lead character, Olive (Emma Stone), is branded a slut through a fake rumor—and instead of letting herself be shamed by it, she profits off it (but never actually has sex). Actually, she calls herself a bimbo ("People hear you had sex once and, bam, you're a bimbo"). The two terms have been interchangeable in pop culture but have very different connotations. "Bimbo" is usually used to describe a conventionally attractive, sexualized, but unintelligent or naive woman. Much like "slut," it implies that these women are interchangeable and easily discarded and that their only value is their sexual appeal. And much like with the reclamation of "slut," "bimbo" has been the subject of a powerful and fun reclamation, led by the Bimbos of TikTok, who embrace the term as describing someone who "radiates confidence, is comfortable in themselves, and doesn't give a fuck about what anyone says to them." But before TikTok, there was also Marilyn Monroe, who was typecast as a breathy bimbo and remains a sex symbol, her almost effortless comedic talent and timing often coming in second place to her trademark beauty.

Going back to *Easy A*, actual virgin teenager Olive becomes the target of slut shaming after she makes a deal with a closeted friend to fake having sex with him so he doesn't get bullied for being gay. They "do it"—meaning they jump around on a bed at a party making obnoxiously comical sex noises—and voilà, he is accepted and high-fived by the jocks, while Olive becomes the school's designated Slut. She is shamed by her peers, lectured by her teachers, and dumped by her best friend. In reaction to this, Olive develops a new business: helping socially awkward dudes in her school gain traction by being allowed to claim they slept with her in exchange for gift cards to various stores, like the Gap, Office Max, and Home Depot. Her reputation tanks, but ironically, Olive starts and ends the film a virgin. Her actual sex life is never really questioned, but it's so easy to brand a teenage girl a slut for having one *alleged* sexual encounter that it becomes a social experiment of sorts. Of course, this is a teenage comedy, so things get messy and get solved by a very public, extravagant declaration of what was really going on.

In *The To-Do List* (2013), Brandy (Aubrey Plaza) is a do-gooder, a straight A student, and a virgin. Before she leaves for college, she decides to approach losing her virginity as a to-do list of tasks. She makes a list (in different colored pens) of all the sex acts she needs to tick off before going to college (it includes French kissing, motorboating, tea-bagging, and all the jobs—hand, blow, and rim). Experimenting with sex doesn't make Brandy into a Slut: she's still valedictorian, she's still studious and organized. However, when she crosses an emotional line (hooking up with a boy one of her friends likes), they are quick to label her a Slut.

In *Diary of a Teenage Girl*, the 2015 adaptation of the graphic novel by Phoebe Gloeckner, the film opens with the gleeful voice-over of a teenage girl in 1975, Minnie (Bel Powley), declaring, "I had sex today. Holy shit!" The film is an exploration of her discovery of sex and pleasure and how she wants to navigate it on her terms. It's designed for a teenage audience, so it was disheartening to see that slut shaming extended to the box office when the film was rated 18 in the United Kingdom, which meant that teenagers would not officially be able to go see the film.

Phoebe Waller-Bridge's characters, both Lulu in her first series, *Crashing*, and the titular character in *Fleabag*, sexualize everything on an almost pathological level: "From her pizza to her father. It's been drilled into her that sex is the most powerful language for a woman."

The confusing messaging about female promiscuity—that one should take advantage of being a sex object and fuck around but then settle down into being a good girl—is delivered at the same time as the message that being slutty is inherently bad, devalues a woman, and will leave her ruined, traumatized, or dead. Olive, Brandy, and Minnie are wondrous examples of teenage girls who prioritize their own comfort above the opinion of others (Olive's choice to remain a virgin counts in my book). Their decisions about sex and the messiness that ensues do *not* leave them ruined or traumatized. Sex is something that they decide to figure out on their own terms, and with the natural selfishness of teenagers, they mess some things up. There is glee and joy in Brandy and Minnie's discovery of sex.

For Waller-Bridge, "There's no such thing as a slut." I disagree. There is such a thing as a Slut, but the screen hasn't always been kind to her.

"Traditionally, the trainwreck starts out as the girl who 'has everything going for her'.... Her implosion is a way of taking her back down a few notches, to where we live."

JUDE DOYLE, AUTHOR OF *TRAINWRECK*

"Cinema has never looked kindly on the woman who is led by her desires."

RYAN GILBEY, *THE GUARDIAN*

The Trainwreck

When men are a mess, they're lovable klutzes. They're kind of hapless, but in a cute way, like a puppy that has stuck its face in a dirty puddle. They're a staple of bro comedies and every single mismatched hotness TV husband in every sitcom. Homer Simpson, Fred Flintstone, Al Bundy, Peter Griffin, the list goes on. They can mess up, over and over and over again, but they'll smile, do one good thing, and then their much-hotter wives/girlfriends will take them back with a "Well, shucks, what am I going to do with you?" shrug. It's a well-documented trope that stems from the very beginning of TV sitcoms.

But when women are a mess, they're broken and damaged and, unless they get their shit together by Act Three, unfixable (and therefore, unlovable). They're sleeping around, so they're sluts; they're drinking and partying, so they're off the rails; they wear provocative, sparkly clothes, so they're vacuous; and they're not that ambitious, so they're lazy. They are Trainwrecks and simply cannot be taken seriously.

The stakes, it almost bores me to say, are as high for women in fiction as they are in real life: the pressure to be a good example and have things sorted out by a certain age; the pressure to always be in control, to never overindulge, to plan ahead. Even the word "trainwreck" carries with it the disappointment of a head shake.

"Trainwreck," much like "bitch" or "slut," is a word rooted in the brand of clickbait misogyny associated with gossip media and celebrity culture. And much like the other two examples, it's become its own archetype, one associated directly with female excess. The Trainwreck is a woman out of control, a hot mess, fun for a while but ultimately not worthy of time, care, or a happy ending. It's familiar terminology to us now after decades of participating in a celebrity culture that profits and punishes any excess in women in the public eye.

While the focus here is not female celebrities, the relationship between fictional characters and the public and that between celebrities and the public are not dissimilar. Whether they are real or scripted, women are expected to set an example. If they deviate from that, if they transgress, they must be punished— preferably with public humiliation and social exclusion. We have a different expectation of actresses who portray these Trainwrecks—we almost want them to be as messy as their characters. There is a tired expectation that women writing about women who are vaguely similar to them in terms of experience are, essentially, writing about themselves. Especially when they are also portraying characters in their creations. Case in point: Lena Dunham as Hannah Horvath on *Girls*, Issa Rae as Issa Dee on *Insecure*, Michaela Coel as Arabella on *I May Destroy You*.

The Trainwreck archetype combines multiple transgressions.

She's never just a slut or just crazy—she's both, and more, at the same time. Not to get too literal, but once the train starts moving, we're told it's impossible for the Trainwreck to get off. She can rarely, if ever, be redeemed. And it's okay to ridicule her downfall, because it is all her own fault, all a result of her choices. In fiction, the trope has expanded in the last decade. Influenced, perhaps, by a new generation of writers and performers who have grown up with Trainwreck celebrity narratives from the noughties and have looked beyond these, there has been, of late, a cultural reappraisal of the outrageous cruelty that female celebrities were subjected to by the media and audiences. This reappraisal has been both outward and inward facing, with many cultural commentators and writers rethinking their own role and how the messages that were delivered to those of us growing up in the era of the flashy grotesquerie of noughties gossip culture have been internalized. It's the women who grew up with these contradictory messages being thrown at them, the ones who were told to love the work but hate the women making the work, who have gone on to create in-depth explorations of the Trainwreck. The most influential of the 2010s was undoubtedly *Fleabag*. But to get to her, we must first understand how her excesses have appeared so far, creating an archetype of a woman gone wild that has become so recognizable it only takes a quick glance at a movie poster to categorize her in our minds.

PARTY GIRLS

What makes a woman messy?

The short answer is excess. Of any kind. The more complicated answer is excess of *fun*. The Trainwreck in pop culture is a sort of deuteragonist of the Shrew. She's fun to be around, a "good-time girl," but ultimately a cautionary tale, a woman who will lead good girls astray if they spend too much time with her. Indulging in pleasure and partying for the sake of it is childish and unladylike. Girl parties should be wholesome sleepovers in pastel-colored pajamas, not drug-fueled benders involving sex with strangers. That's why she's often been the supporting character and not the lead.

The Trainwreck has her pop culture roots in the flappers of the 1920s. A type of new woman that emerged in the aftermath of WWI and prohibition, flappers created the image of a fun-time girl with short hair, a loud laugh, and an insatiable appetite for partying. Clara Bow, a silent film actress who became a star by popular demand, is often said to have embodied the "it factor" and become the first "it girl" of pop culture. The 1927 film *It* explores this magnetism that some people have, the attractive force that will "win all men if you are a woman and all women if you are a man," as author Elinor Glyn put it. Other notable flappers of the era, like author Zelda Fitzgerald and *New Yorker* columnist Lois Long, were known for filling their nights with "jazz, gin and jitterbugging." The flapper, which is an era-specific term that conjures up images of bob haircuts and glittery dresses, didn't last long on the scene—but the image of the frivolous, extravagant, and ultimately doomed party girl would morph in our cultural consciousness into the Trainwreck.

An episode of *Sex and the City* summarizes the way pop culture treats Trainwrecks in a single scene. In the sixth-season episode "Splat!", aired in February 2004, Carrie is attending a swanky New York loft party with her penultimate boyfriend in the series, the Russian, a.k.a. Alexandr Petrovsky (Mikhail Baryshnikov). Aging party girl Lexi Featherston (Kristen Johnston), who is wearing a shiny purple dress, doing coke in the bathroom, and loudly demanding to have a cigarette (despite smoking being out of vogue at this point), falls out the window of a high-rise. Splat.

In an oral history of the episode for *Vulture*, the show's creator explicitly called her a cautionary tale for Carrie. Lexi was a character created to "scare her with what her life could be like if she stayed" in New York instead of moving to Paris with the Russian. "No one's fun anymore! Whatever happened to fun?" rants Lexi, smoking her cigarette near an open floor-to-ceiling window, just before she falls out of said window, "I'm so bored I could die." Lexi Featherston[1] is only onscreen in one episode, and for less than ten minutes, but the message is clear: grow up or die. Trainwrecks never live to see a happy ending, and they make everyone else uncomfortable in the process.

RISE OF THE HOT MESS

Ten years later, in 2014, comedian and soon-to-be-actress Amy Schumer capitalized on the popularity of the term "hot mess" and built on it in her sketch show, *Inside Amy Schumer*. She used it to promote the show's second season, with ads showing the words "Hot" and "Mess" plastered over Schumer's face. It was all over subways and billboards in New York City. Schumer's show was a hit, running from 2013 till 2016, and in its third season received near universal acclaim. Schumer and celebrity guests

---

1   A perfect OTT name for a party girl, a name you can yell in the middle of a loud dance floor and everyone will still hear it.

poked fun at media stereotypes of women with sketches like "Chicks Who Can Hang" and "Last Fuckable Day."

Inspired by Schumer, *Time* magazine traced the evolution of the term "hot mess": "Mess can describe an eccentric person, a large quantity or something both 'praiseworthy' and 'confusing.' Hot can be used to describe someone daring, flamboyant, uninhibited, wild, intense, lustful, sexy or drunk." This definition taps into the essence of the Trainwreck. She's a contradiction, a cocktail of all the attractive qualities in a woman and the excesses she's warned against. She's appealing and likeable—but takes it too far, becoming loud, obnoxious, and attention seeking. She's fun, outgoing, and exciting—but overindulges in booze, drugs, and sex, ending up in sticky situations that are no one's fault but her own. "Trainwreck" and "hot mess" are, in the annals of pop culture, effectively interchangeable terms. They almost always refer to women and contain within them the contradiction of having too many attractive, likeable qualities.

A year later, Schumer would star in the film *Trainwreck*, her first film role and one that aimed for a reclamation of the trope we're talking about here—but instead inadvertently drove it into the white feminist ground, reducing the messiness of the Trainwreck into a fixer-upper, giving us another character who was comically broken but not unfixable. At the time of release, the film was a huge deal and landed squarely in the middle of a time when pop culture's white feminism was reaching its zenith.[2] *Trainwreck* was a huge commercial success—grossing over 140 million dollars

---

2   By the time Schumer followed up *Trainwreck* with her next big screen efforts, *Snatched* (2017) and *I Feel Pretty* (2018), the cultural temperature had started shifting away from white women's problems as a source of comedy.

globally—building on the audience's desire to see exceptionally funny women behaving messily. It's not a coincidence that the film used this term as its title. It's a one-word summary, painting an instant image of a woman we've been taught to pity. You know exactly what you're going to get: a wild woman you can make fun of, the feminized version of a fuckup.

In *Trainwreck*, Schumer is a magazine writer who enjoys drinking and fucking and never lets men stay over. We're introduced to her through a montage of guys that she's kicking out of her apartment after sex, and then see her making out with a guy by a literal dumpster. She fits the bill of the hot mess to a tee. The visual symbol of the Trainwreck is the "walk of shame": last night's makeup, night clothes in the daytime, messy hair, bad breath, or in Amy's case, waking up on Staten Island in a random dude's bed.

While *Trainwreck* promised the sort of ruthless feminist comedy that Schumer had become known and celebrated for through her sketch show, it ended up being a traditional rom-com, using the then-popular appeal of the Trainwreck to get bums on seats. The film pities its own protagonist, though, which considering it used the subversive appeal of the Trainwreck to market itself, makes for a confusing narrative. From the start, Amy is a commitment-phobe. Her dad ranted to her about monogamy when she was a child, and she's grown up to categorically refuse it. The *Little White Lies* review wrote, "She's an expert in the Apatowian art of self-sabotage, careful to accept the love she thinks she deserves and never make herself available to anything more than that." She has a lot of sex and initiates most of it, but we're never really shown that she's enjoying any of it. She's tasked to write a profile on a successful sports surgeon, Aaron Conners (Bill Hader), who becomes her love interest. She beds him but is confused when he expresses real interest ("Did you butt-dial me?" she asks). Of course, they fall in love, they have a conflict, they break up, Amy cleans up her act, she gives an over-the-top public declaration of love, and they get back together. The titular Trainwreck has fixed herself.

The film came on the heels of the massive box office success of *Bridesmaids* (2011)—an ensemble comedy led by another Trainwreck of sorts but of the more depressed kind, not the party kind—which grossed 288.4 million dollars. In *Bridesmaids*, Annie (Kristen Wiig) has lost her business, apartment, and boyfriend. Her bakery went under after the 2008 Recession, and her boyfriend left her soon after. She now lives with two weirdo English siblings and has unfulfilling, casual sex. The commercial success of that film prompted Hollywood to ponder: So women can be funny, huh?[3] And so, in the early 2010s, the Trainwreck became a staple of Hollywood comedy, in part a response to the bro-dominated comedy of the 2000s, anchored by writer-director Judd Apatow (who would direct *Trainwreck* and shepherd *Girls* into production) and his troupe of collaborators. The bro comedy "worked by parodying and subverting clichés of masculinity and genre frameworks; they mocked the inherent self-seriousness at play in sport and action films, but in doing so, they also prodded at their own weakness." —The female-led comedies did a similar thing and centered women who were not all together. The Trainwreck would become a comedy staple

---

3   Carole Lombard would be rolling her eyes from her grave.

before she became the emotional tragicomic heroine. The joke was: Hey, did you know women can be gross and chaotic too? Who would've thunk it.

But the joke was on them, because underlying the rise of this trope was a lesson, once again, on how to be an acceptable woman. Spoiler alert: don't be like them. In their book *Trainwreck*, where they trace pop culture's relationship with Trainwrecks through real-life women and their public humiliation, author Jude Doyle argues that Trainwrecks act like living guidebooks for what women should not do. The Trainwreck, they write, "lets us know when we've crossed the line, because if we act like her, or look like her, or are treated like her, we've almost certainly fucked up."

In fiction, there is an infantilizing element to the Trainwreck. She is often presented as either being in a state of pathetic emotional fixation (you should've grown out of this by now) or as having regressed due to having failed at life (be it at business, love, or beauty). She is either stuck at home or needs to go back to her childhood home for one reason or another. The Trainwreck is a woman who has failed to grow up and who therefore deserves to be punished by her own story. In *Bridesmaids*, Annie is so depressed by the failure of her baking business and her relationship that she doesn't see the possibility of another chance for herself. *The Hairpin's* Arielle Dachille describes the Trainwreck's immaturity as being "her chronic lack of pragmatism and direction, her status as romantically challenged, her absence of self-control—they all give her away as a girl, not yet a woman."

In *Colossal* (2016), we meet Gloria (Anne Hathaway) coming into her apartment the morning after a bender. She's not exactly apologetic, but she does have a story ready for her live-in boy-friend, Tim (Dan Stevens). She had to take a friend somewhere, to a loft, and then she had to wait for her, or take a nap, or something. Her story doesn't really matter, and he doesn't really want to hear it. This is not the first time she's been out partying all night, and it's not going to be the last. "You're drunk, Gloria. You're out of control," he tells her, having already packed her bags and kicking her out. When he leaves for work that morning, her friends rush into the apartment, ready to continue the party. Gloria moves back to her hometown, into her parents' empty home, where she quickly falls into a friendship with Oscar (Jason Sudeikis), a jealous boy she knew in primary school who grew up to be a bitter man, envious of Gloria and anyone who gets more attention than him. The film moves into sci-fi territory, with Gloria and Oscar both becoming huge monsters (she a kaiju, he a robot) when they step into their childhood playground. Their monstrous selves terrorize the city of Seoul, South Korea. Gloria is a mess and an alcoholic, but she's not a bad person. However, the fact that she's a mess gives the people in her life—specifically the men in her life, her ex-boyfriend Tim and Oscar—an excuse to treat her like she's a child. Tim comes to her hometown under false pretenses, berating her for taking a job as a waitress. "Can you guys please not talk about me like I'm not here?" she tells them. Gloria is calm, firm, and, crucially, sober.

OVERSTAYING THE PARTY

Pop culture has generally set the age of thirty as the time limit on fun for women. Annie in *Bridesmaids* is in her midthirties.

Fleabag is thirty-three. Amy in *Trainwreck* is thirty. Abbi and Ilana are turning thirty at the end of *Broad City*. After this point, "funloving" becomes "messy." Too much partying, too much going out, too much wine, cigarettes, drugs of any kind—all of these are signifiers of a woman on the verge of losing control. The older she gets, the more tragic the Trainwreck. Think of Lexi Featherston.

Stories about women in their thirties must focus, we're told, on steady romantic relationships, family, and ascending careers: the balance that women's magazines have sold to us as "having it all." Anything less would be a tragedy. Unless they grow up. And by "growing up," of course, we don't mean emotional growth, self-awareness, or empathy, but rather external signifiers of adulthood like having a partner or a good job. Maybe a child. Elements that denote responsibility.

The Trainwreck lacks stability, understood as a monogamous relationship and/or a family. But this suggests that the only relationships worth considering are romantic ones and completely underestimates friendships—especially those with other women—as central relationships in one's life. The kind of friendship to which romance will always come second—Laura and Tyler's in *Animals*, Fleabag and Boo's in *Fleabag*, Annie and Lillian's in *Bridesmaids*, Abbi and Ilana's in *Broad City*, Frances and Sophie's in *Frances Ha*—they, and not their occasional lovers or significant partners, are the loves of each others' lives.

The lack of definition or societal importance given to these relationships influences the types of stories that have Trainwrecks as protagonists: most are centered on single women and female friendships. If they're single, they must find love or else become unlovable forever. The nuance, intensity, and even toxicity of female friendships has been fodder for many years for Great Cinema, Great Novels, and Great Television—but as with a lot of narratives that center the interiority of women, these stories have been largely swept aside, often classified as "chick flicks," a category derogatory both to women and cinema.

The question at the heart of *Bridesmaids* is not whether Annie will find a guy to settle down with but whether she will salvage her friendship with Lillian. Riding this wave of newly lovable female slackers after the commercial success of *Bridesmaids*, *Broad City* (2014–19) started as a web series before being picked up by Comedy Central and turned into a television sitcom. The show follows the everyday lives of two twenty-somethings, Ilana (Ilana Glazer) and Abbi (Abbi Jacobson). *Broad City* is remarkably low concept, relying entirely on the personality of its two leads and their over-the-top, ebullient love for one another. What separates *Broad City* from other shows about aspirational twenty-somethings trying to make it in a big city is that they're not trying to change themselves: Abbi has aspirations of becoming an illustrator but doesn't really pursue it in earnest until the very last season of the show; Ilana is uninhibited, completely secure in her personality, her sexuality, and her lack of ambition. The core of the show is their devotion to each other and their friendship, which is absolute. Ilana, in some ways, is the natural heir to Samantha Jones, with an added millennial and queer twist. She's promiscuous, noncommittal by choice, and completely in love with herself and her best friend. She's not judgmental and is consistently supportive, but whereas Samantha was a self-made PR power player, Ilana is a slacker.

She likes smoking weed and partying and does not like work, either in practice ("I am so overworked. We all are. Today, I got eight emails") or even as a concept.

Broad City was the feminist equivalent of the bromances that had dominated mainstream comedy for the decade prior, in which the plot was virtually nonexistent and in fact didn't even matter that much because it was an excuse to just hang out with the characters. *Broad City* took the same approach, making the show both a sitcom and an anti-sitcom. It's got catchphrases ("Yas queen") and running jokes (Abbi training Shania Twain) but barely any series arcs. There are no neat endings for anything. It's an extended hang with two characters who just really enjoy each other's company. Although it poked fun at its characters' childishness, propensity for drama, and laziness, it also showed they were loving, loyal, and fun, making the Trainwreck not a trainwreck in every aspect of their lives. Much like their male counterpart, the slacker bro, they were adorable, their messiness forgiven.

Glazer and Jacobson chose to end the show after five seasons. In the finale, when Abbi is about to move out of New York, they do the one thing they hadn't managed to do in their time there: walk across the Brooklyn Bridge. Where other millennial-aimed series end with other relationships supplanting the friendships that seemed so important at the start of the show, Abbi and Ilana affirm their love for each other as "the most beautiful, deep, real, cool-and-hot, meaningful, important relationship of my life."

THE ABSOLUTE WORST

I noted earlier that Schumer's character in *Trainwreck* shares her performer's actual name—Amy—as do Ilana and Abbi on *Broad City*. These stories of Trainwrecks are often exaggerations of the personalities, experiences, or created personas of the women who wrote and, more often than not, performed them. It's a double-edged sword whereby audiences can much more easily connect the character and the creator, while also potentially confusing them, letting their opinion of the performer tarnish their relationship with the character. But while Amy, Ilana, and Abbi all had redeemable, if not aspirational, features, the protagonists of *Girls* (2009–14) were universally unlikeable—by design.

The show created, written, and starring Lena Dunham was greenlighted, famously, on the basis of a one-and-a-half page pitch after Dunham had garnered buzz and awards for her first independent film, *Tiny Furniture* (2010), in which she played a laconic recent graduate. In *Girls*, she plays *another* laconic recent graduate, Hannah Horvath, who has aspirations of becoming "a voice of her generation"-level writer in New York City. Aspirations that are being subsidized by her parents, of course, and the show kicks off when her parents decide to cut her off financially. Hannah is selfish, self-centered, and ignorant of the work it takes to actually fulfill her fantasies ("I'm planning on writing an article that exposes all my vulnerabilities to the entire internet"). Her closest friends are equally reprehensible: Marnie (Allison Williams) is also self-involved, flakey, callous with others, and totally oblivious to her lack of musical talent ("I thought this would just be a nice opportunity for us to have fun together and prove to everyone via Instagram that we could still have fun as a group"); Shoshanna (Zosia Mamet) is naive, is celebrity obsessed, and wants to live a high-end lifestyle while actually flip-flopping around her postcollege career ("I can't be surrounded by your negativity while I'm trying to grow into a fully formed woman"); and Jessa (Jemima Kirke), a free-spirit party girl who dabbles in addiction and makes consistently brash decisions ("I hate when people are early. It's so vile").

Predictably, because *Girls* is centered on the lives of four young women in New York, the show was often compared to *Sex and the City*, but *Girls* allowed its characters to be explicitly messy and deliberately unlikeable. Perhaps too much so. They are all egotistical and entitled to a comical extreme. "They think the world should be just and fair and that they're talented and will eventually find their places in it," writes Guelda Voien. One of the turning points of the show, going from an awkward watch to a full-on hate watch, was when Hannah, having been offered an e-book deal, hears of her editor's death and collapses in tears because no one has told her anything about the future of her e-book. Throughout the duration of the show, Dunham was asked constantly to defend her characters and to comment on their unlikeability. "Walter White and Tony Soprano literally murder people, and everybody's like, 'I love them,' and all we do is be kind of rude and do drugs sometimes and we're unlikable," she told *People*.

The protagonists of *Girls* were unlikeable in deeply reactionary and relatable ways, in that we all know or recognize some of their traits in people we know or in ourselves, but are also too embarrassed to admit it. Relatability isn't fun when the qualities that are relatable aren't admirable. We don't really want to relate to characters that are "messy and rude and confused and awkward and hopeless and stubborn." We turn to our fictions, or at least the fictions billed to us as sitcoms, to see our imagined, bettered selves: their funny comebacks, inside jokes, simmering sexual tension that ends in perfect romance, great apartments, and always ascending careers. That's what the characters in *Girls* expected to happen to them too.

They were also cruel, especially to each other, in ways that only the closest of friends can be. When the series was coming to an end in 2016, think pieces proliferated about how much everyone still hated all the characters, especially Hannah. Commentators confessed to "hate-watching" the show. Hannah Horvath was pitted against actual serial killer Hannibal Lecter in *The Atlantic*'s "#ActualWorst" bracket (she lost). The *Huffington Post* published a graph tracking the likeability of each character. Their likeability had become a cultural obsession in and of itself. The show even addressed this in its third season, with all of the characters piling onto each other about all the things they hate about one another. Shoshanna calls Hannah "a fucking narcissist" and tells Marnie she's "tortured by self-doubt and fear," Jessa calls Shoshanna a "cruel drunk," and Hannah accuses her of being intellectually "unstimulating." They all, essentially, hate one another: "It's not like the four of us have had any real fun together in the last two years."

At the end of the series, they decide they simply cannot be friends anymore. Crucially, they don't want to be. At Shoshanna's engagement party (which comes as a surprise because none of them had actually cared enough to ask about her romantic status), they finally decide to go their separate ways, which they had been doing anyway: "We can't hang out together anymore because we cannot be in the same room together without one of us making it completely and entirely about ourselves," says Shoshanna. And the episode allows us to see them, finally, sort of happy, framing them all dancing on their own.

It took ten years for the discourse around *Girls* to be separated from its creator; there was so much buzz, praise, criticism, and backlash happening all at once, calcifying into a slew of bitter takedowns of the show's creator, the characters, and the show itself. As the *Ringer's* Allison Herman writes: "One could barely make out the show itself through all the chaos surrounding it." *Girls* was an important show; although it was not an era-defining show as much as people wanted it to be, it certainly opened the door for more shows about women who don't necessarily fit in pretty little boxes. Though it was annoying and reductive at its best and downright cruel at its worst, the discourse around the unlikeability of its characters constituted a purging of an expectation we had collectively thought we'd moved past. Its success, and *Girls'* embracing of what Herman calls the gray area somewhere between "empowering and abysmal," opened the door for more stories that had similar aspirations.

TOO MANY COCKTAILS

Animals (2019), adapted by Emma Jane Unsworth from her own novel of the same name, is not about women falling apart due to their penchant for excess but about two friends growing apart, a slow-motion emotional breakup that has no name. When Unsworth's novel was released in 2014, it was an instant best seller. The author bemoaned the lack of hedonistic heroines who weren't healing from some unnamed trauma and were instead just having fun: "There was no recreational joy allowed with drugs or intoxication or in sex. Women who were having a lot of sex were always troubled. Someone in their family had to be dying or have a hole in their heart." The film adaptation came hot on the heels of the success of films like *Bridesmaids*, *Trainwreck*, and the slew of similar movies that come after any film is a commercial success.

Animals is the story of the intense, intoxicating friendship between two Dublin party girls: the American aphorism machine Tyler (Alia Shawkat) and aspiring writer Laura (Holliday Grainger). Their lives are a kaleidoscope of shiny dresses, wine glasses, and nighttime wildlife. In the early hours of the morning they return to their shabby chic house, and they wake up to each other, completely unencumbered, comfy in their own mess (literally *and* figuratively). Even in the cold light of day, with hungover, pale skin, dark circles under their eyes, and mismatched clothing, they're electric. Committed to fun. In one scene early on, Laura wakes up tied to her bedposts—we never find out why—and calls for her friend. Tyler shows up in sunglasses, a mustard kimono, pink pants, no bra, and silver high boots, declaring: "The way I see it, girls are tied up to bedposts for two reasons: sex and exorcisms." Everything that happens to them is just another story.

Growing up, I wanted to be a Tyler, to be the girl who could desire openly and unabashedly, who could lock eyes with the lead singer of a band and take him to the bathroom for an eight-minute quickie. Kate Stables, in her review of the movie for *Sight & Sound*, called her "a vampish mix of Sally Bowles and Marc Bolan." A girl who could wear glittery jumpsuits without worrying about whether they fit or not, secure in the knowledge she looked fantastic whether she did or not. A woman who could use three-dollar words with no hesitation or worry about being branded a pedant.

Alcohol is at the center of most of these stories. In *Animals*, Tyler and Laura's recurring in-joke is collecting the leftover wine from any glasses left unattended and drinking up the swirl when their money has run out. They'll go anywhere that offers free wine and have a one-liter jar of MDMA that they dip into like it's full of wasabi peas. The poster shows the two actresses manspreading on a couch surrounded by half-full wine bottles. They are wearing leather boots paired with bridal gowns—these girls drink, smoke, and spread their legs. Beware of the bad girls. The poster for *Trainwreck* has Amy Schumer chugging on a bottle of booze (albeit wrapped in a brown paper bag). One of the posters for *Young Adult* (2011), mocked up like the cover of a YA novel in the vein of *Sweet Valley High*, sees Charlize Theron's blond bob dangling from the side of the bed, with a hand clutching a bottle of whiskey.

In the dark comedy series *The Flight Attendant*, Kaley Cuoco stars as alcoholic flight attendant Cassie, a charismatic party girl of the skies, jet setting from one city to another while pocketing travel-sized bottles of vodka and bedding handsome men. The series combines the Trainwreck narrative with a whodunnit. After a hot date in Bangkok with a tall, dark, handsome stranger who reads Dostoevsky on a long-haul flight, Cassie wakes up next to his dead body and with fragmented memories of what happened the night before. In the first of a series of bad decisions, Cassie cleans up the crime scene and runs away. Throughout the rest of the show, she tries to uncover what happened to the stranger she spent the night with. While the mystery elements are fun to follow, it's Cassie's grappling with this situation—and herself—that's the heart of the show.

Doreen St. Félix said in the *New Yorker* that Cassie is "steering, but she is not in control." The whole series is about her trying to take control of the steering wheel, but it never becomes a tale of redemption, of going to rehab, meeting a great guy, and getting a dog. Much like Fleabag, who doesn't accept her own grief, Cassie doesn't accept the trappings of her own alcohol addiction and misremembered trauma. Kaley Cuoco plays her with a manic energy. Cassie never wants to sit still, and she cannot handle being alone. She doesn't bother hiding her constant drinking. Her co-workers mostly look away because she's, well, fun. The show introduces her as a woman living a life of extremes and contrasts, going from being the life of the party to waking up on a subway train. Inside her fridge there's only wine, Coke Zero, and pickles. She's always late, unreliable, noncommittal, and running away from problems, people, and memories.

Cassie falls well into the lineage of pop culture Trainwrecks who are at risk of drowning in a hot mess of their own creation, but this time round the show is not unsympathetic toward her. *The Flight Attendant* wants Cassie to get better. In a similar vein to that of *Fleabag*, the show finds a way to get us inside Cassie's head, via a memory palace (a replica of the hotel room where the whole ordeal began), where the show can turn her manic internal monologues into dialogue. When she's in her head, Cassie doesn't speak directly into the camera like Fleabag, but she does speak to a dead one-night stand.

Party girls—like Laura and Tyler, like Cassie—are intoxicating to watch. They have an eagerness to live and to love and, sometimes, just a hint of sadness, a depth of feeling, but it never overwhelms them. But the movies seem to pity them. They are over the top, too much, laughable at their best and ruiners of lives at their worst. While the fictional, alcoholic, bon vivant actors in *Withnail and I* (1987) and real-life (and fictionalized) drug aficionado Hunter S. Thompson in *Fear and Loathing in Las Vegas* (1998) become pop culture icons, inspiring drinking games and quote-along screenings, girls like Tyler are pitied with a somber headshake. They are always a bad influence on others. Could you be the most alluring and the most pitied girl at the party?

When she doesn't fix herself or move on, the Trainwreck is truly a tragic figure. Take Mavis Gary (Charlize Theron) in *Young Adult*, a thirty-eight-year-old former "psychotic prom queen bitch," now a YA ghostwriter living in Minneapolis. Mavis is truly unpleasant. We meet her, in true Trainwreck fashion, facedown on her bed, fully clothed in sweatpants and a Hello Kitty T-shirt. Her apartment is messy, full of Diet Coke cans and empty containers. She doesn't even take her dog out for a walk—instead locking the poor Pomeranian out on her balcony. Mavis actively refuses to believe that anybody could be a good person—or even worse, aspire to be a good person—because for her it's all about appearances. When out on a date with a man who tells her about his volunteering work, she scoffs, replying only with a "Yikes!" Becoming obsessed with reconnecting with her teenage boyfriend Buddy Slade (Patrick Wilson), Mavis impulsively drives back to her small hometown of Mercury intent on getting Buddy back. Meanwhile, Buddy is happily married and has just had a baby. Granted, he is not the brightest guy, but he's a generally affable, kind man who will go out for a drink with a high school ex-girlfriend. Mavis is also, very clearly, an alcoholic. She'll down double whiskeys like they're water and only discards her rank sweatpants when she's about to meet Buddy.

With Mavis being played by Charlize Theron, who is, in the words of *Young Adult*'s director, "intimidatingly beautiful," there is a physical deconstruction of the Trainwreck. Mavis has thinning hair, bad skin, and last night's makeup still on. She's not a Trainwreck because she parties too much; she just doesn't care. She fully believes and trusts that she can rely on her beauty, on cleaning up, getting a mani-pedi and a blowout, and regaining her power over people. An overgrown Mean Girl, she's used to being served. The idea of someone not wanting to be with her or be her is unfathomable to Mavis.

LOVABLE FUCKUP

Being a Trainwreck is fun transformed into a fault: playing dress-up, indulging pleasure for pleasure's sake, without a plan, with abandon. Being a Trainwreck is being messy, and being messy as a woman means being both threatening and pathetic.

Fleabag is both and neither, at the same time. The titular character from Phoebe Waller-Bridge's hit BBC show (initially a one-woman stage show) moves from one expectation to another in a narrative dance that gains new layers on every watch. *Fleabag* leaned into every single element of the Trainwreck and subverted them all.

Fleabag's central conflict is internal, a mix of grief and guilt over losing her best friend, Boo. She slept with Boo's boyfriend, and although Boo never found out it was her, the infidelity led to her accidental death. We don't find this out until the last episode, but this is always on Fleabag's mind, popping up in the form of flashbacks to their moments of friendship, the kind where you create a bubble of inside jokes and naked emotional intimacy, the kind where you can ugly-cry without a second thought.

Fleabag wears multiple masks, and each one is systematically torn down as the show progresses. At first, Fleabag is pure chaos with a chic bob. When we meet her, she's barely holding it together. She compulsively antagonizes her family, her boyfriend, and strangers, even those trying to help her. She brings sex into everything ("I'm not obsessed with sex; I just can't stop thinking about it. The performance of it. The awkwardness of it. The drama of it. The moment you realize someone wants your body. Not so much the feeling of it"). She looks down on her boyfriend Harry, even breaking up with him out of boredom or because her flat needs a clean. Her tiny guinea pig-themed café is on the brink of going out of business, but she won't ask for help or even open the bills when they arrive. She's plummeting toward disaster, trying to expedite its arrival by avoiding dealing with any of it.

To be blunt, Fleabag is not having a nice time, and she's kind of an asshole. That's okay, though. She's *written* as an asshole. She's constantly confrontational and seems to be allergic to basic niceties, bulldozing through every situation, determined to be the antihero of her own story. However, she is also grappling with the intense pressure of performing coolness, of having it all together without ever asking for help, as all the feminist lectures she's

attended have taught her. Her guilt manifests in self-destructive
behavior, or perhaps this tendency to self-sabotage was always
there. On a date with a guy who doesn't feel comfortable going
back home with her, who tells her he likes her, she just replies,
"You're a dick," then steals twenty pounds from him and leaves.
Instead of asking for help, she turns up at her father's house late
at night, screaming into his letterbox: "I have a horrible feeling
that I'm a greedy, perverted, selfish, apathetic, cynical, depraved,
morally bankrupt woman who can't even call herself a feminist,"
she tells her father, who replies simply, "You get that from your
mother."

But Fleabag is not irredeemable. She has a hard time and
doesn't know if she's equipped to change. She helps a random
drunk woman who's passed out at a bus stop. She's kind to her
sister, Claire, who she envies for being the image of perfect,
controlled, successful womanhood (Claire has "two degrees, a
husband, and a Burberry coat") while also seeing through the
polished facade to the messiness in Claire's life. Meanwhile,
Claire envies Fleabag's charisma, her appeal, her—for lack of
a better word—likeability. It angers her that Fleabag is witty,
funny, and attractive even when she's a mess. The other characters in her life don't know how to support her, deepening
her sense of loneliness. She calls her dead best friend's phone
repeatedly, perhaps bringing herself up to confess her transgression against Boo, perhaps just to hear her friend's voice again.
She is asked many times throughout the show, "Are you okay?"
and her reply is always, "I'm fine," even though it's very clear
to everyone—even the drunk woman semipassed out on the
sidewalk—that she is very much not fine. *Fleabag* is not about

unruliness, it's about accepting the general messiness of everyday life and the very specific brand of messiness that comes with being a millennial woman.

The entirety of *Fleabag*'s first season is a study in unlikeability. All the characters, especially the women, dislike each other and themselves. Fleabag, most of all, doesn't like herself. Her frequent breaking of the fourth wall—speaking directly to camera, to us, the audience—become less a series of winking jokes on rewatch and takes on a more self-loathing taste, the inner monologue of a woman who hates herself but needs to cover this feeling up even to herself. Waller-Bridge, speaking on the podcast *The Guilty Feminist* with host Deborah Frances-White, said that "the relationship between her and the camera is a relationship with her and the idea of being judged." Fleabag's harshest judge is herself, and at the end of the first season, her barely held together exterior falls down.

Fleabag hasn't really been shown much kindness—especially by those closest to her. The final episode is a compilation of humiliations: her stepmother makes her serve drinks at her sex-hibition art show; her ex-boyfriend has fully moved on and rejects her awkward come-ons; her fuck buddy dumps her after their date to focus on his feelings for another woman; and her sister disavows her because she believes Fleabag kissed her husband. Infantilized endlessly by all of them, she plays up her role as the designated hot mess, causing a scene. The series ends with the first honest moment of the show: Fleabag, after wandering alone at night with her tear-streaked makeup all over her face (the image that would become synonymous with the show and a perennial presence on mood boards everywhere), confesses to the same loan manager she antagonized in the very first episode that she fucked up her business, her family, and her best friend, all because of her obsession with sex:

> *Fleabag: And sometimes I wish I didn't even know that fucking existed. And I know that my body, as it is now, really is the only thing I have left, and when that gets old and unfuckable I may as well just kill it. And somehow there isn't anything worse...than someone who doesn't want to fuck me. I fuck everything...except for when I was in your office, I really wasn't trying to have sex. You know, everyone feels like this a little bit, and they're just not talking about it, or I'm completely fucking alone...which isn't fucking funny.*
>
> *Bank Manager: Right, well... I should probably, erm... I should probably, erm... I should probably...*

[He appears to leave but actually he's getting something.]

> *Bank Manager: People make mistakes. It's why they put rubbers on the ends of pencils.*

Fleabag hit a chord because it does what most stories about Trainwrecks never do: Fleabag is given a chance to get better on her own terms. She takes the Trainwreck and shows us the emotionally rich landscape of her mess. She doesn't miraculously form an attachment that promises to "fix" her and get her up to society's standards of a put together woman (we see through Claire that this is a mirage), but she gets a fighting chance. When we next see Fleabag, she's still a mess (blood running down her

nose, her family furious with her once again), but she's actually
doing better. She's stopped having meaningless sex, her guinea
pig café is booming, and her relationship with her sister is
becoming more open, more honest. She does fall in love with a
priest, but, hey, nobody's perfect.

Ultimately, Trainwrecks are hungry characters. And female
hunger, whatever shape it takes, has always been scrutinized, chastised, and punished. They're thirsty for experiences, booze, excess,
and freedom. Booze or drugs or sex may not satisfy their particular thirst, but stories that treat their party girls with the same generosity that we afford to our male fuckups are starting to appear
more frequently. Writing about *Animals* for the *Independent*, critic
Clarisse Loughrey summarizes it: "You'll find no life lessons here.
Laura and Tyler are free to pursue their desires, to whatever end."

What makes Trainwrecks so endearing, actually, is their honesty about their lack of direction. Pop culture has ways of simultaneously elevating fun, gregarious women and punishing the
ones who appear to be wayward or directionless. Anything that
strays away from a narrow path of acceptable, ladylike issues is
teetering too close to the edge of becoming a Trainwreck. There
is so much familiarity in the act of desperate clinging on to something that worked for a while—a friendship, a lifestyle—because
it's absolutely terrifying to take a next step when everything
around you seems to drill in how easy it is to fuck up and how
unsalvageable a mistake can be for a woman. But the Trainwreck
in these stories, especially in the ones penned by women, is not
a figure of pity but one of forgiveness. Watching them mess up
may be explosive fun, but seeing them acknowledge their mess
and move on without letting it define them is cathartic.

"She's zany, but in a cute way!"

"You've seen the madwoman before. She's your ex-girlfriend with smeared red lipstick refusing to quiet her anger during an argument. She's the former wife trapped in the attic whose machinations have been branded unfit for society. She's every woman who has been called 'too much.'"

The Crazy Woman

There is no greater compliment to a film than having a universally recognized phenomenon named after it. "Gaslighting" is a term that's everywhere today, diluted to within an inch of its original meaning, a runner-up in the Oxford University Press's "most popular new words" in 2018. The term describes the manipulation of someone to make them question reality, their perception of it, and their own sanity. And it started with a movie, *Gaslight* (1944). Well, not quite. The term itself originated in a medical journal in 1988, but it was popularized, like many things, through film. The Hollywood version was a remake of a 1940 British film of the same name, itself based on a play from 1938, titled *Gas Light*.[1]

In the film, Paula (Ingrid Bergman) marries the dashing Gregory (Charles Boyer) after a short but intense romance. He insists they relocate to London, where she doesn't know anyone.

---

1 Let's quit complaining about Hollywood running out of ideas. It's old news, literally.

Things start to go missing; she hears footsteps coming from their empty attic and sees lights flickering. Paula is accused of being a kleptomaniac and is increasingly confined to her house by her preoccupied husband. She becomes a nervous wreck, a shell of her former self, isolated, paranoid, constantly trembling. In a clever twist that will not surprise today's audiences, it turns out it was the husband all along. He isolated her from everyone around her and crafted situations that would make her question her perception of reality so he could eventually institutionalize her against her will and steal jewels belonging to her late mother (who he also murdered, by the way). While Paula gets away in the end, we don't get to see the lasting effects of such a traumatic ordeal.

The scariest part of *Gaslight* is how easily we believe that unusual or abusive behavior is all an exaggeration on the woman's part. We'd rather think a woman crazy than believe that there's something bigger at play, and when a woman is presented to us as crazy, her entire worldview is negated before she even utters a word.

THE ROOTS OF HYSTERIA

There are a lot of things I've not done, a lot of things I've not said, for fear of coming off as crazy. I guarantee that every single woman has thought herself to be going crazy at least once in her life. It's the ultimate technique in making women doubt their own experiences.

This is not an accident. The roots of our social and cultural obsession with deeming women crazy go back millennia. Hysteria comes from the Greek word "hystera," meaning "uterus." Victorian physicians used hysteria as a catchall illness for women who were not behaving well in one way or another. It was very specifically a female disease because it was related to the uterus, which was deemed to be at risk of roaming wild around a woman's body and wreaking physiological and psychological harm. There was no cure. If a woman didn't like sex, or liked sex too much, she was hysterical. If she was depressed, or manic, or suffered any form of mental illness, or basically deviated from the very strict constraints of what made up the Victorian ideal of womanhood, she was hysterical.

Even though we no longer have the same attitudes toward women, the Victorian legacy of the hysterical woman remains alive and well, especially in the fictions that we create.

Writing for the *Guardian*, journalist and former "Mind Your Language" columnist Gary Nunn summarizes this lasting legacy:

> Let's invent a character. This person is quirky, outspoken and highly intelligent—sometimes to the bewilderment of those around them. If he's a man, he's a "bearded eccentric intellectual," "misunderstood" or a "tortured genius." But what if our invented character is a woman? My guess is that she would be described as "shrill," "unhinged," "depressed," "bonkers" and almost certainly "hysterical." We seem to describe hyper-intelligent women and men using different value judgments.

BUNNY BOILER

Fast forward to 1987, when another movie would become such a cultural behemoth that it would inspire a theoretical framework of interpersonal relationships (whereby the attractive qualities in a person eventually turn toxic and lead to a breakup), birth a character that would terrify all the men in America, and define the era's image of the Crazy Woman: *Fatal Attraction* (1987).

In the film, publishing executive Alex Forrest (Glenn Close) is a cool-as-fuck eighties broad. She's got the blond perm, bold lipstick, shoulder pads, and leather jacket. She's got a cool job, she's literate and cultured, and she lives in an open-plan loft in the Meatpacking District in New York City. She's independent, listens to opera, smokes, and dances like nobody's watching. Her mistake: she really wants to sleep with Michael Douglas.[2]

The attraction between Dan Gallagher (Michael Douglas) and Alex is immediate and undeniable. They lock eyes at an industry party and enjoy a harmless little flirt in a room full of people. Dan, at this point, is flattered. Alex is visibly turning heads, and easily rebuffs other men's attention. She chooses him. They bump into each other once again in a meeting, which would make a great meet-cute if it weren't for the annoying question of Dan's wife and child. For all intents and purposes, he is a content family man. And yet—he makes the decision to go out with Alex for lunch.

"As a lawyer, you must be discreet. Are you?" Alex asks. The way she looks at him, in that pause, the screen might as well have been set on fire. Their sexual chemistry is irrefutable.[3]

"Am I what?" He is bemused, struggling to catch up.

---

2   I'm fascinated by the subgenre of eighties cinema in which women really, like *really*, want to fuck Michael Douglas and risk their lives, their careers, and their sanity for it. Case in point: *Fatal Attraction, Disclosure, Basic Instinct.*

3   The shocking part was how much Glenn Close had to fight for this role, mainly because she was not considered sexy enough. The studio didn't even want her to audition.

"Discreet?"

This entire scene, by the way, Dan is holding a match to light Alex's cigarette.

It just so happens that Dan's wife is out of town for the weekend, so that innocent lunch turns into a two-day fuckfest. They go out, have tons of sex, make spaghetti, and generally have a great time. Then Dan has to go back home, and Alex gets upset. She gets clingy, tries to get him to stay by slashing her wrists. From that moment, Dan creates distance; at first politely, then firmly, then radically. Alex calls his office relentlessly, then his home. Her attempts at getting his attention increase in desperation: she feigns being a potential buyer of his apartment so she can meet his wife, Beth (Anne Archer), tells him she's pregnant with his baby and planning to keep it, sends him tapes filled with rabid verbal abuse, pours acid on his car, and goes to his suburban home and kills his daughter's pet rabbit by boiling it. At her worst, Alex kidnaps his daughter, taking her from school. She returns the girl unharmed, but the panic of her missing child causes Beth to get into a car accident. Alex decides she needs to kill Beth, seeing her as the only thing standing between her and Dan's being together. She attacks her at their home, but ultimately, it is Beth who ends Alex, shooting her through the chest. Alex dies, and Dan saves his marriage.

Fatal Attraction caused a furor. It was the biggest film of the year, grossing 320.1 million dollars, and spent eight weeks at the top of the U.S. box office. Director Adrian Lyne would spend the first two weeks of the film's release standing in the back of theaters, watching the audiences' reactions, lapping up the audience participation, the yelling of "Kill the bitch!" at the end. Women went to hairdressers asking for "a haircut like Alex Forrest." Men rang up director Adrian Lyne to say, "Thanks a million, buddy, you've ruined it for us." A slew of copycat, similarly titled thrillers were released (*Dangerous Affection, Fatal Confession, Deadly Illusion*). *Saturday Night Live* did skits (including one where Glenn Close reprised her role as Alex Forrest, this time attending a support group meeting where she freaks everyone out). Years later, Tom Hanks's character would summarize the pop culture phenomenon in *Sleepless in Seattle*: "It scared the shit out of me! It scared the shit out of every man in America!"

Alex Forrest became *the* eighties villain, *the* female villain. A fearsome, uncontrollable Crazy Woman, reduced by reinterpretations and spoofs to a woman obsessed who couldn't deal with rejection. But Glenn Close, who portrayed her (and terrified every man in America), never saw her as a villain. Alex was not a Crazy Woman; she was a human being struggling. Giving an address to the Oxford Union in 2018, Close said: "Alex is a soul in crisis and in need of help. And for reasons that are only hinted at in the screenplay, she's incapable of a mature and sustaining relationship and is destructive to herself and others." In every single interview or revisiting of the film, she's steadfastly held on to this view. Speaking to the BBC's Film Programme in 2018, she talked about rewatching the film in the wake of the reckoning around female anger: "It would be wonderful to tell the same story from her point of view."

There is a palpable sadness to Alex, something raw and brittle that lies underneath the one-liners and the leather jackets. Her obsession with Dan isn't really about Dan at all. When she declares she wants to keep the baby and demands he take responsibility, the shock of his rebuttal is not due to it's being a rejection of her but rather it's being a rejection of responsibility.

He was the married man and made the decision to have an affair. And yet here she was, losing her sense of self, demanding a crumb of accountability.

It was also, initially, meant to be an entirely different film. Based on the short film *Diversion*, written and directed by James Dearden, it was meant to be precisely about a married man taking responsibility for an affair and the harm that affair inflicted on both his lover and his wife. It was not going to be a film that would blame the other woman, or the wife for pushing the husband into the arms of another, but would rather explore the husband's accountability. That movie would never get made because—I wish I were making this up—the husband was deemed *too unlikeable*. During the development process, Dearden was pushed to soften the husband and make Alex more extreme, more aggressive, more obsessed. Studios refused to let Dan be a cheater, because they wanted audiences to feel for him. Michael Douglas, already attached to the project, also refused to play a "weak, unheroic character."[4] The husband was reframed as a victim, and Alex as the Crazy Woman.

The thing is, she was designed to be relatable. Sherry Lansing, the head of Paramount Studios at the time and coproducer of the film, said: "All of us have made a call in the middle of the night when we shouldn't have, or driven by somebody's house when we shouldn't have. I've never boiled a rabbit, but I've made phone calls."

"It's going to go on and on until you face your responsibilities," Alex tells Dan. In a line delivery that is as menacing as it is indignant, she says, "I will not be ignored, Dan." Dan pities her, calling her "sick." "Why? Because I won't allow you to treat me

---

4   Joke's on him, though, because even as it is, Dan is a weak, unheroic character.

like some slut that you can just bang a few times and then throw me in the garbage?"

The film and the reactions to it, both positive and negative, were quick to demonize Alex Forrest. But there were two people making decisions at that lunch, and only one of them was married. The cultural reaction to *Fatal Attraction* tells us so much about how people still love to hate and fear the Crazy Woman. The term "bunny boiler," which became synonymous with an unhinged woman, came from this film. Close and Douglas were on the cover of *Time* magazine in November 1987 in a long piece that explored the zeitgeisty phenomenon of the film. That same article dubbed Alex "a creature of insatiable lust and leeching possessiveness." There was a significant change in the film after the initial test screenings. Initially, Alex was going to kill herself and leave Dan's fingerprints on the knife, incriminating him for her murder beyond the grave (remind you of anyone? *Cough cough, Amy Dunne*), while listening to the opera *Madama Butterfly*, which is an ongoing motif throughout the film for her. Test audiences hated it. They wanted Alex punished. Despite a lot of protests from Glenn Close (she complained for weeks, and really fought against the changes, she cared so deeply about Alex), the production reshot the ending, having Alex killed not by Dan but by Beth, the untarnished woman, a beacon of "chic domesticity" (as *Time* called her).

Feminist writer Susan Faludi, in her groundbreaking book of essays *Backlash*, condemns the film as widely misogynistic and emblematic of a particular misogyny of the 1980s, one that condemned the single, career-minded, modern woman who had erupted after the third wave of feminism with the best, most wide-ranging tool available: the movies. The ending of *Fatal*

Attraction, the pointed choice of having Beth kill Alex in her home, was decried by Faludi: "It's a nightmare from which he [Dan] wakes up sobered, but unscathed. In the end, the attraction is fatal only for the single woman."

Audiences loved to hate Alex and used her as a cultural scapegoat for the dangers of singledom, independence, and careerist or sexually emancipated women—but, much like Glenn Close, I love Alex Forrest. The film portrays her downfall into obsession in a slick, compelling way, the layers of coolness and success that she's wrapped in at the start being broken down one by one. Her black leather outfits and smoky eye makeup are replaced with shapeless white gowns reminiscent of a psychiatric institution, her cool industrial apartment becoming more a cold cell. She is not the villain of the film, and neither is she the victim of it. Perhaps at the time, the shock to the system of seeing a woman like Alex Forrest on the screen was too much, but *Fatal Attraction* contains in itself a whole other film in the margins, in Alex's silences. I, for one, would like to see that film Glenn Close wants to make from Alex's perspective.

UNHINGED WHITE WOMAN

The Crazy Woman is a woman obsessed. The object of her obsession is often romantic, but not always. Even with Alex Forrest, you could argue that she's obsessed with an ideal that has been sold to her, an ideal that Dan inhabits and doesn't appreciate: the wholesome family life, big house, cute kid, pet bunny. She's also been sold the ideal of modern womanhood, the smart, independent, sexy woman's life she inhabits—but which is also turned against her. How is she supposed to win?

In *Single White Female*, both the Crazy Woman and the object of her obsession are women. The 1992 psychosexual erotic thriller starred Bridget Fonda as Allison "Allie" Jones, a software engineer who finds a beautiful rent-controlled apartment in an Upper West Side building[5] and needs to find a roommate pronto because she's just caught her fiancé cheating on her. She puts out a personal ad ("SWF seeks same," which was actually the title of the novel the film is based on) and meets Hedy (Jennifer Jason Leigh), who seems like a perfect roommate at first. While Allie is a self-possessed, successful woman, Hedy is her polar opposite: she's mousy, demure, and introverted. They quickly bond in the way you would with someone you're sharing a living space with—but Hedy starts to edge closer to something a little different. She gets jealous and resentful when Allie reconciles with her fiancé and they decide to move in together. It's implied she murders Allie's dog by pushing him out of the window. Allie is not oblivious to these things, but she only realizes the extent of Hedy's obsession when the latter gets a makeover to look exactly like her. Hedy gets her hair dyed and cut to match Allie's, changes her style to match hers, and even goes to a club masquerading as her. Hedy takes this role-play to a new level when she sexually assaults Allie's boyfriend under the guise of being Allie—and then murders him with Allie's stiletto. Hedy's obsession with Allie is not really about Allie at all. Allie is an image, an idealized version of modern femininity that is right there in front of her but still unattainable. A rejection from Allie, for Hedy, is bigger than

---

5   Another subgenre I'm obsessed with: the rent-controlled, spacious apartments that only exist in the fictional New York of the movies. They're always spacious, airy, bright, with floor-to-ceiling windows, and *always* have a killer living in the building.

just one person. In one scene, she tells her: "You're in a different league—I know that. You have this great personality, you've got this great style, you run your own business. You're always going to find somebody. You've got to be stupid to think that you won't."

Like with *Fatal Attraction*, there is much left unsaid about Hedy—she embodies a particular Crazy Woman that is so riddled with inadequacies and self-hate that she wants to be anyone other than herself.

A millennial spin on Hedy appears in the 2017 film *Ingrid Goes West*, where the titular Ingrid (Aubrey Plaza) is so obsessed with Instagram influencer Taylor (Elizabeth Olsen) that she moves to town, dyes her hair to match Taylor's, and kidnaps her dog as a ploy to ingratiate herself into her life.[6] They start off by being friends, but inevitably it is revealed that Ingrid has fabricated almost everything about her life and her personality specifically to appeal to Taylor. It's also—we know from the very first scene—not the first time she's done this.[7]

"I thought we were friends," Ingrid tells Taylor, which is a one-sided statement. "You are a sad, pathetic, and very sick person," Taylor spits at Ingrid, her words echoing Dan's in *Fatal Attraction*. Taylor confesses her deception on Instagram ("I'm just tired of being me") and eventually gets a happy ending, or a twisted version of one. She gets the followers she wanted: digital acceptance and support.

In *Trainwreck*, Jude Doyle writes of our own parasitic

---

6   It's always about killing pets and matching hair. To quote Fleabag: "Hair is *everything.*"

7   She crashed the wedding of another influencer, who she had previously become fixated on.

fascination with the Crazy Woman: "They're where sexual over-abundance and emotional overabundance collide and merge into something that is both, and neither, and worse than either." The Crazy Woman, even the obsessive, is very, very tired. In *Fatal Attraction*, *Single White Female*, and *Ingrid Goes West*, the Crazy Woman is villainized for trying to fit (in her own, unhinged way) into the mold she was told she needed to fit into. And in her own way, she's tired of being ogled but not seen. Alex, Hedy, Ingrid—they're all accused of being lonely to the point of being sick. They all suffer from a terrorizing type of loneliness, that of a woman alone, being told from all sides that she's unfit for love.

YOU LIKE YOUR GIRLS INSANE

There is one type of Crazy Woman that we love to see, one that's culturally acceptable, even tantalizing. The melancholic chic type, the skinny, sad white woman who wallows beautifully, who makes depression seem chic. In the 1966 French film *Une femme est une femme*, star Anna Karina, looking down demurely yet defiantly, says: "There's nothing more beautiful than a woman in tears." Karina's words perfectly sum up what would materialize a few decades later. In 1999, two films would set a blueprint for white girl sadness: *Girl, Interrupted* and *The Virgin Suicides*.

In the former, our lead sad white girl is Susanna (Winona Ryder), a troubled teenager who has engaged in an affair with her parents' older married friend and attempted suicide. A lot of the girls in the institution suffer from eating disorders, including anorexia, bulimia, and binge eating. Many of them self-harm in one way or another. Some have suffered extreme trauma in childhood.

One is a pathological liar, another is just gay. The standout among the ensemble is Lisa (Angelina Jolie), a hurricane of attitude that behaves like the entire place would collapse without her. "Lisa thinks she's hot because she's a sociopath," we're told. But Lisa's not a murder-y kind of sociopath. She's cruel and cunning but mostly she's hateful. Yet we never really fear Lisa. And we never quite pity her either. Played by Angelina Jolie with a scissor-cut short fringe and a tatty leather coat, her savage putdowns of the other women around her hits us like a brick, but because she's not actively obsessing over any one person, or murdering pets, we give her a pass.

Susanna, at first, is a sort of spy. She ends up in the institution because she had attempted suicide and because of her "generally pessimistic attitude," which is completely at odds with her WASP-y upbringing and the expectations placed on her. Later on, she is diagnosed with borderline personality disorder (and told it's particularly common among young women). She's repeatedly told by others, and tells herself, that she doesn't really belong there, not with these proper crazy women. There is no real plot to *Girl, Interrupted*; it's a mood piece about the Crazy Woman, or different versions of them, the particularities of female craziness all displayed for us to gawk at and, perhaps, see ourselves in. It's a pick'n'mix of crazy. Each of the ensemble characters is diagnosed explicitly; we're given a specific reason why they're there. Crucially, they are never turned into villains. At the end of her time at the institution, Susanna's voice-over offers a note of empathy for all the girls confined to these institutions: "Have you ever confused a dream with life? Or stolen something when you have the cash? Have you ever been blue? Or thought your train moving while sitting still? Maybe I was just crazy. Maybe it was the sixties. Or maybe I was just a girl…interrupted." It's a melancholic but reassuring note to end on, a note for all girls who fear turning into crazy women.

The film was a passion project of Ryder's, who both starred in and produced it (she had acquired the rights to Susanna Kaysen's memoir and tried for seven years to get the project off the ground). The reviews were middling, and the film was often considered unfavorably compared to the much lauded male-centric *One Flew Over the Cuckoo's Nest* (1976). Roger Ebert complimented Ryder and Jolie but bemoaned that their performances needed a film with "more reason for existing."

Susanna and Lisa are two opposite ends of the spectrum of white woman sadness. Lisa is manically sexual, teasing a hapless ice cream parlor employee, blowing strangers, and over-sexualizing every situation. She's so detached from her body that she sees it as a tool—and others as objects that occasionally serve a purpose. She eggs on a fellow patient, Daisy, to suicide, mocking her self-harm, her disordered eating, and her implied incestuous relationship with her father with naked cruelty:

Help me understand, Daisy. Because, I thought you didn't do Valium. Tell me how this safety net is working for you. Tell me that you don't take that blade and drag it across your skin and pray for the courage to press down. Tell me… how your daddy helps you cope with that. Illuminate me. I bet…with every inch of his manhood. They didn't release you because you got better, Daisy. They just gave up. You call this a life, hmm? Taking daddy's money, buying your dollies and your knickknacks, eating his fucking chicken, fattening up like a prize fucking heifer. You changed the scenery but not the fucking situation. And the warden makes house calls. And everybody knows. Everybody knows...that he fucks you. But what they don't know... is that you like it. Hmm? You like it. But hey man, it's cool. Whatever. A man is a dick is a man is a dick is a chicken is a dad a Valium a speculum, whatever. Whatever. You like being Mrs. Randone. Probably all you've ever known, huh?

Lisa mocks Daisy even in death, reacting to the discovery of her body with a simple "What an idiot"—and proceeds to take money out of her pockets. Lisa's viciousness, though, is sort of acceptable, because she's never leaving the institution.

You see, the only Crazy Woman that we are told is permissible, even if she was of the sad white girl variety, is a dead crazy woman or a forever imprisoned one. We last see Lisa looking through the barred windows, tied to a hospital bed, the world safe from her madness.

MELANCHOLIC CHIC

In a kind of zeitgeisty kismet, Sofia Coppola's *The Virgin Suicides* would come out the same year and was also bemoaned by critics. Coppola made her debut with a film that centered girlhood and teenage crazy girls. But they weren't crazy in an institutionalized way: they were sad in a way that only waifish, beautiful girls could be sad.

There is a mythology that is built around Crazy Women, which is the central conceit of *The Virgin Suicides*. We are told the story of the Lisbon sisters, five beautiful blond girls who all end up dying by suicide after months of being confined to their home by their conservative parents, who are still reeling after the loss by suicide of their youngest daughter, Cecilia.

The film, in the same vein as the book it's based on, is told through the perspective of observers, not the Lisbon sisters themselves. The sisters—Therese, Mary, Bonnie, Lux, and Cecilia—are beautiful enigmas to decipher for the group of young teenage boys, their neighbors, who try to piece together the sisters' personalities and lives from afar. After all the girls die via a suicide pact, the boys buy up as many of their possessions as they can at a yard sale. The narration, delivered by their middle-aged selves, continues to ponder the enigma of these girls. Watching both these films as a teenage girl, their influence was immense. These were the first representations of an unhappy emotional landscape I'd encountered, one that tried to visualize the inner world of teenage girls, dreamy and not yet disappointed with the world.

Jude Doyle traces the visual history of the Crazy Woman beyond cinema back to paintings depicting women confined to the legendary Parisian institution la Salpetriere, "half-clothed, unhinged, somehow both sexually titillating and fundamentally abhorrent, grotesquely exposed and irresistibly available." A direct line can be traced from these images to *The Virgin Suicides*, to the overexposed paparazzi photos of female celebrities, and to the music videos of Lana Del Rey, perhaps the contemporary poster girl of white girl sadness.

Whether Del Rey, the musical persona created by Elizabeth Grant, is a real or an exaggerated personality, I don't know, and perhaps no one ever will, but it is a persona that has stuck in the public ever since her single "Video Games" went viral in 2011. The rise of Lana Del Rey coincided with the rise of Instagram and Tumblr, two social platforms that relied on images, on mood, and on snippy, lowercase aphorisms. The aesthetic of her videos cannot be separated from the melancholic chicness of her lyrics, all of which are a combination of suicidal ideation, reminders of her sadness, lusting after dangerous or violent men, fetishization of abusive relationships, and generally looking pretty and feeling bad. The entirety of the video for her single "Summertime Sadness" is composed of different shots of Lana jumping off a cliff, looking fabulous and chic. Further leaning into this persona, in a now infamous interview, Del Rey told a *Guardian* journalist, "I wish I was dead already." Lana Del Rey is like a lost Lisbon sister, uncomfortable in her own skin unless she's wanted by men, unless she's being watched.

The thing about white girl sadness is just that—sad girls are always white and they're always sexy because they're so sad. They fetishize death, "something they don't have to worry about—at least not systematically," writes Safy-Hallan Farah in her newsletter "Hip to Waste." Their sadness and, sometimes, their suicides become enigmas that increase their appeal, like the mysterious pedestal that the neighborhood boys put the Lisbon sisters on. The troubling implication is that mental illness in women is only acceptable (desirable, even) if it's beautiful—and a very specific type of beautiful at that—embodying a frail chicness that slots perfectly into the social narrative that white women must be protected at all costs, that their sadness can never be ugly, that Crazy Women are only crazy if they're not hot.

WHO'S BEHIND THE CRAZY EYES

It's only recently that anyone other than white women have been allowed space onscreen to portray mental illness. In Jenji Kohan's groundbreaking series *Orange Is the New Black,* based on the memoir of the same name by Piper Kerman, the vulnerable white woman is used as a Trojan horse with which to tell the stories of all the women around her. The fictional Piper Chapman (Taylor Schilling), a bougie woman with a master's degree and a soap-making business, ends up in prison, where the carefully constructed layers of her likeability and appropriateness are chipped away until we meet—and hate—the real Piper. It's not her we want to talk about, though. Piper quickly becomes an object of fascination for Suzanne "Crazy Eyes" Warren (Uzo Aduba), who nicknames her "Dandelion" and makes sexual advances to her as well as showing genuine kindness. Before we learn more about Suzanne, she's used as the go-to Crazy Woman who will respond with violence if rejected. She was, essentially, a variation on Alex Forrest, an unstable woman who cannot handle rejection. The *Guardian* even described her as inviting "pity, shock, reproach and belly-laughs." The Crazy Woman, again, was meant to be mocked and pitied, not understood. Her crazy is not to be treated; it's to be ogled.

But the more the show created space for Suzanne's story to unfold, the more it invited empathy. Crazy Eyes was, in fact, crazy—but she wasn't violent, not deliberately so; she was suffering from mental illness and placed in a prison instead of being given support. Her personality is cheerful, intelligent, and kind, and as *Orange Is the New Black* peels away at the layers of prejudice, we see that Crazy Eyes has been systematically wronged by the people around her. "You deserve to be in a facility that can help you with your cognitive difficulties," her adoptive mother tells her. But that facility is not a prison. The series lures us in by our preconceptions of what a Crazy Woman looks and behaves like and then completely calls us out on it, with Aduba's performance gaining additional pathos in retrospect.

CRAZY IS A QUESTION OF PERSPECTIVE

One of pop culture's most pervasive takes on the Crazy Woman is the crazy ex-girlfriend, one that can be traced back to Daphne du Maurier's disembodied ex-wife Rebecca, seen only as a painting in Alfred Hitchcock's adaptation from 1940. Alex Forrest, in her own bombastic way, was the crazy ex who wasn't even a girlfriend, as *Fatal Attraction* constantly reminded us. The crazy ex is a constant in thrillers, always shown as a delusional, obsessive woman incapable of seeing reality. Reality, of course, being the male character's point of view.

In Rachel Bloom's *Crazy Ex-Girlfriend*, this sexist trope and easy blanketing of a rejected woman as "crazy" is creatively reinvented as something that expands all the cinematic clichés associated with a woman's states of happiness and distress. Rebecca Bunch (Rachel Bloom) is a success story: a Harvard- and Yale-educated big shot lawyer who impulsively quits her job after getting a promotion and moves to West Covina, California, committed to the idea of reconnecting with her summer camp boyfriend Josh Chan (Vincent Rodriguez III).

The premise pokes fun both at the Crazy Woman trope, which is mostly present in thrillers, and at romantic comedies, where women are usually only "crazy" in a sexy, fun way that's fixable with a night out and a new love interest. A likeable crazy woman is "zany, but in a cute way," never struggling in a consistent, ongoing way, like Rebecca is.

Where *Crazy Ex-Girlfriend* succeeds is in showing that the girlfriend part is totally irrelevant, actually. The story was never about Rebecca finding or reconnecting with or keeping Josh Chan; the story was always about Rebecca learning to deal with her mental illness and expunging other people's ideas of what success, professional and romantic, looks like for her. All the things she has achieved—an Ivy League education, a powerful job, a big salary—are meaningless because they aren't the thing that she thought she wanted—Josh Chan. She runs away from her promotion not because she's in love with Josh Chan but because it's a knee-jerk reaction to being in a situation she doesn't actually want to be in. In the end, subverting the traditional rom-com structure that the show had been playing on throughout its entire run, she doesn't pick any man. She chooses to give herself some time to get used to managing her mental health. Like Josh Groban sings in the show, life doesn't always make narrative sense.

Crazy is often the default insult for women who exist in ways that upset the status quo; women who have been hurt, women who are tired and overwhelmed, and women who suffer from any form of mental illness are all lumped into this one big bag of "crazy."

It's off-putting and confusing to see the Crazy Woman be so feared and so sexualized. Before the contemporary conversation about mental health and the destigmatization of therapy and medication, this toxic combination almost made it sound appealing. Which adds a "right" and a "wrong" way of mental and emotional distress to the list of things that women need to get right. In the same way that party girls are considered appealing for a while, the idea of being the "right kind" of crazy also becomes something to aspire to. Combined with the dreamlike style of Sophia Coppola's *The Virgin Suicides* and the fetishized melancholy of Lana Del Rey, mental illness is not coded as a condition that deserves attention, empathy, and treatment but rather as a personality trait. An aesthetic, even.

The weird romanticization and sexualization of the Crazy Woman has seeped so far into our own understanding of ourselves that it informs how we experience mental distress too. It becomes a performance even in our most intimate moments. These films and shows, these characters, have been informed by centuries-old culture that has used mental illness, overindulgence of emotions, and irrationality as blanket excuses to imprison women—literally, figuratively, and narratively. We're trigger-happy about calling women "hysterical" if we disagree with their views or simply do not want to entertain their version of a story unless it fits into a sexy narrative.

To quote writer Rayne Fisher-Quann's excellent essay on her over romanticizing of her own manic-depressive episodes: "I put on mascara before crying so I'll look the right kind of sad when I see myself in the mirror. I think about how nothing feels real at all if it doesn't look like the movies."   .

"The thing about Amy is that she could never have been a man. She's purely female. People don't like me saying that, but it's true."

ROSAMUND PIKE, ACTRESS

"You should never tell a psychopath they are a psychopath. It upsets them."

VILLANELLE, *KILLING EVE*

"All I want is for Villanelle to get exactly what she wants and fuck everyone else."

JORDAN CRUCCHIOLA, JOURNALIST AND PODCASTER (@JORCRU)

The Psycho

I've always had a fascination with psychopaths onscreen. It's a type of abject attraction that's akin to poking at what could potentially be a wasp's nest. It might sting, but I can't help but poke and poke. I'd be terrified to meet a psychopath in real life (chances are we all have, though), but behind the protection of fiction and a screen—I'm riveted. I've devoured every serial killer-based film and series I can, read the biographies, listened to hours of true crime podcasts, watched intensely questionable YouTube videos and every new Netflix true crime documentary. I've rewatched *The Silence of the Lambs* every year, as my own sort of holiday classic, and if stressed out, I'll turn to *Zodiac* as my comfort blanket movie. I see it as a safe peek inside a psychology so far removed from my life, so totally inconceivable morally, that it's the cinematic equivalent of bungee jumping. These characters' choices, their violent minds, in the hands of capable filmmakers become even more seductive. The dance between the killer and the detective trying to capture them is the best flavor of macabre. At some point, though, probably during another rewatch of *The Silence of the Lambs* and the intellectual-erotic face-off between special agent Clarice Starling and the imprisoned Hannibal Lecter, I realized that I'd not seen a female psychopath of that caliber yet onscreen. Where were the female Hannibal Lecters?

I didn't know what I wanted until I saw it. I wanted a female character who relished being a Psycho, who was watchable, and who the film never wanted me to pity. Someone who was not overexplained—and especially someone whose violence was not justified by trauma. I didn't want to have to endure a woman's pain as an explanation for why she gleaned satisfaction from killing. There is a whole genre dedicated to this,[1] but this wasn't the type of psychopath I was looking for. Could a violent woman exist? And was it fundamentally a terrible thing to want to see stories about violent women?

Violence in men has always been assumed to be part of their nature. In 2021, the Office for National Statistics released an analysis that claimed that 93 percent of killers convicted of murder and manslaughter between March 2018 and March 2020 were men. According to data gathered by Radford University and Florida Gulf Coast University, only 11 percent of all recorded serial killers in the last century were women. The

---

1   Rape revenge films, which take the trauma of a sexual assault as a motivating impulse for a character to take revenge on the perpetrators; it's a controversial subgenre, borne out of exploitation and horror cinema, but one that is considered cathartic for many survivors of assault and audiences at large. In these films, violence begets violence, and assault against women is always a horrifying, never a titillating event.

first ever academic paper on the phenomena of female serial killers was written in 1985, by criminologist Eric Hickey. Even as I write this, with true crime mania eating itself and a renewed conversation taking place about the epidemic of violence against women, I'm waging an internal debate over whether I wanted to see violent women onscreen to redress the power imbalance as a fictional form of retribution or for some other morbid reason. Even as kids we're told to find a woman if we're lost, and I always worried about this: What if the nice lady was just as bad? Violent women reacting to violence are plentiful, but I wanted to see them play with their prey like a cat. I didn't want to know about their childhood just yet. I wanted to enjoy the thrill of watching them and being afraid of them. Fictional killers in the vein of Hannibal Lecter were charming, intelligent and playful and seemed to materialize fully formed. Born violent, voracious, self-groomed, and hiding in plain sight. To quote Hannibal himself: "Psychopaths are not crazy. They're fully aware of what they do and the consequences of those actions."

ENTER AMY DUNNE

Almost twenty years after Gillian Flynn's novel *Gone Girl* was published, we're still trying to decide whether Amy Dunne is a psychopath, a sociopath, a femme fatale, a woman scorned, or something else entirely. No antiheroine has ever been more of a Rorschach test for morality than her. It's impossible to define Amy Dunne as one thing. She's unbearably smug, annoying, fearsome—and yet compelling. Her narcissism, entitlement, and ruthlessness are terrifying—and so damn watchable. The novel was a monster hit, selling over twenty million copies, and Gillian Flynn adapted it herself into the film of the same name directed by David Fincher and released in 2014.

Flynn, who'd already published two successful novels (*Dark Places* and *Sharp Objects*, both featuring troubled female protagonists), wanted to intentionally write a female villain who is unmistakably *female*. Flynn was vocally frustrated by the assumption that all women must be, by their very nature, good and nurturing, as well as by the lack of development of female villains in literature. Her frustration echoes what I felt rewatching *The Silence of the Lambs* for the umpteenth time. Female characters, it seemed to her, could either be good or psycho bitches ("I don't write psycho bitches. The psycho bitch is just crazy—she has no motive, and so she's a dismissible person because of her psycho-bitchiness"). The "psycho" part in Flynn's psycho bitches refers, I think, to a certain impulsive messiness that make them easy to dismiss as characters; a literary dismissal that echoes the gendered accusation of being "too emotional." Psycho bitches are the stuff of soap operas—they're entertaining but, ultimately, paper thin. They're a grotesque vision of what female villainy could look like—loud, sloppy, sentimental, and easily dismissed.

Flynn, who identifies as a feminist, has railed against the cycle of you-go-girl feminism that demands all women—real and fictional—be resolutely unimpeachable. A less than virtuous woman, even if fictional, will be accused of being antifeminist. There is a palpable obsession in cultural criticism with labeling a fictional character as a feminist or not, and by extension, with labeling the author as a feminist or a misogynist. Upon *Gone Girl*'s release (the film version), *Time* magazine ran a story titled simply "Is *Gone Girl* Feminist or Misogynist?" The question is tiring. More than one thing can be true at once: *Gone Girl* can be a feminist text and Amy Dunne can sure do a lot of unfeminist things. But allowing her to exist without burdening this fictional murderess with having to be a feminist role model is, in itself, a feminist act. A character like Amy is primed to become a symbol that can be pulled in all directions and used to prove a myriad of differing points, with ample ammunition on all sides.

When we first meet Amy Dunne (Rosamund Pike) in the film adaptation of *Gone Girl*—let's call her Diary Amy, as she refers to herself, for clarity—we are seeing a fictional version of her, one fabricated by her for the purpose of creating the perfect image of female fragility. The film's opening and closing shots are of Amy's face turning to the camera, looking up at her husband. At the start, we get her husband Nick's (Ben Affleck) voice-over: "When I think of my wife, I always think of the back of her head. I picture cracking her lovely skull, unspooling her brain, trying to get answers." In one fell swoop, we are presented a familiar narrative: a wife-victim and a husband-murderer. We're settled in our expectations, so used are we to seeing women presented as victims—past, present, and future ones—it would not be surprising for Amy Dunne to be destined to be another dead blond of cinema.

Diary Amy is a charming, smart, beautiful woman who falls in love with a charming, smart, handsome man who quickly reveals himself to be not so charming, not so smart, and not so loyal. It's a familiar story, and throughout the narration of Amy's diary we experience her perception of things interspersed with the live criminal investigation into her disappearance. We're trying to piece together who Amy Dunne is at the same time as we're trying to find her. On the surface she is a perfect victim, and the amount of effort and interest that her disappearance generates confirms a very bleak reality: missing women only matter when they're beautiful, rich, and white. It's a real phenomenon, Missing White Woman Syndrome, which sees the distribution of attention and media coverage offered to missing persons cases (or other violent crimes) overwhelmingly benefit upper- and middle-class white women and girls. Amy's town is plastered with images of her smiling face, with rapturous pity parties for anyone who'd ever come in contact with her. Diary Amy is a fiction, knowingly playing into the idea that when presented with a thrilling story of a missing woman, we would not assume that she could ever be in control or—least of all—be the actual killer. We are culturally trained to trust her.

When Real Amy reveals herself halfway into the film, with the adapted Cool Girl Monologue, the film's equivalent of that of a Bond villain's evil plan exposition speech, she pulls the rug out from under all of us:

Men always say that as the defining compliment, don't they? She's a cool girl. Being the Cool Girl means I am a hot, brilliant, funny woman who adores football, poker, dirty jokes, and burping, who plays video games, drinks cheap beer, loves threesomes and anal sex, and jams hot dogs and hamburgers into her mouth like she's hosting the world's biggest culinary gang bang while somehow maintaining a size 2, because Cool Girls are above all hot.

This monologue, both the book and movie versions, is incisive. It is arguably one of the most important monologues of contemporary pop culture. In this moment, Rosamund Pike's performance shifts completely. The bright-eyed, witty Amy from the start of the film is transformed into (or more appropriately, revealed as) a cold, efficient machinator. Her voice shifts, erasing all traces of sympathy or hurt. The meet-cute and honeymoon phase of her romance with Nick, written in a deliberately maudlin manner, is now remembered with anger ("He took my hope, my dignity and my money"). Real Amy is not mad about Nick cheating on her: she's mad about the offensive predictability of it all, the gauche ickiness of a married middle-aged man having an affair with a twenty-something woman. She's mad that he made her mediocre.

Who Amy is changes entirely depending on who her audience is. When she's speaking to her version of Nick, she's deferential, victimized, trying so hard to keep this marriage afloat, paranoid about being in danger. When Real Amy, in hiding, befriends a couple of poolside stoners, she is vaguely homey, leaning into an idea of female bonding. After she is outsmarted and robbed by them, this snag in her plan forces her to reach out to former boyfriend Desi (Neil Patrick Harris) to come and rescue her. She's playing a different role here—one of a damsel in distress in need of saving from a brutish, abusive husband, pandering to Desi's years-long obsession with her. But she becomes trapped by him, and here comes the single scene that elevated Amy Dunne from a modern manipulatrix and made her a shock to the cinematic system.

In order to escape from Desi's high-tech house, Amy gives an agonized, blood-dripping performance as a rape victim for the cameras dotted around the house as Desi leaves for work. She penetrates herself with a bottle, creating injuries consistent with rape. When her captor returns, Amy is dressed in white lingerie only, and speedily takes Desi to bed. When he is about to climax, she reaches beneath a pillow, and in a split second slits his throat, keeping him inside of her while the blood covers her.

I'd never seen a woman kill onscreen in this way before. Seeing Amy Dunne commit murder left no wiggle room for interpretation. She was a precise, clinical, deliberate killer. There is no doubt and every second is accounted for. Desi, in life and in death, was a vehicle to meet a need. With Amy there is no sentiment, only a tick box on a to-do list. Fake rape. *Check*. Kill Desi. *Check*. There are only two scenes of graphic violence in *Gone Girl*: the fictional account of Nick hitting Amy and the very real murder of Desi by Amy. Films have taught us to be used to the former, but not the latter.

If you read her as a feminist character, Amy's rightfully angry—her husband, Nick, is cheating on her, underappreciates her, empties her savings account, and is generally an asshole. She feels cheated, like she should be entitled to her money and her time back. Her anger is instantly relatable to any woman who's been wronged by her partner, and her "Cool Girl" speech—a pivotal point that readjusts our perception of the story entirely—is a searing "Fuck you" to the sort of fictional ideal of a woman created by male screenwriters who want a fuckable drinking buddy. The Cool Girl is a trope created by decades of pop culture, showing us all the things women should avoid being and all the performances they should balance—all for the benefit of men. And it took a fictional character to draw our attention to it. A fictional Psycho. Once Real Amy lets us in on her ruse, our relationship as an audience with her gets complicated. She's not just a type-A, detail-obsessed, ruthless, entitled narcissist. She's all the things misogynists think women are capable of; she takes advantage of a system unfairly set up to her advantage and looks down on other women. She doesn't seem that feminist anymore.

Who would want to play a woman like that?

Turns out, everyone.

After the film rights had been acquired by Reese Witherspoon's production company (with the initial intent of Witherspoon playing Amy herself), Amy became one of the most coveted roles among Hollywood A-listers. But it would be the English actress Rosamund Pike who would land it. Pike, who had been consistently recognized for her work across both commercial action movies and prestige dramas, had not yet had massive mainstream recognition of the size that would come with leading a project of this size. Before she got cast in the Fincher film, Pike had played Bond girl Miranda Frost in *Die Another Day* (2002) and had supporting roles in *Pride & Prejudice* (2005), *An Education* (2009), and *The World's End* (2012), but she wasn't yet a household name. The benefit of casting a relative unknown in this role was that there was room for the audience to project our own ideas onto her. Pike's performance trades on the same type of assumptions that Amy takes advantage of: that a beautiful, smart, competent woman would never be the villain. She is too good to be a villain, too put together to be a Psycho—but she could conceivably be a victim. Amy was counting on us to cast her as the victim so she could get away with her plan in plain sight. "It's a version of being a woman that isn't contained in any way," said Pike in an interview. "She's extreme."

Gone Girl's success inaugurated a wave of crime books and thrillers with unlikeable, dangerous female characters. It made "crazy female psychopaths" popular. Being a villain was a cute twist. What no other book or film could tap into in the way *Gone Girl* did was our expectations—or the lack thereof. Now we expected the female protagonists to be psychopaths (or sociopaths, or narcissists—Amy has been diagnosed in every which way). It's not that they weren't there before—but now they *sold*. With this commercial success came the film adaptations. The tide had shifted such that A-list actresses were pursuing these roles instead of avoiding them. Charlize Theron took the lead in the artless adaptation of another Flynn book, *Dark Places* (2015). Emily Blunt played an alcoholic witness to a murder in *Girl on the Train* (2016). Amy Adams took on the agoraphobic protagonist in *The Woman in the Window* (2021; she also played another Flynn character in the excellent 2018 miniseries *Sharp Objects*). The genre was so commonplace that in early 2022 we got the spoof version *The Woman in the House across the Street from the Girl in the Window*, truly the death rattle of any cultural moment.

When I write about the dearth of violent female Psychos onscreen, I'm only being half-facetious. Of course there have been plenty of violent women onscreen before Amy Dunne (especially in the realm of genre and exploitation films)—but none struck a cultural chord as widely as she did. In the realm of horror and exploitation filmmaking, there were mythical versions of the violent woman camouflaged as monsters. Their violence was a pathology, explained away by their monstrous condition, and their monstrosity in itself was a metaphor for some undesirable trait. Though witches, succubi, panther-women, and gorgons represented menaces to polite society, they couldn't help it, and they were usually killed before the end credits. In thrillers, even the most scheming of villainesses didn't get their hands dirty—at least not onscreen. In Henri-Georges Clouzot's *Diabolique* (1955), the mistress and the wife of a man conspire to kill him. Although we see his body, we never see the act of murder. Their villainy is still mostly verbal. It's the intention that makes them fiendish, the thought and the plotting. The actual killing remains unseen, so we can still sleep soundly. It's almost impossible to compare Amy to any other female onscreen killer before her, because there are none. She is singular and radically visible. Her singularity comes from her entitlement. She doesn't kill because she's traumatized or angry—those are not the explanations of her violence. She lets us see her kill—because there is nothing to apologize for or be ashamed of. In their book *Dead Blondes and Bad Mothers*, Jude Doyle compares Amy to the titular Rebecca from Daphne du Maurier's book and Alfred Hitchcock's famed adaptation, *Rebecca* (1940), who haunts and tortures her widower and his new wife from beyond the grave, her wickedness seeping into their skin. While we never actually see Rebecca, we get front row seats to Amy's machinations. We get to see her side and hear her internal monologue. This access to and prioritization of the Psycho's interiority is a staple of thriller fiction and has usually been reserved for men onscreen through fiction and seemingly endless fictionalizations and documentary explorations of real-life killers. Amy Dunne is a violent creature, full stop. Is it contradictory that this simplicity seems so liberating?

Hannibal Lecter, whose multiple screen iterations depict him as an aesthete with cannibalistic predilections, draws pleasure from being a wolf in sheep's clothing in high society—as does Amy. But their disguises are different: he is a successful, appreciated, desired psychiatrist who hosts dinner parties for his wealthy buddies, getting off on feeding his foodie pals chunks of his victims; meanwhile, Amy is a highly educated but modestly accomplished woman who loses her job in the recession and is trapped in a dissatisfying marriage; her disguise is that of a mistreated woman. Are their motivations that different, though? They want to live a life that is attuned to their refined tastes. They care more about aesthetics than they do about human life. Mediocrity is offensive to them.

We can explain away our fascination with killers and psychopaths onscreen as a desire to justify wickedness. These characters are usually motivated by trauma, sex, or an unnamed deep, dark desire. Our voyeurism compels us to keep watching to try to see if this movie, this series, this podcast will unlock something that will help us understand. Just think of how many different versions of Ted Bundy we've seen, all trying to uncover how someone could simultaneously be hot and a killer. When an explanation, a villain origin story, is lacking, it's so much more perverse. It opens up the terrifying possibility that violence is simply another want. A predilection.

Whenever we've seen a woman murder onscreen, it's usually out of desperation, revenge, or greed. One way or another, it's about survival. We need a direct justification because a woman, simply put, could not be inherently evil. Could not be violent by nature. Not murderous just 'cause. What's so controversial about Flynn's character is precisely this: she is a truly scary female villain, a woman capable of real violence, created with the knowledge that this violence would have to be different from what we've seen before, needing to be deliberately distinct from male violence. "Female violence is a specific brand of ferocity. It's invasive," Flynn wrote in an essay for Powell's Books' Medium page. "Libraries are filled with stories on generations of brutal men, trapped in a cycle of aggression. I wanted to write about the violence of women."

Amy Dunne's violence is a grotesque meld of her femaleness and her complete disdain for everyone else. There is no reason for it, really. No big trauma that can be used to exonerate or explain away her actions. Nick is an asshole, sure. He's predictably middlebrow in every way. An unambitious writer, inattentive and slobbish. He cheats on Amy and adds insult to infidelity when he uses the same moves he used on Amy years before with his mistress. While he may be tacky in his failings, he's not a villain. Amy's parents are fake and self-absorbed, using their daughter's life to create a fictional, more successful, and very lucrative version of her called "Amazing Amy" (the first fictional Amy, arguably). They are vampiric instead of caring—but none of these relationships are justifications for the extremity of her actions.

The first half of Fincher's film is, in essence, a study of Nick's unlikeability. From that first menacing shot of him stroking Amy's head and fantasizing about cracking open her skull, he is quickly defanged. Nobody really likes him or his shitty grin,[2] but

---

2   The casting of Ben Affleck as Nick Dunne is an act of metacasting genius, capitalizing on the actor's own push-and-pull, like-me-hate-me relationship with his public persona and the media. He started off as an indie darling, picking up an Oscar for cowriting the script for *Good Will Hunting* with his childhood buddy Matt Damon, and then became a failed leading man, better known for his real-life romances than his roles, before reinventing himself again as a solid director and...Batman.

you'd hardly conduct a ninety-eight-step plan to set someone up for murder because they never do the dishes. He's flawed in very basic ways, and it's his lack of specialness that Amy finds so insulting. He had sold himself to her as someone better, someone more interesting, and throughout their marriage had revealed himself to be someone simpler. What others might call compromise, Amy Dunne sees as an unacceptable failing of character. Just as Lecter is offended by rudeness, Amy is offended by mediocrity. Her drive is to win, at everything ("What's the point of being happy if you're not the happiest?"). Nick makes her into a loser by being himself. And that she simply cannot abide.

The second half of the film is a chilling dissection of, as Flynn puts it, the violence of women and the systematic ways Amy weaponizes other people's perceptions of her. She plays into different female stereotypes: the cool girl, the battered wife, the rape victim, the traumatized survivor, the besotted partner, the dutiful daughter. It is a knowing kaleidoscope of semidisguises on Flynn's part: "I see Amy as someone who knows all the tropes and the stories about being a woman and is not afraid to use those stories to get her own way." Once Nick realizes who she really is, the only opportunity to defeat her is to peel away these personas. His lawyer, Tanner Bolt (Tyler Perry), tells him: "Make them stop seeing her as America's sweetheart and start seeing her for what she is: a mindfuck of the first degree."

Gone Girl, and Amy in particular, was the subject of much controversy upon the film's release. People labeled it unfeminist and Flynn was accused of misogyny. Critics accused it of setting back female representation. The more successful or visible an unlikeable woman is, the bigger the backlash. It's a direct parallel to the level of (negative) influence this character is expected to have. The accusation behind this kind of backlash is always: How dare you write a bad woman, an evil woman, a woman who lies and kill! How dare you, as a woman, show us in that light, in the darkest light. How dare you go against your own. "I've grown quite weary of the spunky heroines, brave rape victims, soul-searching fashionistas that stock so many books," said Flynn at the time. "I particularly mourn the lack of female villains—good, potent female villains. Not ill-tempered women who scheme about landing good men and better shoes (as if we had nothing more interesting to war over), not chilly WASP mothers (emotionally distant isn't necessarily evil), not soapy vixens (merely bitchy doesn't qualify either). I'm talking violent, wicked women. Scary women."

But are the critics annoyed at Amy's villainy, at the fact that she was created by a female writer, or that she tricked them for half the book/film and then revealed herself? Are we really angered by the possibility of a female villain or because she called us out on our own preconceptions of female fragility?

There is a running joke among true crime nerds that claims there are fewer female serial killers because women are better at not getting caught. Amy, covered in Desi's blood, dramatically returns to Nick, literally falling into his arms in front of a gaggle of reporters, relieved to be back with her beloved husband, a damsel saved. She absolves him of public scrutiny as they embrace for the cameras, while he whispers, "You fucking bitch" in her ear. It's a bullet through the image of a perfect husband and a perfect marriage.

Amy weaponizes her body as though it's not her own. She

fakes rape (not once but twice). At the end of the story she inseminates herself with Nick's sperm, locking him into their marriage. If the Bitches from earlier in the book weaponized their femininity as a tool of manipulation and seduction, Amy straight-up bludgeons the notion of womanhood, leaning into every misogynist's paranoia about women lying and performing victimhood in order to get their way.

Let's be crystal clear here: Amy is not a feminist, nor is she written as one, nor does she at any point pretend to be one. Flynn pries open the limitations of female villainy through her: Amy Dunne is not girlbossing murder; there is no great big trauma that justifies her choices; there is no precedent for her manipulations. And that is the point. She is belittling to everyone she considers beneath her—especially other women: when she talks about Nick's mistress, she describes her as "a bouncier cool girl"; she uses her well-intentioned neighbor Noelle as a tool in her plan; she looks down on the woman she befriends at the motel when she's in hiding, even spitting in her drink when she makes a remark about Amy's disappearance. Is it internalized misogyny or is she just a Psycho? Which would be worse?

Author Mary Gaitskill, in her *Bookforum* review of Flynn's book, taps into this nastiness as the most astute way of visualizing the extreme tiptoeing around how women are allowed to be: "She's just amplifying an attitude that's shoved in front of us all the time." Women are only allowed to step out of line when they have been "scorned," which fits into an individual, emotional response. We are culturally trained to dismiss and deride women who lose control of themselves and of their lives and, concurrently, to fear women with too much control over themselves.

Amy lives in the in-between of these two fears. For the first part of the film, she fools us. And by the time we realize it, we can't stop watching. She's not lost control in the slightest, so we don't know how to place our reactions to her.

The fact that both the author and the actress were, and still are, subjected to questioning about their so-called responsibility for breathing life into a character as vile as Amy Dunne is pointedly and pathetically predictable. Women who create unlikeable—or worse, psychotic—female characters are asked to shoulder the morality of their characters. If Flynn wrote Amy, then she must also be just like Amy, right? If Pike gives a brutally powerful performance as Amy, she must also be a Psycho. The divide between the word and the writer becomes so much blurrier when the latter is a woman.

I'M YOUR BIGGEST FAN

The same accusations of irresponsible writing were not thrown at 1990's *Misery*. Based on a Stephen King novel and adapted for the screen by William Goldman, the story concerns a popular romance novel writer, Paul Sheldon (James Caan), who gets stuck in a snowstorm after finishing his first "serious novel," putting an end to the series of books that had garnered him much commercial success but very little critical respect. After he is hurt in a car accident, kindly local nurse Annie Wilkes (Kathy Bates), who also happens to be his number one fan, saves him and nurses him back to health—at first. Mad that Sheldon's latest novel kills off her favorite character Misery Chastain, she imprisons him in her home and forces him to write another novel for her. Turns out she's not just a fan but also a full-on serial killer. Through her own scrapbooking she is revealed to have been acquitted of dozens of murders that she committed in the hospital where she was working as the head nurse.

In a structure not dissimilar to *Gone Girl*, the first half of the film has us believe that Annie is just a harmless eccentric. Bates plays her as an uptight, buttoned-up, lonely woman with bouts of anger and depression. She will not tolerate swearing (though she's A-okay with murdering babies and hobbling her favorite author). In his review, *New York Times* critic Vincent Canby writes that "Annie is the sort of person who believes there's enough ugliness in the world without adding obscene language." Her obsession is not so much with Paul as it is with his creation, the *Misery* novels, and she's unable to separate the fiction from the author. Whereas Amy is a kaleidoscope of personality, Annie doesn't really have a particularly strong identity, so she latches onto things. She's the blueprint for a type of toxic fandom that demands authorship rights from their favorite pop culture artifacts as a form of reward for their love and commitment.

Annie is both cheery and cold. Bates, who at that point was mostly known for her work on the stage and not the screen, had the benefit of being a fairly new face for cinemagoers. Every choice in her performance as Annie came as a shock. At first, she makes you think of your first grade teacher, a kind figure in overalls that you never, ever want to upset. The idea of her being angry seems inconceivable. We see the kindly Annie, the depressed Annie, and, finally, the real Annie—a controlling and violent being with an intricate vision of what she wants but who is unable to create it herself outside of forcing people to bend to her will.

Does the film let Annie be anything but a Psycho Bitch (as per Gillian Flynn's definition), though? We're getting Annie at her lowest, removed from her profession, even removed from her killings, and exercising what control she can over a trapped, injured man. Even though, superficially, she is in control of Paul—after all, it is her house, she's able-bodied while Paul is injured, she's got medical knowledge and primes Paul with pills—the film mocks her as a prudish, old-fashioned, unimaginative psychopath. Her backstory as a serial killing nurse as well as her public trial and acquittal are revealed through newspaper clippings that Annie dutifully keeps in a scrapbook. But we never really see her as anything more than a circumstantial threat. She's only scary on her turf. Outside her house, Annie Wilkes is kind of a sad sack.

Unusually, Kathy Bates's performance was rewarded by the Academy with a Best Actress Oscar.[3] She plays Annie as a contradiction both physical and emotional: she's a controlling Psycho one moment, a giddy fangirl the next; a lonely spinster surrounded by stuffed toys and eating snacks in bed in one scene, and a chilling, cruel, grand dame in the next. One review noted this physicality, writing that Bates "seems to tower over her hostage, looming over the camera like a hulk despite only standing at 5ft 3in."

In the end, in a brutal, extended fight scene, Annie is defeated. More than that, she is humiliated, repeatedly, by Paul. He lures her into thinking they're going to die together and that he loves her but then takes extra pleasure in stuffing the pages of his

---

3   Unusual only because horror films rarely fare well with awards bodies.

burning manuscript in her mouth. Paul really, really hates Annie. He might be traumatized, but he kills the Psycho and makes sure to take pleasure in it—and with him, the audience.

There is an allure that neither Amy Dunne nor Annie Wilkes have—nor are they aiming for it. Neither of them is fuckable. Women onscreen, femme fatales and beyond, are always there to excite, at least a little bit. Film theorist Laura Mulvey's oft-misquoted theory of the male gaze is based on this very simple notion: that women onscreen have, for the most part, been positioned as objects to be looked at, to be desired, by heterosexual male viewers. But what happens when a murderess, a Psycho, becomes a sex symbol? How can we reconcile being afraid of a Psycho and desiring her?

HERS IS BIGGER

Basic Instinct (1992) is not a subtle film. It wears its intentions on it sleeve: the film starts and ends with a sex scene. In both, a blond woman is seen straddling her lover. The first sexual encounter quickly turns into a murder scene, the little death becoming death itself with a few swift stabs of an ice pick by the anonymous blond. The crux of the film is a criminal investigation led by San Francisco police detective Nick Curran (Michael Douglas), who predictably becomes sexually infatuated with the lead suspect, Catherine Tramell (Sharon Stone), determined to both find the killer and prove her innocence. The possibility of Catherine being the killer is planted in our minds from the very beginning: we see, after all, a svelte blond woman stabbing a man during intercourse—and then we meet two svelte blond women: Catherine and her part-time girlfriend Roxy (Leilani Sarelle).

Catherine is highly educated (having two master's degrees, one in psychology, another in literature, a detail that's thrown out in lieu of further characterization) and extremely wealthy in her own right, having inherited a fortune. She becomes a suspect when the murder from the opening matches a murder in one of her novels to a tee. And because she's played by Sharon Stone—who is not only beautiful but struts with the big dick energy exemplary of a kind of eighties wealthy hedonism—her attractiveness means that people are more inclined to find excuses for her behavior ("She's got 100 million bucks. She fucks fighters and rock stars and she's got a degree in screwing with people's heads," muses Nick, almost impressed).

Catherine's new book is about a "detective who falls for the wrong woman." "I'd have to be pretty stupid to write a book about killing and then kill him the way I described in my book. I'd be announcing myself as the killer," she declares in the middle of her interrogation by the police. Catherine is more offended at being perceived as stupid than at being seen as a killer.

In that scene, she's unblinking, toying with the way the roomful of policemen are looking at her, some visibly sweating every time she moves her leg. She is a tease of the homicidal kind, with Stone messing with the men surrounding her like a cat pawing at a mouse it can't be bothered to kill. It seems almost too easy for her. *Basic Instinct*'s interrogation scenes mirrors the one at the end of *Gone Girl*, wherein Amy is being interrogated by a roomful of police officers. Both Catherine and Amy play into the role of victim with the police when it's convenient for them, activating their instinct to protect white women, who are considered vulnerable by default. In *Gone Girl*, the only one casting doubt on Amy's tale of perfect victimhood is the sole female detective, Rhonda Boney. In *Basic Instinct*, even though she's the lead suspect, Nick never sees Catherine as a threat. Even though she tells Nick directly to his face that she uses people ("I'm a writer. I use people for what I write. Let the world beware"), she isn't listened to because it is impossible to believe that she's not a damsel in distress.

While the film frames Catherine as a sex-crazed femme fatale, she is a serial killer with a clear pattern (the sexual encounter, the white scarf, the ice pick). It's clear but it is still offscreen—we never see Catherine actually *commit* the violence (which, every time I watch *Basic Instinct*, is almost a disappointment). There is something radical in a woman choosing violence for violence's sake and not for revenge.

Similarly to Kathy Bates, and to Rosamund Pike later on, Sharon Stone was not a household name when she played Catherine. Only six weeks before she was cast in the film, her manager had told her she wasn't getting jobs because "everyone said I wasn't sexy. I wasn't, as they liked to say in Hollywood at the time, 'fuckable.'"[4] In her memoir, *The Beauty of Living Twice*, Stone recalls how much the production took out of her: "I had walked in my sleep three times during production, twice waking fully dressed in my car in my garage. I had hideous nightmares." During the shooting of the first sex-murder scene, she worried she had actually killed the actor, that the retractable ice pick had not been retractable after all. Stone was, in fact, the thirteenth

---

4   I'm sorry, what?

choice to play Catherine Tramell. Everyone else the filmmakers had approached had rejected the role. She had fought for it. Stone, who was thirty-two at the time of casting, had been working for years but had not yet broken out in a big way. The film would make her into a star—but would also condemn her to being a sex symbol.

The film collapsed all the clichés and possibilities of the erotic thriller into one single story. It was a commercial juggernaut, directed by the Dutch master of horn Paul Verhoeven (who'd already made *RoboCop* and *Total Recall* and had caused a national polemic in his native Denmark for his explicit early films). In direct contrast with Verhoeven's satirical sensibilities was the writer, Joe Eszterhas, who'd made a name for himself writing flashy, high-concept, highly sexualized films like *Flashdance* and thrillers like *Jagged Edge*. Not a sliver of subtext between them. Hordes of erotic thrillers would continue being produced after *Basic Instinct*, a lot of them directly imitating it in title, theme, or style, but the genre would never reach such heights of mainstream success again.[5]

The critics at the time savaged the film. Roger Ebert called it "a worthless scrap." Rita Kempley described it as "panting peep at the misperceptions and clichés surrounding female sexuality." It was boycotted by queer activists who resented that two bisexual women were presented as psychopathic killers. It's pointless to debate whether *Basic Instinct* is high art or low art (or both). It had an impact. It made Stone into a star and defined, for better or worse, her career. *Basic Instinct* forwent the shadowy morality

5   Not even when Eszterhas and Stone reteamed for the high-rise erotic thriller *Sliver* (1993).

of the femme fatale and made her explicit. A hedonist. A horn-dog in pursuit of pleasure above all, even if pleasure meant murder. As Stone writes in her memoir, "Women championed that movie; men were obsessed with a woman who could make it stop. She was their favorite."

But for all the impact and controversy of Catherine Trammel and Amy Dunne, they were not pop culture poster girls: they were warnings. It wouldn't be until the glammed-up assassin Villanelle that we would get a Psycho with a catchphrase that would capture the collective imagination.

MY FAVORITE PSYCHO

Villanelle does not have the self-control of Amy Dunne, but she has *style*. We first meet the accent-shifting assassin making faces at a young girl in a café in Paris. She travels the world, going from Paris to Vienna to London in the first episode alone. She cares about fashion, that most female of pastimes, wearing a pink Molly Goddard gown to therapy, a blue linen dress for a job in Tuscany, and a set of silk pajamas for every day of the week. She speaks several languages—cracks jokes in Italian, mocks an old lady in French, pokes fun at her handler in Russian, and flirts in English. She's got a shabby chic apartment in Paris, with only Moët Chandon champagne in the fridge and a secret armoire filled with disguises, weapons, and wigs. She lip-synchs to Roxette on car rides, despises Crocs, and has an obsessive crush on the MI6 agent who is tasked with capturing her.

All of this with glowy, no-makeup makeup and a messy ponytail. If it weren't for all the murdering, Villanelle could be any aspirational rom-com heroine. And perhaps this is why she struck a nerve. She's the glamorous, fun take on the Psycho, unmarred by an inciting traumatic incident. Villanelle appeared at a time when the cultural true crime obsession was at an all-time high (true crime documentaries have risen in popularity massively over the past five years, regularly charting for weeks in the top ten most viewed shows on Netflix).

As far as murderesses go, the professional female assassin is a familiar archetype in action cinema (think Anne Parillaud in *Nikita*, Meiko Kaji in *Lady Snowblood*, Geena Davis in *The Long Kiss Goodnight*, Charlize Theron in *Atomic Blonde*, Saoirse Ronan in *Hanna*, Zoe Saldana in *Colombiana*, Uma Thurman in *Kill Bill*, Angelina Jolie in *Mr. & Mrs. Smith*, *Wanted*, and *Salt*, Jessica Chastain in *Ava*; the list goes on). However, she's rarely a Psycho—she's a professional. Killing is her job, and usually the plot revolves around her being very good at it but wanting a way out. More often than not, the female assassin plays into a very masculine fantasy of a physically overpowering woman who is still vulnerable, still someone to save. It's a "badass" spin on the damsel in distress, intimidating in a sexy way. Jodie Comer knew this was the trope when she first read *Killing Eve*: "When I first read 'assassin' I kind of rolled my eyes and imagined her in six-inch heels and leather pants, using her sexuality to get herself out of situations." But while she is a sexual being, her sexuality is never a tool she deploys.

While she is indebted to the femme fatales of the 1940s and 1950s, Villanelle is a millennial evolution of them. She doesn't need to seduce her targets—or the audience—to be lethally charming. Unlike the murderous women who have to hide their true nature, Villanelle is absolutely explicit about who she is and how much she enjoys playing at humanity.

Villanelle makes killing fun. All the while a millennial Psycho (both the character and the actress were born in 1993), she texts about murder in emojis (bus, dead eyes, smiling ghost, thumbs up). She's annoyed by her employers, like a lot of us are, but loves the job itself. She jokes about killing someone "for free" and ponders going freelance. She's vocal about how much she loves killing and relishes her reputation even among other assassins (the Ghost—a fellow contract killer who uses techniques that are the complete opposite of Villanelle's—calls her "the demon without a face"). She wants to wear beautiful clothes, eat good food, and take a bath after a long day at work. If the long day at work involves shooting or stabbing some people, so what? When asked by Eve Polastri, the MI6 intelligence agent played by Sandra Oh, what she wants, it's not world domination or eternal life or becoming the head of the secret assassin organization that employs her. It's "Nice life. Cool flat. Fun job. Someone to watch movies with."[6]

While Villanelle is all excess, Eve is all restraint. From the very first episode she is drawn to Villanelle, talking in almost fanlike terms about her kills ("She's outsmarting the smartest of us and for that she deserves to kill everyone she wants"). She's *impressed*. When Eve successfully captures the Ghost, she's almost disappointed ("She kills people for a living; you'd think she works in accounts!"). The Ghost, played in the show by Dutch-Korean actress Jung Sun den Hollander, is Villanelle's

---

6   No joke, Villanelle's living aspirations mirror my own: good light, high ceilings, excellent water pressure.

opposite: she hides in plain sight, posing as a cleaner, banking on being an invisible laborer that her marks will not even acknowledge, using safe and quiet ways of eliminating her targets, remaining invisible and immemorable. Eve, like us, is sort of deflated. Where's the pizzazz? We're here to see assassins toy with their prey before slitting their throat!

There is an attraction that fictional—and real-life—psychopaths hold over us. While the textbook definition of a psychopath tells us they're incapable of empathy, seeing people as mere objects that either serve a purpose or do not, we still, in the back of our minds, think that perhaps we might be the exception. Like how Clarice Starling drew the attention and respect of Hannibal Lecter, like how Eve Polastri becomes a source of fascination for Villanelle, maybe we'll be the one that charms the psychopath too.

Like a child, Villanelle loves performing empathy. But she always, always reminds us that there is nothing behind the smirk. She trips a woman in a bar and overacts helping her up, smirking all the while. Working on an assignment for Eve and the MI6, Villanelle needs to go undercover to expose an organized criminal. She poses as an American addict named Billie, a pink-haired persona she creates to ingratiate herself into her mark's family. As part of this, she goes to an AA meeting, where she delivers a monologue that, as a performance of a performance, is perhaps a peek into the depths of Villanelle:

> I have real trouble telling the truth. I don't understand the concept, actually, but somebody told me it was important. Most of the time, most days, I feel nothing. I don't feel

anything. It's so boring. I wake up and think, again, really? I have to do this again? What I really don't understand is why everyone else is not screaming with boredom. I try to find ways to make myself feel something. Doesn't make any difference. No matter what I do, I don't feel anything. I hurt myself—doesn't hurt. I buy what I want—I don't want it. I do what I like—I don't like it. I'm just so bored.

Jodie Comer delivers this monologue almost entirely in close-up, the camera closing in on her as the tears build up in her eyes. Is this Villanelle's facade breaking down? Is this the real thing here? She's touching—but at this point in the show we should know not to trust her. We've been here before. She's told us many times over that she feels nothing, that she is a pure Psycho. In a conversation with Eve, she warns her: "Don't speak to me like that, Eve. I like you but I don't like you that much. Don't forget: the only thing that makes you interesting is me." Be careful, she's saying, because this cutesy charming side of me that you enjoy rooting for is a facade that can quickly fall. Villanelle is driven by pure id, so surely this is just another performance. And yet we gladly lap it up.

Until Villanelle, there wasn't really a fandom around a Psycho. She's the antagonist, the villain, the boogeyman of the show turned into a pop culture mascot by fans. I have a wish list on Etsy with *Killing Eve*–themed folksy art: knockoffs of her pink dress and teddy bear T-shirt; birthday cards and posters with illustrations of Jodie Comer and Sandra Oh; charm bracelets with things Villanelle loves, like Paris and croissants and shoes; stickers of her catchphrases; "Sorry Baby x" in Villanelle's cursive made into stickers, neon signs, cards, and mugs; a car air freshener with Jodie Comer's face on it.

Comer, as Villanelle, charmed audiences and critics alike. Jia Tolentino wrote in the *New Yorker* about her "mercurial, unassailable charisma." Hannah Giorgis talks about her appeal in the *Atlantic*: "She doesn't meet the entertainment industry's perpetually moving goalpost of female characterization, likability, yet she is nearly impossible to not root for." Comer's performance is a slippery one, switching within nanoseconds from one accent to another, one faux personality to another. She's got a bright, airy beauty that's unthreatening but undeniable. Show creator Phoebe Waller-Bridge has been explicit that Villanelle "never ever uses her beauty." She is never a seducer—she's a killer. Giorgis adds to this: "She is no heroic femme fatale that slashes throats in the name of justice—simply a woman who knows her pretty face can be a potent anesthetic to her targets' flight instincts."

It's in the in-between moments that we see the maskless Villanelle, quiet moments that are filled with dread at her getting caught. The boldness of the show is that we see Villanelle's world and her methods, but although we get a front row seat, we're never allowed in. It would be, to quote Eve, "too basic bitch for her" to be explained away by a single traumatic incident, a single reason for her being the way she is. We know she lost her mother early on, and we know she developed a sexual obsession with a former teacher (who shares the same kind of thick, wild hair that Eve has) and killed and castrated her husband out of jealousy. We know she spent some time in a Russian prison before getting recruited into the high-powered agency known as the Twelve. But the show never tries to explain away her Psycho-ness, because that would make her much less interesting, and much less watchable. It's impossible to separate Villanelle and our reaction to her from the decade in which she came to the screen, a decade infected by the rhetoric of girlboss feminism, Instagram aesthetics, and the idea that we can build a life that is glamorous and fun and not filled with fear. Perhaps Villanelle struck a chord because she is so deliciously unafraid to move in the world and so unwilling to compromise on her desires, vio-lent as they might be.

A GIRL WALKS HOME ALONE AT NIGHT

We can accept that female characters kill, but only when they have a reason to kill, and only when they're not actually enjoy-ing the killings. When I try to understand the appeal and lack of female Psychos—why the murder of Desi by Amy Dunne was so much more chilling to see than it was to read, why we get so much glee from Villanelle's sadism—I come back to the lack of restraint these characters show in those violent moments. When you walk through life measuring every step, calibrating every smile, and designing every action based on how people might react to it, it's such a strange relief to see a character indulge in her impulses. Since *Gone Girl*, there has been more exploration of female Psychos within different genres, tapping into what it might look like to be a natural-born psychopath *and* a woman.

Thoroughbreds, the debut feature from playwright Cory Finley, shows us two upper-class teenage girls who have no great trauma but experience a general inability to feel emotions, guilt or otherwise. Amanda (Olivia Cooke) and Lily (Anya Taylor-Joy) rekindle a childhood friendship based on a radical honesty about the performance (or lack thereof) of feelings. Amanda is blasé about this, not in a confessional sort of way but completely matter-of-factly: "I really don't feel anything. Sometimes I feel hungry, or tired, but joy, guilt, I don't really have any of those.... I have a perfectly healthy brain, it just doesn't contain feelings." Meanwhile, Lily, who is initially bribed into hanging out with this teenage psychopath, is using her to get away with the murder of her stepdad, who she despises. On the surface, both teenage girls are poised, polite, smart, cool operators in their upper-crust world. Both Lily and Amanda are all surface, and Lily has gotten really good at reflecting back whatever is needed in any given moment. The camera films them straight on, even when Lily drugs Amanda and, offscreen, stabs her stepdad, later on covering her with his blood. They are both skilled imitators of sentiment, but only Lily sees it as a superpower instead of a hindrance.

In her second feature, *Titane*, which picked up the highest prize at the 2021 Cannes Film Festival, the Palme D'Or,[7] French director Julia Ducournau creates a female psycho killer *designed* to not have an explanation for her rage but rather to have her violence built into her. As a child, Alexia is badly hurt in a car accident and has a titanium plate implanted in her head—this doesn't alter her disposition, but it sets the basis for an affinity with metal that borders on the fetishistic. When we next meet

---

7   Only the second time a female director has picked up the award (the first being Jane Campion for *The Piano* in 1992), and it was for a genre film. What a time to be alive.

her as an adult, Alexia (Agathe Rouselle) is an exotic dancer at car shows and moonlights as a serial killer. When a male fan approaches her in an empty parking lot, he first demands a selfie, then a kiss on the cheek, then forcibly kisses her on the mouth. In the hands of another filmmaker, this would be the start of a rape scene. But Ducournau has her character stab the man through the ear with her hairpin. Alexia doesn't even blink. In a follow-up scene, she hooks up with a girl and then, out of nowhere, stabs her with the same hairpin in the face. In a sequence more akin to a dance scene than a murder spree, Alexia hunts down and brutally stabs all the girl's roommates—comically exhausting herself when more roommates keep popping up.

Ducournau deliberately wanted to "reverse the idea that a woman is a designated victim, and to show that women feel violence too and they can express violence too." In one of my conversations with the writer-director, she recalled reading a survey about how many women had experienced instances of being insulted or harassed on the Paris subway at any point in their life. The answer was 100 percent. Alexia came from a desire to create a character whose very core was violence, inseparable from her femaleness, but which was not excused by any one event. The director wanted to create a character who would retaliate to violence with violence, outside of the idea of vengeance.

All these women, these Psychos, are uniquely female and uniquely sadistic. Amy Dunne demands perfection fed to her—and to all of us—for eons, even if it is artificial. And Villanelle has successfully separated morality from audience enjoyment. We like to watch her kill, so we'd like her to keep killing, please, for our entertainment. We don't really judge Villanelle—in fact, the shipping of (i.e., wish for) her and Eve's romance is a guiding force of the *Killing Eve* fandom.

These characters have their hold on us because they are unafraid. Villanelle is the scary thing walking down a dark alleyway. In one episode, she trails two young women. They notice someone following them and panic, try to run away, till they bump into Villanelle—the very person who was chasing them. They instantly relax. After all, she's a young woman, just like them. She's not a threat. Correction: she's not our *idea* of a threat. It's a scene familiar, both onscreen and off, to many women, evoking a particular kind of spidey sense, an alertness that has become mundane to anyone who's ever been afraid of walking alone on the street. Villanelle has never felt that fear. And oh how much fun that is to see.

"Throughout my career, executives would say: 'A nice girl doesn't force her opinions on people. A nice girl smiles and waves and says thank you.'"

TAYLOR SWIFT, *MISS AMERICANA*

Sarah Marshall: "It's hard to hate John Lennon. It's easy to hate women apparently, always."
Mike Hobbs: "Also the terrible behavior of men is always seen as sort of intrinsic to their character. Well, like, 'John's going to be John.'"

YOU'RE WRONG ABOUT PODCAST,
"YOKO ONO BROKE UP THE BEATLES"

The Shrew

A while back I was speaking to a man on a dating app, on which I had my profession set as "writer." Inevitably we talked about movies. He asked for my opinion on a film. I shared it, making a joke about how much I disliked the movie. He started to get offended, as if my opinion negated his. Not because I'd said anything about him, or even because he liked this particular film, but because I elaborated on my own opinion. I was being too much of a smart-ass about it. And then the conversation ended.

This harmless encounter gave me pause, and it made me overthink this interaction way more than it deserved. We never met (a rare sign of good judgment from me), but I remember this moment because it conjured up a feeling I'd been trying to suppress for years, especially in my work: "Dumb yourself down or they will get angry." In other words: "Don't be a nag."

Knowledge and intelligence come in different shapes and frequencies, but there is a universal lesson that girls are instilled with: you need to be smart, but just the right amount—for girls, there is such a thing as being too smart, at which point you become a know-it-all—and never, ever, be smarter than the man you're speaking to, because that will make you sound shrill.

Smart girls are girls who keep quiet. Smart girls who want to show off their smarts get put in their place with these admonishing terms: "nag," "know-it-all," "shrill." It's an invisible line and we're taught through movies and TV that the invisible line is in a woman's words as much as her actions. Perhaps this is the most difficult chapter to write, because that line is different for everyone. The daggers of "nag" or "shrew" or "shrill" can be pulled out at any moment, and for any reason, because they merely define a woman who is speaking her mind—especially when she has the audacity to speak her mind in public. In her chapter on the word "shrill" in *Pretty Bitches*, lawyer and journalist Dahlia Lithwick writes, "We criticize female voices in the public sphere chiefly because we aren't certain that women have the authority to lead public thinking."

In her book *Women & Power*, classicist Mary Beard opens with a stark notion: that from the very beginnings of Western civilization, women have been told to shut up because their voice—their actual, physical ability to speak—was antagonistic to authority. The disempowering of women in culture begins with taking away their voice. Literally. All these words—nag, shrill, shrew, harpy—relate to the sound of a woman's voice. There is no context in which they are perceived as positives. So when we think of a nagging wife, or a shrill woman, we imagine a woman talking incessantly, a woman who won't shut up, a woman who just doesn't know her place. "Shrill," writes

Lithwick, "is the polar opposite of persuasive. It is importuning and nagging and small."

We are not accustomed to, and have no real framework for, what a powerful woman sounds like beyond trying to make herself sound like a man: lower voice, steadier tone, less feminine expressions, less girly, more gravelly. When Marge Simpson needs to tell Homer something important, she rehearses "her less nagging voice." Much has been written about Theranos founder Elizabeth Holmes's faked baritone voice, which was imagined in the TV series *The Dropout* as a sort of villain origin story moment, with Elizabeth (Amanda Seyfried) staring at herself in the mirror, repeating the phrase "This is an inspiring step forward" until she perfects the deeper-sounding pitch that will, she expects, make her sound more authoritative. In the 2020 documentary about her, *This Is Paris,* media icon Paris Hilton starts off by parodying her own baby voice ("How many voices do I have?") before switching to her natural timbre. The higher a woman's voice, the less authoritative it seems, regardless of what she is saying.

A Shrew is a woman who speaks her mind but has to constantly negotiate how she does it in order to avoid being seen as a Shrew. Because when the Shrew speaks, she is annoying, and the audience wants her to shut the fuck up. It really doesn't matter whether she's right or not. It's the sort of thing that builds up till you don't notice it anymore and start shutting yourself up too. Movies have conditioned us to automatically despise the two extremes of the female voice: she's either quiet (read: meek; read: she should speak up for herself) or she's too loud (read: shrill; read: she needs to chill out a bit). Onscreen, these two extremes have manifested as the "nagging wife" and the "ambitious smart-ass." The difficulty of writing this chapter is that this means that the Shrew can be literally any woman who speaks—and be punished for it. Sometimes by her own story, other times by her audience.

SHREWS COME IN TWO SIZES

The template for the contemporary Shrew comes from Shakespeare's contested comedy *The Taming of the Shrew*, wherein the main plot revolves around the breaking of an unruly woman's spirit to make her fit for marriage. Katherina "the Cursed" Minola has been played on the big screen by Mary Pickford in 1929, Elizabeth Taylor in 1967, and, in her teen edition, by Julia Stiles as Kat in *10 Things I Hate about You* (1999).

This nineties teenage update on the Shrew codes her as an angry feminist, a sort of proto-pick-me girl who is disdainful toward everyone and quite self-righteous. Kat is presented to us as an antiheroine because she's "not like the other girls," meaning she's more concerned with reading *The Bell Jar* than vying for boys' attention. She's not interested in fashion or popularity and is comfortable being by herself, indulging in her own interests. However, not even she is immune to the crinkly smile of Heath Ledger. There are many problems with Kat's characterization in the film—her total lack of intersectionality, despite preaching about feminism; her judgmental dismissal of feminine women as flighty or superficial; her inability to communicate without hitting someone—but she was, in this era of teen movies, a protagonist unlike any we'd seen before.

Perhaps this pick-me attitude, which I'll admit resonated with me as a teenager who was very much similar in her tastes, has aged the worst. Kat's dismissiveness toward all other women who do not share her particular interests, putting herself above them, is a by-product of the very same patriarchal structures that she protests.

As in the Bard's play, Kat is hated by everyone—in the nineties edition this is because she's a somewhat obnoxious, angry, outspoken feminist. She's openly contemptuous of everyone around her (especially high school boys), except her Shakespeare-obsessed bestie. In order to date her sister Bianca (Larisa Oleynik), a girly girl who operates well within the high school social system, new boy Cameron (Joseph Gordon-Levitt) hatches a plan whereby he gets the smug, rapey model Joey (Andrew Keegan) to pay the smug, scary outcast Patrick Verona (Heath Ledger) to date Kat.[1]

Much like the Mean Girls of other nineties teen movies, Kat is introduced to us via her reputation and how other people perceive her. "Miss I-have-an-opinion-about-everything," her English teacher calls her. "A bitter, self-righteous hag who has no friends," says Joey. Her sister calls her a "complete psycho." Cameron uses the more politically correct term "difficult woman," tiptoeing around what he really wants to say: "She's a raging bitch." Everyone around her mocks her, both teasingly ("Made anyone cry today?") and cruelly ("Why can't you be normal?"). Kat has learned to respond to both in the same cutting, mocking way. But while the rest of the school rolls their

---

1   There are a lot of smug men in *10 Things I Hate about You*, but only some of them are attractive. And when I say "some," I mean only one: Heath Ledger.

eyes when she speaks, Patrick is left speechless. When he has a comeback that is worth her time, and her attention, she starts to listen. A lot of the criticism of her, keeping Beard's idea in mind, comes down to Kat's talking a lot. She questions her teacher. She talks back to her bullies. She even snaps back at Patrick when he stumbles into the wrong class: "I guess, in this society, being male and an asshole makes you worthy of our time." She is mouthy.

As a girl, the Shrew is the antithesis of the Trainwreck in that she knowingly sacrifices, or avoids, the trappings of partying. The confusing push-and-pull of girlhood means that Kat has all the ingredients of a popular, well-liked girl, but she's reviled. We learn in the film that, as a freshman, her first sexual experience was with Joey, and she regretted it so much it pushed her away from doing anything based on peer pressure. She did what people expected her to do, betraying what she really wanted to do. With the double-edged sword of being a teenage girl, she is punished either way. The downfall of her likeability, and what defines her, is her aggressive smugness. In the teen world, Kat the Shrew is told constantly that she needs to relax, to chill, to shut the fuck up. There is so much emphasis on her being quiet and adaptable that her actual faults are skimmed over. The real lesson Kat needed to learn wasn't to be "tamed" but to be more forgiving of herself and of others, especially other women. Like all teenage girls, she defines herself by what she likes, not by who she is yet ("Thai food, feminist prose, and angry-girl music of the indie-rock persuasion"), so Patrick seduces her based on that. It's curious that the vitriolic hate she receives from her peers as a teenager, or young girl, is transformed into something more insidious when she grows up. The teenage Shrew's arc is not to be tamed by others but to make decisions for herself, to hold herself accountable, and to embrace the parts of herself others told her she needed to eliminate.

What happens to the Shrew when she grows up?

THE SKYLER EFFECT

It's easy to confuse an actor with their character. In some ways, it's almost a compliment to their craft that they embody a character so fully that the lines between the real person and the character become blurred. Some actors have built entire careers on playing variations of the same role over and over again.[2] Some actors have clearly stipulated no-gos in the types of roles they will take on, either based on a particular public image they want to maintain or due to personal reasons.

On the other hand, other actors will make a big deal out of disappearing into a role, of transforming their body, face, and voice or disrupting their own life in order to become the character they're portraying. The industry and audiences usually reward these efforts with accolades, success, and fame. They see it as a sign of commitment to the role, a striving for authenticity. Robert De Niro put on twenty pounds of muscle and then sixty pounds of extra weight to play boxer Jake LaMotta at different stages of his life in *Raging Bull* (1980). Christian Bale has transformed his body multiple times for roles, dropping sixty pounds to become a skeletal figure in *The Machinist* (2004) and then

---

2   Looking at you, Robert Downey Jr.

bulking up by one hundred pounds to play Batman. Charlize Theron put on thirty pounds, bleached her eyebrows, and wore prosthetic rotting teeth to portray real-life murderess Aileen Wuornos in *Monster* (2003). Their efforts often become part of the star's mythos, and they also help us separate the artist from the character. But then, sometimes, when it comes to actresses who don't have a cemented public image yet—one that has already established a likeable persona for them—there can be backlash when the lines between performer and character blur. Not just against the character they portray but against the actor themselves.

Anna Gunn, who played Skyler White, the wife of chemistry-teacher-turned-meth-kingpin Walter White, in the revered show *Breaking Bad*, is not the first but arguably has been one of the *most* vocal actors about the vitriol she's received for playing one of the most hated characters in modern TV history. So much so, that the irrational hate that audiences feel toward some female characters has been dubbed "The Skyler Effect": "a female character judges the male protagonist's bad behavior in a completely rational way, and the audience hates her for it," writes Marion Johnson in the *Huffington Post*. When she was cast on the show, Gunn had been working steadily since the early nineties, mostly in TV, but none of her previous projects had broken out in the same way as *Breaking Bad* did. The same happened for Bryan Cranston, who portrayed her onscreen husband and who'd by then been known mostly for his comedic roles, especially the hapless, power-walking dad Hal on *Malcolm in the Middle*.

The premise of *Breaking Bad* is quite simple, and quite simply genius. A mild-mannered, frustrated high school chemistry teacher is diagnosed with terminal cancer. Worried about his family's well-being after he's gone, he turns to cooking meth to build a solid nest egg for them. The thing is, he gets really good at it, and he finds that he enjoys being a drug lord. So what started off as a desperate measure quickly turns into a vocation, with all the complications that come with, you know, operating a drug cartel. While Walter is busy becoming a drug kingpin, Skyler, his wife, is unaware of his secret dealings at the start of the show. When she does find out, she tries to stop him. She even tries to leave him and at one point is essentially held hostage in her own house. Eventually, she starts helping him, using her accountancy and administrative skills to help better manage the practicalities of a growing drug business. Skyler effectively makes a deal with the devil who's already sleeping in her bed.

Skyler White subverted the character of the mob wife and the nagging wife. She transformed from a devoted wife in a suburban marriage into a morally compromised partner, held hostage by a husband putting her and their children in mortal peril. Skyler's acceptance and participation in Walter's drug schemes is both an exhilarating character arc and a portrait of a woman's moral descent. None of it black or white. Every single character on *Breaking Bad* is or becomes morally compromised.

But—and this is the bit that often gets forgotten—before she became Walter's reluctant accomplice, her husband lied to her, threatened her, broke into her home after she'd kicked him out, and in one episode, kidnapped their baby daughter in order to force Skyler to stay with him. Before she found out her husband was actually the Man Who Knocks, Skyler was a character already written to both lean in and subvert the nagging wife trope. She was consumed with making sure their life was on track; she's a pragmatist and has no qualms about making tough, unglamorous decisions in order to provide (she'll take a part-time job while pregnant; she'll accept money from her well-off sister to pay for her husband's cancer treatment). She will do anything it takes and this somehow made her unlikeable, a Shrew, a know-it-all do-gooder who was smothering Walt.

The more Walt descended into and rose up in the drug world, and the more he became truly himself, the more audiences hated Skyler. She was seen as an impediment to his plans and ungrateful for everything he was doing (ostensibly) for their family, simultaneously a killjoy for Walt's meth-dealing shenanigans and a hypocrite for helping him be better at his meth-dealing shenanigans. Skyler White was a do-gooder and wrongdoer, somehow at the same time.

While Anna Gunn was picking up awards for her work on the series, including two Emmys (she was nominated three times), audiences despised Skyler and, by extension, Anna. Critics and audiences saw Skyler as "inept, high-pitched, and whiny." Headlines called her "the worst character in TV," a "cold and emotionless nag," and a "henpecking woman," and claimed that she was "too far gone." She was a "hypocrite" and a "killjoy." There were vicious Reddit accounts dedicated to hating Skyler. Facebook groups and entire websites were set up to revel in Skyler-hate. On Facebook, almost 26,000 people liked the "I Hate Skyler White" group. Memes were made that said, "I'm not always a bitch—just kidding, I always am," or "Skyler is my favorite Breaking Bad character—said no one ever," even "Why the fuck does no one kill this bitch?" Audiences despised her with an intensity that didn't touch any of the other characters, no matter what they did. Walter literally murdered people and yet the majority of the vitriol was directed toward his wife for being annoying. At a public Q&A, early on in the show's run, an audience member asked Anna Gunn the question, "Why is your character such a bitch? I mean, Walt is working and he's doing this for his family." Skyler was the carping "ball and chain" wife that was getting in the way. She was annoying, she was shrill, she didn't get or appreciate all the "hard work" that Walter was putting in for their family so she didn't deserve the rewards it brought. She should just shut the fuck up or get the fuck out if she didn't like it. To the public, Skyler White was the ultimate Shrew, and there is no nuance or empathy allowed for Shrews.

The show's fan base also criticized the show's creator, Vince Gilligan, for defending the character and Gunn. In an interview with *Vulture*, he addressed the strange and strangely intense response directed at Skyler and directly at Gunn at public Q&As. Gilligan called out the people who virulently detested Skyler but sided with Walt as "misogynists, plain and simple." It seemed to baffle Gilligan how much people sided with Walt while seeming completely unable to sympathize with Skyler:

> People are griping about Skyler White being too much of a killjoy to her meth-cooking, murdering husband? She's telling him not to be a murderer and a guy who cooks

drugs for kids. How could you have a problem with that? She's got a tough job being married to this asshole.

Skyler was trapped, in her house, in her marriage, and in the dangerous criminal game that she did not choose to be dragged into ("I can't go to the police, I can't stop laundering your money, I can't keep you out of the house, I can't even keep you out of my bed"). The hate got so intense that Anna Gunn wrote an op-ed in the *New York Times* where she addressed, and tried to rationalize, why her character was so reviled.

Skyler was a complicated character, "morally compromised" in her own way, wrote Gunn. But she "hasn't been judged by the same set of standards as Walter." She compared the reaction to Skyler to that directed at Carmela Soprano (wife of Tony on *The Sopranos*) or at Betty Draper (wife of Don on *Mad Men*): "Could it be that they can't stand a woman who won't suffer silently or 'stand by her man'? That they despise her because she won't back down or give up? Or because she is, in fact, Walter's equal?" In fact, Skyler in some ways was more skilled than Walt at a different part of his own game. She was more measured and strategic and extremely good at laundering money. If she was as ego driven as Walt, they would've made perfect partners, but instead she was also criticized for being good at the drug business.

But that rationalizing didn't keep people from wanting to kill her—"her" meaning Anna—as a way to make the character go away. The Skyler effect was not the first time dislike of a female character reached the level of a cultural shorthand and audiences confused the actress with the character. The fact that *Breaking*

Bad (and *Mad Men*, for that matter) arrived on television during the late noughties, when fandom had solidly migrated online, is crucial context. Online message boards, Twitter chatter, and memes were fodder for this toxic fire. With the show becoming more widely available through Netflix during its run and after it ended, this gave this online hate a second life, which would inevitably reach Gunn. She couldn't help but be aware of the hate, how it was engaging fans online—a vitriol quantifiable by likes and shares is hard to avoid.

I HATE BRENDA

Before they become nagging wives, Shrews are teenage upstarts. In the 1990s, the most hated TV character was also a woman— a teenager, actually: Brenda Walsh of *Beverly Hills, 90210*, as played by Shannen Doherty. On the show, Brenda Walsh was a transplant from Minnesota mostly concerned with finding her footing in a new high school. Initially, she was written as a strong-willed, grounded teenager who wants to be popular and liked, has a crush on the Beverly Hills bad boy Dylan (Luke Perry), and feels out of place among the rich teenagers of her new milieu. Usual hot, teen girl stuff. Although her character started off as a do-gooder, tabloid reports of Doherty's brattish and demanding on-set behavior seemed to seep into her onscreen character, and Brenda started being more impulsive and self-absorbed, as if the writers wanted to make the real-life Doherty lean into the worst parts of her public self through the character of Brenda. The more audiences heard about the way Doherty allegedly behaved onset, the more they hated her onscreen. Stories about her "increasingly petulant" and "brat-tish" behavior were a mainstay in tabloids at the time. It was said she was hated by all her fellow cast and crew, was mean to publi-cists, and often had extreme demands like requiring exactly ten bottles of Evian to wash her hair or refusing to walk across the road to a set (forcing a car to pick her up, make a U-turn, and deposit her at the door).

This gossip (whether true or not) and its impact were enlarged by the fact that the show itself was a major pop culture phenomenon that catapulted its young actors to stardom. In its second season, *Beverly Hills, 90210*'s ratings almost doubled, and by the end of season four (coincidentally the last season before Doherty departed the show) it was being watched by 21.7 mil-lion viewers. Very soon, though, the cool thing was not just to be a *90210* fan but a Brenda anti-fan. There was an "I Hate Brenda" fan club, which included a hotline (the "Brenda Snitch Line," for gossip about either Brenda or Shannen); they made T-shirts and bumper stickers and published the "I Hate Brenda Newsletter," which reached over seven thousand people in the pre-internet era. "We will not stop until Brenda is off the air," the founders of the club told the *Los Angeles Times*. There was even a band who put out a six-song album called *I Hate Brenda*. In the same year that *Time* magazine ran a cover story titled "Year of the Woman," *Glamour* magazine crowned Shannen Doherty the "Prima Donna of 1992."

Outside of her role as Brenda Walsh, Doherty also played Mean Girl/aspiring bitch Heather Duke in *Heathers*. Although that film would not be commercially successful, it would con-firm what the public was keen to believe: Brenda was a bitch, and so was Shannen. The actress—who was in her early twenties at this point, having taken on the role of Brenda at just nineteen—seemed to lean into this public perception, appearing on the cover of *People* magazine as "TV's brashest 21-year-old," and even satirized herself in the 1993 *Saturday Night Live* sketch "Salem Bitch Trials," appearing as a woman put on trial for being a "stuck-up bitch."

"I met her on the road with the Devil, and she didn't even introduce me," she's accused by a villager. Like in all court dramas, Doherty delivers a speech imploring common sense: "Why is it when a man speaketh his mind, he's admired and made judge. But when a woman displays forthrightness, she's accused of being a bitch." She is judged and sentenced because, although her words make sense, her delivery is deemed bitchy: "Your eloquent plea doth not fall upon deaf ears. However, your words would sway greatly more had they not been delivered in such a bitchy manner! You shall be burned!"

It's a hilarious sketch, and one in which Doherty poked fun at the allegations of her own bad behavior. Perhaps if Doherty's rise to fame had come a few decades later, we would've been able to acknowledge and respect her forthright approach to her own troubles. In the 1990s, though, you were either a bitch or a good girl, likeable or unlikeable. Doherty would leave the show in 1994 and would effectively disappear from the screens until her return on another Aaron Spelling show, *Charmed*, in 1998. The identification of Doherty with her *90210* character was so strong that the controversy followed her onto this new set too, and after three seasons, her character on *Charmed* was killed off. Doherty, unlike Gunn, leaned into and made lighthearted fun of the rumors circulating around her—but no one else thought it was funny. To the public, it was a confirmation that they were right in hating Brenda and Shannen alike.

CANNOT WAIT FOR PEOPLE TO HATE ME

I'd love to say that this has changed. It has and it hasn't. Another mob wife of the small screen, Wendy Byrde (Laura Linney), is receiving a substantial amount of hate for her portrayal of a devious, scheming wife of a drug lord in *Ozark*. There are entire Reddit threads dedicated to hating Wendy, but there's also some talk about how they love to hate her. Meanwhile, other actresses are also embracing the appeal of the Shrew. Shalita Grant, who plays the mom-influencer Sherry Conrad in the third season of *You*, has gleefully given interviews where she jokes: "I cannot wait for people to be like, 'I hated you.'"

There is a different tonality to the type of hate directed toward, say, the glamorous bitch versus that directed toward the Shrew, who might be morally superior but is lacking in charisma. Her lack of pretense or glamour makes her unattractive, thereby costing her the only currency she had. Shrews are more easily dismissed than Bitches despite embodying more traditionally feminine attributes and often being the moral compass of a flawed partnership; but they are more easily hated because they are not fuckable enough. And most of all because Shrews will *not shut up.*

In this way, this archetype is the most insidious one of all. You are damned if you speak too much—too loud, too opinionated, too annoying, too naggy, too shrewy—and you're damned if you don't speak—too meek, too weak, no backbone, no character. So what, then, is a congenial middle ground? Maybe it just doesn't exist. The abuse these characters—and the actresses who play them—have received is revealing, but it will not shut them up. The worst possible outcome of hearing any of these words, or of hearing any of these characters being labeled as Shrews, is silence.

"I don't like to smile unless I have a reason."

DARIA

Bus Driver: "You girls watch out for those weirdos."
Nancy Downs: "We are the weirdos, mister."

THE CRAFT **(1996)**

The Weirdo

Nobody wanted to be the weird girl in school. I did. I always gravitated toward the weird girl or was the weird girl. The early and mid-2000s, an era that feels in many ways like an extension of the nineties with the added complication of a nascent online culture, were a contradictory cesspit of misogynistic and empowering narratives. In the same way that you cannot separate sex from the pre-Code era in Hollywood, you cannot separate the Weirdos from the commercialization of alternative culture during the late 1980s and nineties. The rise of grunge aesthetics and riot-grrrl feminism melded with the early noughties' online girl culture, creating a small but impactful cross section of onscreen Weirdos that stood firmly within mainstream screen culture but off to the side of the frame.

The pick-me attitude was a strange defense mechanism spawned as a reaction to and reflection of mainstream pop culture, a confused middle finger to the chick flicks with white-backgrounded posters and the straight-haired, summery stars that wore low-rise jeans and were hyperfeminine.

The Weirdo girl was rarely the main character, but for the misfits among the audience, she was often the most memorable one.

STRANGE AND UNUSUAL

What makes a weird girl weird, exactly? The instant image conjured up is a girl of the goth persuasion. A black-clad, surly creature with niche interests, often morbid in nature. Pale, antagonistic and off-putting, she loves cemeteries, vintage cameras, and dark eyeliner. Generally speaking, the weird girls of film and television were not coded as evil, just strange. Ordinarily, she'd be a throwaway, underdeveloped character, almost for comic relief, like Ally Sheedy as the basket case in *The Breakfast Club* (1985), who squeals behind her dark bangs or creates art with her dandruff in the last row of detention, or the comically over-sexed goth Tosh in *Urban Legend* (1998), who doesn't mind her roommate being in the room while she's having sex but draws the line at the lights being on. Yet as grunge and Gen X alt culture infiltrated the mainstream, so did the Weirdo. With music videos by bands like Nirvana and Soundgarden propelled through MTV, films about young adult ennui like *Reality Bites* (1994) and TV shows about teenage angst like *My So-Called Life* (1994–95) and later on *Freaks and Geeks* (1999–2000), the Weirdo became an unlikely protagonist.

The Weirdo is not so much defined by her unlikeability as she is by being in opposition to her environment, which explains why she's so attractive for rebellious teen girls. Unsurprisingly, the Weirdos of late eighties and nineties cinema would become the first poster girls of Tumblr era alt-girls. For anyone who found themselves outside of the teen social hierarchy, or confused by it, these characters provided an emotional and aesthetic respite. In a sea of bandeau tops and swirly-pattern dresses, a character dressed in head-to-toe black lace in the middle of summer either repelled or enthralled. Sometimes a bit of both.

There is a protective shell to weirdness. These characters' antagonism can be read as a form of power, a defense mechanism, and a way to distinguish themselves from others. The Weirdo is a solitary character, often alone either by choice or by force, but she craves a tribe deeply. Romance is rarely her prime objective[1]— it's friendship, any connection that will work as a soothing balm on the feeling of isolation. So when the Weirdo finds a group to belong to, it takes on something of a mystical resonance. It's not a surprise, then, that most pop culture Weirdos are teenage girls or young adults. Teenagehood is, after all, a time when we're trying to figure out our identity. When combined with the ingrained appeal of the occult, the rise of alternative culture, and the rich visual legacy of the witch in pop culture, it feels inevitable that the nineties gave us a film like *The Craft* (1996).

Watching the film for the first time—and every time since then, if we're being honest—it holds that persuasive power of being extremely specific and totally universal at the same time. Which is, in a way, what it feels like being a teenager. Your experiences are of a seismic magnitude; things considered small from an adult perspective feel end-of-the-world huge, like they were

---

1   Excluding Angela (Claire Danes) and her infatuation with blue-eyed Jordan Cat-alano (Jared Leto) on *My So-Called Life*.

never before experienced by anyone else in the same way. And simultaneously, there is a desperate desire to find someone who feels exactly the same as you do. I thought of Nancy Downs, played by Fairuza Balk in *The Craft*, many times during my high school life: the way she cocked her head and her unblinking stare, more quietly threatening than any magic. Her purposeful walk through a hostile high school corridor, eyes directly firmly ahead of her. I thought of the way she stared directly into her bullies' faces instead of looking away, like I did when I had to face my own bullies. Nancy Downs was intense and unhinged, but she was also kind and hurting. For teenage girls feeling everything all at once, she was everything. Like *The Craft* itself, Nancy Downs exists in the middle of the very rare Venn diagram of feeling extremely of its time and yet completely timeless, acutely relevant to whatever moment someone finds the film.

The plot of *The Craft* concerns the coming together of a coven of teenage witches, all classmates at a Catholic high school. Sarah (Robin Tunney), a transplant from San Francisco, is recovering from a recent suicide attempt. Her arrival and powers catch the attention of a gang of outsiders: Nancy, Bonnie (Neve Campbell), and Rochelle (Rachel True). They join together to summon Manon, a pagan deity that gifts them with powers that enhance those elements in their lives where they feel the most powerless.

Magic in *The Craft* is presented as something material, organic, seeped in a secret tradition that the girls have had to learn and that connects them to the world around them but also feels entirely theirs. Alongside the craft, magic exists as a natural power that is passed on genetically—but this is rare, and Sarah (who got it from her mother) is the only one of the girls who is a natural-born witch. The magic of *The Craft* is based on rituals, a clawing back of some semblance of power by three wounded and disempowered characters (I'm excluding Sarah here).

There is no Satanism, or even any direct references to Wicca. The filmmakers created a new god for the young witches to worship: Manon ("It's like God and the Devil. I mean, it's everything"). The filmmakers consulted real-life Wiccan practitioners to respect the authenticity of their practice (Fairuza Balk, a practicing Wiccan in real life, got so involved in her research that she bought an occult store that still operates to this day).

The teenagers have very little in common with one another outside of their interest in the occult and are connected mainly by how they are each othered in their own way: Sarah is dealing with depression and grief; Rochelle is the only Black girl in her school and the target of racist bullying; Bonnie has deep shame issues around the scars that cover her body; and Nancy is suffering from neglect and abuse on all sides. They are all outcasts, Weirdos, in different ways. Beyond magic, it's their otherness that binds them together. There has been criticism of the film for pitting the girls against one another when Nancy becomes the default villain—a manic, power-crazed creature just short of foaming at the mouth—but it makes sense, since Nancy is the most powerless of the quartet. In their high school, her barriers are up, all bravado and morbid knickknacks (she casually kneels against the noose she keeps in her locker while people stare). But when she leaves school, home is not the safe place it should be. Nancy's entire body is in defense mode. She's easy to anger because it's the only language the people in her home—the adults meant to protect her—will understand. Even when left by herself, Nancy is not relaxed; she cowers. There is no care or gentleness in her life: at school, she's called a slut and a witch, and people point fingers and stare; at home, her mother is drunk and yelling, and her stepdad tries to cop a feel as she squeezes out of the shower. When the girls ask Manon for favors, they ask for the things that will help them mend what they see as being broken in their lives: Rochelle wants to get her racist bully off her back; Bonnie wants to heal her body; and Sarah wants the boy who rejected her to want her. With the exception of Rochelle's request—which betrays a simplistic take on racism that seems to believe it's a case of one bad apple and not an entire structure that allows this behavior—their requests to their deity are child-like patches on their problems. Nancy, though... Nancy asks for power. Magic for her is a source of internal and external power she doesn't have access to in any other way.

This is when the film itself turns against Nancy. She gets greedy and she can't handle it; she's drunk on the opportunities that Manon's power gives her, some of them for herself, but mostly for others: her stepdad suddenly dies from a heart attack while assaulting her mother, and they both inherit money from his life insurance; she camouflages herself as Sarah to get back at Chris, who attempted to assault her friend ("The only way you know how to treat women is by treating them like whores, when *you're* the whore! And that's gonna stop!"). But even all of Manon's power doesn't give Nancy what she *really* wants. Instead, it severs her connection to the one thing that grounded her, the one caring space she knew: her coven. In a final showdown between Sarah and Nancy, with Bonnie and Rochelle siding with the latter, it's a magical take on the type of psychological warfare that only teenage girls are truly capable of. ("You know in the old days, if a witch betrayed her coven…they would kill her".) The Weirdos' infighting is laced with poisonous barbs aimed straight at each other's underbellies: Nancy tells Sarah to kill herself; Sarah in turn tells Nancy that even Manon, her only solace and the source of her power, has rejected her. Nancy is defeated not just supernaturally but emotionally. She's left totally alone, her powers bound by Sarah and in a cell in a mental institution.

Witchcraft has always been a metaphor for female power, both in its natural form—secret knowledge—and in its supernatural one—actual powers over reality. The witch represents a fearsome take on feminine power so of course she is either vilified or ridiculed. While the rise of the alternative aesthetic was a timely, easily monetized and broadcast rebellion, the turn to the occult in times of despair goes back centuries. In times of crisis, women (and increasingly not just women but queer and nonbinary folk too) turn to the occult. It might manifest in different ways potion making or spell casting or TikTok tarot readings—but the elemental ambition remains the same.

Until *The Craft*, witches onscreen were either straight villains (*Black Sunday, Suspiria, The Witches, Blood on Satan's Claw*) or romantic comedy heroines (*I Married a Witch, Bewitched*). "To market it," said Fairuza Balk in an interview at the time of the film's release, "they have to distort it and make it into something evil or stupid." By contrast, *The Craft* channeled the dissatisfaction and anger of teenage girls into a kind of post-new-wave, lightly occult-inspired visual aesthetic that has had many direct rip-offs.[2] The seriousness with which the film took magic was tantamount to the seriousness with which it took the girls themselves. The film struck a chord. It performed well at the box office and has lived on through countless sleepovers, finding a devoted cult audience that continues to chant, "Light as a feather, stiff as a board" to candlelight.

Sarah, Bonnie, Rochelle, and Nancy would become icons for outcast girls—and magic a supernatural solution for their sense of disempowerment. Writing in 2018 for *Refinery29,* Anne Cohen pointed out that *The Craft* was taking a look at dark, taboo themes like "bullying, racism, poverty, body issues, abuse, suicide, sexual assault and otherness in a way that doesn't feel like an after-school special." Giving these issues a (literally) supernatural weight gives them the seriousness that often gets denied to teenager's issues, "while arming its characters with unusual tools to cope."

Unsurprisingly when it comes to films about teenage girls, the original reception for the film was tepid at best. It had been marketed as "*Carrie* meets *Clueless*" and failed to impress critics at the time, who saw it as flashy but insubstantial. The *Chicago Tribune* critic Michael Wilmington said it had "more flair than depth, but not much of either," and Roger Ebert seemed to look down on the film's protagonists:

> Their classmates don't like them, which seems strange,
> since they have messy hair, slather on black lipstick, wear
> leather dog collars, smoke a lot, have rings piercing many

---

2   Fox's *Charmed* TV series used not only a similar concept but also the same font, montages, and music for its theme song, "How Soon Is Now?" Other films that directly lift from *The Craft* include *Little Witches* (1996) and *The Covenant* (2006).

of the penetrable parts of their bodies, sneer constantly, and, in short, look like normal, popular teenagers.

This is, to be honest, mostly about Nancy. She's the only one who wears dog collars and has a nose piercing. So strong is her screen presence that we cannot but paint the rest of the girls with the same goth brush.

But these teenage Weirdos weren't the first of their kind.

ARE WE THE WEIRDOS?

When Lydia Deetz (Winona Ryder) arrives with her parents at their new house, she's wearing an all-black getup with a wide-brimmed black hat and peering at the world behind a clunky Nikon camera. She's drawn to the spiders breeding in the house and the dark staircase that leads upstairs to a locked attic where—because this is *Beetlejuice* (1988), after all—she'll meet the ghosts of a recently deceased couple, the Maitlands (played by Geena Davis and Alec Baldwin, a most wholesome pairing of very tall actors who make for very unspooky ghosts). Lydia is able to see them because, while "live people ignore the strange and unusual, I myself am strange and unusual." While the title character is the stripy suit-wearing demon Beetlejuice, the real standout was always Lydia, the dramatic, oversensitive teenager who befriends the ghosts in her house.

The film, though a fairly cutesy family comedy, arrived bang in the middle of the rise of new-wave music and goth culture. Lydia's dreary outlook is reminiscent of Siouxsie and the Banshees lyrics. In any other film, Lydia would be a background gag, a running joke to emphasize the wholesomeness of the main, more conventional leads. In *Beetlejuice*, she is not only the heroine but is also the only (living) character capable of empathy: she's able to see the ghosts in their new house because she's curious, probing around the attic, and she's not afraid of them. Instead, she asks them questions. Beyond the costuming of the Weirdo, it's her empathy that always stands out.

While Lydia is ostracized by her father and stepmother, Wednesday Addams is the gothic golden child of the Addams family. Although there was a sitcom that ran for two seasons (from 1964 till 1966) based on the *New Yorker* cartoon series by Charles Addams, it's the 1991 feature film that has permeated pop culture and where Wednesday played a much more significant role.

In the film, the Addams clan is composed of patriarch Gomez Addams (Raul Julia), an independently wealthy bon vivant completely unconcerned with money or competition; his wife Morticia (Angelica Huston), who he adores; and their children, Wednesday (Christina Ricci) and Pugsley (Jimmy Workman). For comedic appeal, the horniness of the parents is exaggerated, as is the role of the children, who are aged up into preteens who don't really attend school and instead spend most of their time experimenting with weapons of varying degrees of deadliness.

The entire appeal of the Addamses is that everything about them is meant to be morbid and scary—but they're not actually. Their house is a gothic mansion that's falling apart, with creepy staircases and hidden rooms. Their housekeeper, Lurch, looks like Frankenstein's monster's cousin. Their butler is a disembodied hand. There are cobwebs everywhere, and Morticia cuts off the heads of roses after they bloom.[3] While the whole premise of the Addams Family was that they were an inversion of the All-American Nuclear Family™, the joke was on everyone but the Addamses: they were a generally happy, well-adjusted bunch who just happened to be Weirdos. It was the rest of the world that was conniving, greedy, and mean. The Addams' weirdness was kooky, but beneath the black outfits and pale makeup, what was *actually* wrong with them? Gomez and Morticia's marriage was effervescent, they were devoted and demonically horny for one another. Wednesday and Pugsley were constantly playing with each other, and when their family hit financial troubles, they tried to pitch in by selling toxic lemonade. The Addams are a unified front that the outside "normies" cannot pierce through.

At the time of making *The Addams Family*, Ricci was a working child actor, having made her debut in the family drama *Mermaids* (1990) with Ryder herself and Cher as their messy mother. In a case of a cinematic passing of the baton, Winona Ryder's take on the Weirdo inspired Ricci's, who went on to play Wednesday Addams the year after *Mermaids*.

Wednesday had a deadpan tone of voice and a uniform of tight braids and a black dress with black tights. A terrifying, tiny icon who'd stare daggers into adults and other kids alike, Wednesday was a quiet blueprint for future alt-girls everywhere, a beacon of confidence, absolutely secure in who she was, from the style to the tone ("This is my costume. I'm a homicidal maniac. They look just like everyone else").

In the sequel *The Addams Family Values* (1993), where we see

---

3   Frankly, this is my dream family.

more of Wednesday's interactions with the "normal" world as a teen girl, this contrast between her and the rest of girlhood is empha-. sized, and she is particularly scathing. When a Mean Girl tries to bully her, she snaps back, unfazed ("Is that your bathing suit?" the Mean Girl asks. "Is that your overbite?" Wednesday responds). It's in these moments that the Weirdo's individuality reveals itself as a strength, not a weakness. Moonfaced and stern, Wednesday only cracks a smile when she's about to electrocute her brother.

Lydia, Nancy, and Wednesday coexisted in the same era, cementing the nineties as a thriving time for the onscreen Weirdo. Only a year after *The Craft* was released, *Daria* began airing on MTV. A spin-off based on a supporting character in the animated sitcom *Beavis & Butthead*, Daria Morgendorffer is a deadpan, smart-ass teenage girl who looks like a down-to-earth take on Wednesday Addams, with the same acerbic wit. She dresses unfashionably (always in her green jacket and combat boots), wears her big glasses, and doesn't make any effort to fit in. In fact, she makes fun of the entire idea of "fitting in." Daria's smug, anti-girly girl humor was the signature of the show. She wasn't necessarily angry; she was more quietly resentful of everyone else's stupidity. "[Her] sarcasm proved so extreme it amped way past wiseass into some scary dimension of its own," wrote Emily Nussbaum on the eve of the show's finale in 2002.

The end of Daria's reign would also mark the start of a new pop culture era, one populated with intense, hyperfeminine figures. The 2000s were the era of a new type of bombshell, and the Weirdo would be relegated to a supporting role. The noughties-dominating wave of hyperfemininity included an obsession with female virtue and virginity, glittery OTT personalities, and a sense of fake access to or faux ownership of actresses that would make the sort of earnestness that characterizes the Weirdo completely out of place. Everyone's lives—especially actresses'; the younger and the messier they were, the better—were fair game. The 2000s were the era of the Trainwreck, and it wouldn't be till the late 2010s that we'd see a resurgence of the Weirdo trope in a big, brash way on our screens.

UNHINGED AND UNPUNISHED

Harley Quinn is a newer addition to the canon of Weirdos, and one that has made a zany, mismatched brand of femininity her aesthetic and her core selling point, especially once her big-screen adaptation became divorced from the figure of the Joker. It's curious to note that Harley Quinn was born of the screen and not the comic book page. She was originally created as a one-off sidekick to Batman's forever antagonist, the Joker, for the acclaimed show *Batman: The Animated Series*. Created for the screen, she evolved and grew in popularity in comic book form, and now she's had three live-action, full-throttle iterations in the DC universe: *Suicide Squad* (2016), *Birds of Prey* (2020), and *The Suicide Squad* (2021).[4] In each one, she's been portrayed by actress Margot Robbie, who has playfully called Harley a "bottomless pit of issues."

It was Robbie's portrayal of Harley in *Suicide Squad* that garnered the most fan support and critical acclaim in a film that is otherwise, to put it bluntly, quite boring. In her first introduction

---

4   Don't get me started.

onscreen, she's seen hanging from a straitjacket she's fashioned into a kind of hammock ("That is a whole lotta pretty and a whole lotta crazy," a guard tells us). She's crazy, we're told, because she fell in love with the Joker and he forcibly subjected her to electroshock therapy, which irrevocably damaged her. There's a neon-pink sign that appears, establishing her as a "total wild card." The entire characterization the film gives her is—sigh—that she's crazy but crazy hot too. The journey of Harley Quinn begins with her as a tired, over-the-top caricature of the Crazy Woman, but she is transformed into a Weirdo.

While *Suicide Squad* shows Harley as little more than a sexy lapdog to the Joker (in one scene, she's literally called over with a whistle), it's when she detaches herself from the green-haired villain that she comes into her own. In a history of the character written for *Vulture*, a Harley Quinn superfan defended Harley's messiness as a key to her appeal: "She doesn't make choices that are smart or good for a woman, but she gets to make those choices. Men are allowed to be fuckups in all kinds of characters, and women aren't. We have to be idealized. She gets to not be."

Fans' adoring response to this character has only increased in strength with Robbie's portrayal. DC Comics copublisher Jim Lee referred to her as "the fourth pillar in our publishing line, behind Superman, Batman and Wonder Woman." Harley Quinn is also only the second female character (behind Wonder Woman) to get her own standalone movie, which is huge considering how long it's taken the Marvel Cinematic Universe to have a female-led standalone film.[5] After more than a decade of female

---

5   The first was *Captain Marvel* (2019), followed by the much-delayed *Black Widow* (2021), a character that appeared as early as *Iron Man 2* (2010).

insanity being presented as, mostly, white girl sadness, the live-action Harley Quinn is an explosion of high-femme weirdness, which separates her from the Crazy Woman. Her worldview is twisted, violent, and filled with neon colors, glitter, and stuffed animals. But it's also bodily. Harley contorts herself; from that very first voyeuristic sequence, she seems to enjoy pain (her torture scene in *The Suicide Squad* takes on a semi-erotic tone), and she's sexually active.

Let's hold on to this for a moment. In *Suicide Squad*, Harley is obviously crudely sexualized by the film and by all the male characters she's surrounded by. There are shots of her bending over, shots of her licking her prison bars suggestively, shots of her changing clothes. Outside of Margot Robbie's fiendish performance, the film seems to see her as nothing more than unstable T&A. It's performative, limping sexualizing that's straight out of a 2002 music video. The camera lingers over her body, and all this time her costume is a pair of glitter booty shorts and stiletto Converse. The shots of Harley's backside were peppered all throughout the marketing materials for the film. We're told that she's sexually liberated, but she never actually has sex, the film just oversexualizes her for the titillation of the audience. Her subsequent big-screen outings course correct this portrayal, with Harley continuing to be sexually open, unabashedly horny, and, it's implied, fluid. In *The Suicide Squad*, she gets a brief new romantic interest in President Silvio Luna, a fictional dictator who tries to woo her into marriage, but after an explosive quickie, Harley shoots him point-blank in the chest, having learned to see red flags in a man at this point ("I made a promise to myself that the next time I got a boyfriend, I'd be on the lookout for red flags. And if I saw any, I'd do the healthy thing—and I would murder him"). Like other Weirdos, Harley's real interest isn't in romance; it's in belonging.

Even her violence is goofy, leaning into the comic book aesthetic pure (KAPOW!) vibes. Her gun shoots candy-colored gas, bean bags, and confetti bombs. Of course this is not how real violence works, but the directors of both *Birds of Prey* and *The Suicide Squad*, Cathy Yan and James Gunn, respectively, make us see it from her distorted point of view, with cartoon flowers erupting from wounds instead of blood. That's how Harley sees violence. It's as *The Suicide Squad*'s production designer, Beth Mickle, called it, "Harley Vision."

In *Birds of Prey*, Harley has been dumped by the Joker and does what we've all done in one way or another after a bad breakup: she gets some new tattoos, cuts her hair, and gets a pet. This is a woman who thus far has been defined by her relationship with a man. Remember, even her creation, even her name, is a feminized response to the Joker's (the harlequin being a colorfully dressed comic relief character in Italian commedia dell'arte). Her brand of supervillain Weirdo might be unique, but her problems—a toxic relationship, a bad breakup, a struggle to make friends—are all too common.

"A harlequin's role is to serve," she says, "an audience, a master. A harlequin is nothing without a master. And no one gives two fucks about who we are beyond that." Her journey involves realizing that she is her own creature and that her openheartedness is not a flaw but a strength. Harley is "the asshole no one likes" because she's been in the Joker's shadow for her entire life (at least as Harley Quinn), and she is mocked by other women around her for it ("Some people just aren't born to stand on their own," they say about her as she carries out margaritas for them). The difference between Harley and us is that she does what we'd secretly want to do—she throws the tray of margaritas at them and leaves. The boldness of Harley Quinn is not her glitter blazer or bizarro tattoos; it is that she genuinely won't sacrifice her inner happiness for other people's idea of her. Beneath the antics is a big heart.

Harley is treated as a joke by others. Every time she's underestimated, she seems to enjoy her violence all the more: she giddily beats up a gaggle of policemen in a puff of pink and blue smoke; she'll roundhouse kick a man and break his knee; a running joke in *Birds of Prey* involves a stream of forgettable henchmen looking to take revenge on the grotesque shenanigans she inflicted on them (like tattooing a joker's smile on one particularly burly dude).

Once she is removed from the Joker, Harley is a joyous explosion. By herself, Harley finds joy in small things: a perfect cheese-and-egg sandwich, a glitter-encrusted fanny pack. The clashing prints, sequins, candy-colored hair, short shorts, and glitter socks are not just wacky for wackiness's sake. This is Harley simply enjoying the things that she enjoys for herself, just because, no justification needed. "I'm a princess," she says, marveling at her own reflection in a puffy, glittery red dress. This is the "feminine uncanny" that Emerald Fennell was exploring in *Promising Young Woman*: "This idea that just because you love Britney Spears doesn't mean you couldn't cut someone's face off. Just because you wear pink doesn't mean you're not filled with murderous rage." Just because Harley likes to wear sequin pants and bright lipstick doesn't mean she won't jump on a guy's legs and break both of them.[6]

As Harley, there is a physicality to Robbie's performance that goes beyond the badassery expected of action heroines. When

---

6   Which she does in *Birds of Prey*.

she roundhouse kicks someone, she's doing it with her entire body. There's a glee to Harley's brutality that Robbie captures through her wide, Cheshire cat-like grin. She smiles not to seduce or entertain anyone but because she's enjoying the fuckery of it all so much. It's rare to see such glee from a character—especially one in a comic book franchise, which have largely gone down the gritty route established by *Batman Begins* (2005)—who enjoys the thrill of everyday madness more than that of a villainous plan.

In her red flag speech in *The Suicide Squad* she says, "The music you like ain't real music at all." Tearing up, she remembers what it was like to be under someone's thumb, what it meant to erase herself to fit into a mold someone else had cast for her. Harley evolves from the villain's henchwoman into a character in her own right, her own Weirdo, when she is allowed to roam free and enjoy her egg and cheese sandwiches unencumbered.

WE'RE ALL WEIRDOS NOW

What makes the Weirdo is not the aesthetic or the deadpan or bizarro humor. It's her contentment with being exactly who she is. A woman who is not concerned with what everyone thinks of her is a woman who is happy in her unruliness. A woman not concerned with likeability, we're told, is a Weirdo. Why though? It brings me so much joy to see someone enjoy the things they do, earnestly, giddily even. The urge to put down women for what brings them joy is not merely masculine. Because we're told constantly that there is one right way to be a woman, everything else must be the wrong way. Everyone who does not fit in the perfect ladylike mold must be a Weirdo. It is so difficult to not hear someone else's voice in your head. So easy to fall into the dynamic of shrugging off the things that feel right to you. "I know it's dumb, but I like it" is a go-to. When people around you keep telling you that you're weird, it's easy to internalize that as meaning that you're "wrong" or "basic." The Weirdo is always her own success story, defined by her own set of expectations.

These characters, though coded as Weirdos, are proud of this difference. It might come from a place of hurt, like Nancy Downs or Harley Quinn, or smart-assery, like Daria or Lydia Deetz, but it's an unshackling. What we always find is a big heart, a non-judgmental nature that is welcoming to strangers, even protective of them. There's a kindness to Nancy when she tries to magic away Bonnie's scars, when she warns Sarah about the dangers of Chris's pathological slut shaming. There's kindness in the Weirdo.

This whole chapter is a bit of a cheat, because being defined as a Weirdo is not about being liked by others but rather liking yourself. It's about embracing yourself—who you are and how to be that person. This might mean enjoying trips to the cemetery, or it might mean pairing sequins with stripes. This is a personal process, and each Weirdo is their own galaxy. I think often of how I trained myself—very deliberately—to stop looking around me, to stop looking to see if others are looking at me, to stop trying to decipher their expressions (were they judgmental? Were they approving? What was I doing right? What was I doing wrong?). A few years back, I got the word WEIRDO—all caps—tattooed on the back of my arm as a reminder to not look back, or around me. I watch these performances and I notice that Nancy, Daria, Lydia, Harley—they never look around them. For the Weirdo, there's only looking ahead.

The Death of Likeability

This book really shouldn't exist. Writing about unlikeability seems old-fashioned, superfluous, or even dopey at this point.[1] Even the word itself should've been retired from production rooms, script meetings, and reviews.

And yet—films and shows centering unlikeable female characters are still being questioned, still being canceled, and the likeability of their characters is still being equated with a lacking in the storytelling. And yet—storytellers are being equated with their characters, with actresses being deemed unlikeable by the brainless power of association with characters they've played. Equating the likeability of a fictional female character with the quality of the storytelling is a reductive, moronic moral equation. We should demand that our characters be compelling, competent, and complicated.

Surely we should be done with the notion of likeability at this point. We should be done with the word and the nonsensical set

---

1   I'm sure my editor loved reading this bit!

of parameters that separate being likeable and being unlikeable, a set of rules that seemingly only applies to and affects women.

Surely we should be able to separate the actresses that play complicated, messy characters from the fictional characters they embody.

Surely we shouldn't demand these fictional women be aspirational, always, and all the time.

Surely women onscreen can be bad people and good characters.

Surely we're beyond thinking of art as an instruction manual for living.

And yet—we're not.

I'd like to not use the word "unlikeable" ever again. Let's retire the word altogether. Let's find another, better term, because we're now—finally, thankfully—experiencing a rise in pop culture that centers layered, imperfect women with wants, desires, and flaws. Some of them are criminal or murderous; others, more mundanely annoying. Perhaps most impressively, these characters are no longer being positioned as aspirational figures (except in the occasional tacky marketing campaign) but as, simply, full-fledged characters. There are so many, in fact, that it would be impossible to write about all the films (and, mostly, TV shows) that have come out since I started writing this book. Some films and shows are bringing this amorphous concept of unlikeability to the forefront by design now, trying to make it into a selling point ("I'm Cruella, born brilliant, born bad and a little bit mad").

Archetypes and tropes will always be there, but they're meant to be shortcuts, not rules. We can't avoid being influenced by the stories we see onscreen, but we also have the power to influence the stories that are made. It's not as black-and-white as being led into certain actions because we see a character do them, but it builds up. If we're told enough times that ambition makes a woman a bitch, we're going to learn to bottle that ambition up. If we only see stories about upper-class melancholic white girls being depressed, we might think that they're the only ones allowed to get sad.

Likeability is a moral trap.

I don't want characters to be "goals," I don't want them to be "strong" or "role models" or "inspirational"—I want them to just be great characters. I don't want to bend over backward trying to find redeemable aspects or excuses for their actions. It's not a question of perception but of permission. The pleasure of watching unlikeable female characters is watching them make choices, following their intentions, and using their agency. Even when they don't get away with it, they have an intention; they're not passive. We might not always get what we want, but we always *want* something. And while women are mostly taught to temper their desires, curb their hunger, stop wanting quite so much, watching these characters unleash their wants is such a joy.

Characters like Fleabag, like Annalise Keating, like Villanelle and Eve Polastri, like Bridget Gregory, like Cassie, like Amy Dunne—they don't fit into a single box. They break open the conventions and the stereotypes, sometimes forcing a conversation, other times quietly getting on with business. We don't need to like them. We don't even need to understand them. We just need to want to keep watching.

In the process of writing this, I knew I wanted to end the word "unlikeable." I want to finish it off, explode it in all directions, and unpick exactly why it just doesn't make sense anymore. I wish I could say this applies in the same way to real life as it does to fiction. But, as I hope I've showed over the last however-many pages, unlikeability is too small a notion. It simply cannot contain the richness and layers of the characters we're seeing on our screens now.

Most importantly, we now have the language and the tools to go back through the history of cinema, the history of television, and revisit characters we once dismissed as Bitches, Crazy Women, Trainwrecks, Sluts, or Shrews.

Likeability is too silly a rulebook. It limits the characters and limits our imaginations. We shouldn't have to squint and read between the lines to give breadth to characters. It's truly sad that there hasn't yet been a book breaking apart the tropes and character archetypes that we've so long just brushed under the same dirty rug called "unlikeable female characters."

When I was pitching this book, I was asked a question: What do you want the readers to take away from this? Simple as it sounds, it's empathy. I'd like us to allow our female characters the same amount of empathy and grace that we allow all other characters. With all the talk around representation, we have not yet allowed our fictional women much leeway to be as messy, flawed, or downright evil as fictional men without making it into a headline or a joke.

I maintain we are living in a moment when unlikeable female characters are thriving not in spite of but because of their unlikeability. But every year, with every big release, it still comes as a surprise. It's still a shock to the system to see women transgress onscreen, even if what they're transgressing is a made-up rule to begin with.

Our embracing of these characters, their financial and awards successes, their cultural impact—these should be reason enough to call it quits on this antiquated notion of "likeability." We can and should move beyond reductive expectations, because being unlikeable is just *one* character trait.

I'd like to end this with a quote from Glenn Close, a figure who has appeared several times throughout this text, an actress who has breathed life into many of the characters I've discussed over these past ten chapters, the mad and the bad, and has always spoken about empathy: "The women I have played—other than Cruella—who have consistently been called 'villains' or 'bitchy' all have reasons for their behavior. I'm not saying that their behavior is always acceptable, but they exist in the gray areas of life where we all live." There's no room for "likeability" in the gray areas of life, and there shouldn't be any on our screens.

An Unlikeable Watch List

Over the course of this book, I've cherry-picked films to dive into the different tropes of unlikeable female characters. There are so many more films and TV series made in and outside of Hollywood that could've been covered, referenced, and nit-picked, but that would've made for too many pages for my gentle editor to comb through. So if this book sparks an interest in diving deeper into the mercurial topography of the unlikeable female character, here is a chronological, nonexhaustive recommendation list:

---

* *Daughter of the Dragon (Lloyd Corrigan, 1931)*
* *Red-Headed Woman (Jack Conway, 1932)*
* *Baby Face (Alfred E. Green, 1933)*

* *I'm No Angel (Wesley Ruggles, 1933)*
* *Female (Michael Curtiz, 1933)*
* *Dangerous (Alfred E. Green, 1935)*

---

* *The Letter (William Wyler, 1940)*

* *The Little Foxes (William Wyler, 1940)*

* Doña Bárbara (Fernando de Fuentes, Miguel M. Delgado, 1943)
* La mujer sin alma (Fernando de Fuentes, 1944)

* The Wicked Lady (Leslie Arliss, 1945)

---

* Harriet Craig (Vincent Sherman, 1950)
* Traicionera (Ernesto Cortazar, 1950)
* Gun Crazy (Joseph H. Lewis, 1950)
* Sunset Boulevard (Billy Wilder, 1950)
* The She-Wolf (Maria Plyta, 1951)

* Susana (Luis Buñuel, 1951)
* No Man's Woman (Franklin Adreon, 1955)
* Diabolique (Henri-Georges Clouzot, 1955)
* The Violent Years (Ed Wood, 1956)

---

* When a Woman Ascends the Stairs (Mikio Naruse, 1960)
* Santo Contra las Mujeres Vampiro (Alfonso Corona Blake, 1962)
* Cleopatra (Joseph L. Manciewicz, 1963)

* Marnie (Alfred Hitchcock, 1964)
* La tía Tula (Miguel Picazo, 1964)
* Who's Afraid of Virginia Woolf? (Mike Nichols, 1966)
* Les Biches (Claude Chabrol, 1968)

---

* Wanda (Barbara Loden, 1970)

* The Blood on Satan's Claw (Piers Haggard, 1971)

* The Bitter Tears of Petra Von Kant (R. W. Fassbinder, 1972)
* Mahogany (Berry Gordy, 1975)
* Adoption (Marta Meszaros, 1975)
* Son nom de Venise dans Calcutta desert (Marguerite Duras, 1976)
* Opening Night (John Cassavetes, 1977)
* The Bitch (Gerry O'Hara, 1979)

---

* Body Heat (Lawrence Kasdan, 1981)
* Deprisa, Deprisa (Carlos Saura, 1981)
* Gary Cooper que estás en los cielos (Pilar Miró, 1981)
* Love Letters (Amy Holden Jones, 1983)
* Dance with a Stranger (Mike Newell, 1984)
* She's Gotta Have It (Spike Lee, 1986)
* Black Widow (Bob Rafelson, 1987)
* Dangerous Liaisons (Stephen Frears, 1988)
* A Short Film about Love (Krystof Kieslowski, 1988)

---

* Mermaids (Richard Benjamin, 1990)
* High Heels (Pedro Almodóvar, 1991)
* Raise the Red Lantern (Zhang Yimou, 1991)
* Basic Instinct (Paul Verhoeven, 1992)
* Betty Blue (Jean-Jacques Beineix, 1992)
* Crystal Nights (Tonia Marketaki, 1992)
* Death Becomes Her (Robert Zemeckis, 1992)
* Guncrazy (Tamra Davis, 1992)

* Betty (Claude Chabrol, 1992)
* Dolores Clairborne (Taylor Hackford, 1995)
* La Cérémonie (Claude Chabrol, 1995)
* To Die For (Gus Van Sant, 1995)
* Set It Off (F. Gary Gray, 1996)
* The Long Kiss Godnight (Renny Harlin, 1996)
* Alma gitana (Chus Gutiérrez, 1996)
* Bound (The Wachowskis, 1996)
* Citizen Ruth (Alexander Payne, 1996)
* El tiempo de la felicidad (Manuel Iborra, 1997)

* Jackie Brown (Quentin Tarantino, 1997)
* Under the Skin (Carine Adler, 1997)
* The Sopranos (1997–2007) TV
* Traps (Vera Chytilova, 1998)
* Elizabeth (Shekhar Kapur, 1998)
* The Last Days of Disco (Whit Stillman, 1998)
* Cruel Intentions (Roger Kumble, 1999)
* Rosetta (Dardenne Brothers, 1999)
* Jawbreaker (Darren Stein, 1999)

---

* 28 Days (Betty Thomas, 2000)
* La comunidad (Alex de la Iglesia, 2000)
* Baise-moi (Virginie Despentes, 2000)
* Fat Girl (Catherine Breillat, 2001)

* Wit (Mike Nichols, 2001) TV
* The Piano Teacher (Michael Haneke, 2001)
* Morvern Callar (Lynne Ramsay, 2002)
* Thirteen (Catherine Hardwicke, 2003)

* The Brave One (Neil Jordan, 2007)
* Mad Men (2007-2015) TV
* Breaking Bad (2008-2013) TV
* Julia (Erick Zonca, 2008)

* Frozen River (Courtney Hunt, 2008)
* Fish Tank (Andrea Arnold, 2009)
* Nurse Jackie (2009-2015) TV

---

* Crime d'amour (Alain Corenau, 2010)
* Easy A (Will Gluck, 2010)
* Carmina o revienta (Paco León, 2012)
* Stories We Tell (Sarah Polley, 2012)
* Girls (2012-2017) TV
* Veep (2012-2019) TV
* Scandal (2012-2018) TV
* Zero Dark Thirty (Kathryn Bigelow, 2012)
* The Bling Ring (Sofia Coppola, 2013)
* The To-Do List (Maggie Carey, 2013)
* Gone Girl (David Fincher, 2014)
* How to Get Away with Murder (2014-2020) TV
* Broad City (2014-2019) TV

* Spring Breakers (Harmony Korine, 2015)
* Diary of a Teenage Girl (Marielle Heller, 2015)
* Assassination (Choi Dong-hoon, 2015)
* Elle (Paul Verhoeven, 2016)
* Lady Macbeth (William Oldbroyd, 2016)
* The Love Witch (Anna Biller, 2016)
* Insecure (2016-2021) TV
* Raw (Julia Ducournau, 2016)
* Fleabag (2016-2019) TV
* Thoroughbreds (Cory Finley, 2017)
* Atomic Blonde (David Leitch, 2017)
* Sarah Plays a Werewolf (Katharina Wyss, 2017)

* *The Handmaid's Tale (2017–) TV*
* *The Beguiled (Sofia Coppola, 2017)*
* *Marlina the Murderer in Four Acts Mouly Surya, 2017)*
* *Julia Ist (Elena Martín, 2017)*
* *I, Tonya (Craig Gillespie, 2018)*
* *Fugue (Agniezska Smoczynska, 2018)*
* *Destroyer (Karyn Kusama, 2018)*
* *Succession (2018–) TV*
* *The Favorite (Yorgos Lanthimos, 2019)*
* *Hustlers (Lone Scafaria, 2019)*

---

* *I Hate Suzie (2020) TV*
* *I May Destroy You (2020) TV*
* *Hacks (2021 -) TV*
* *Titane (Julia Ducournau, 2021)*

ACKNOWLEDGMENTS

I'm most grateful to my dear friend Ruby McGuigan, aka my Estelle, who read the proposal and the many versions of this book and pushed me to finish it when I thought I couldn't. Thank you to my agent Silé Edwards, whose very first late-night email and continuous enthusiasm made this book possible. To my editor Erin McClary, I appreciate your kind edits, patience, and support; the pull quotes were crucial in convincing me not everything I was writing was shit. Thank you to Gaylene Gould, for first planting the idea of this book in my head in a corridor in BFI Southbank, and always for your support and generosity. To my friend Jordan Crucchiola, for every single hour we've spent talking at odd hours between London and LA, for reading this book when it was at its roughest, and for being the most enthusiastic about everything. And to Sean Backhurst, for your enthusiasm for every word, your adorable messiness, and for going to the big Foyles to see where this book would be living.

SOURCES

INTRODUCTION: HOW NOT TO BE A GIRL

Anne Helen Petersen, *Too Fat, Too Slutty, Too Loud* (London: Simon & Schuster, 2017)

Rachel Vorona Cote, *Too Much: How Victorian Constraints Still Bind Women Today* (London: Sphere, 2020).

Elizabeth Wurzel, *Bitch: In Praise of Difficult Women* (London: Quartet Books, 1998).

A BRIEF AND INCOMPLETE HISTORY
OF THE UNLIKEABLE FEMALE CHARACTER

Richard Lawson, "Showtime Cornering the Market on 'Ladies with Problems' Shows," *Gawker*, March 24, 2010: https://www.gawker.com/5501286/showtime -cornering-the-market-on-ladies-with-problems-shows.

Elena Nicolaou, "What Women in Film Can Learn from the 'Manless Eden' That Was Hollywood's Silent Era," *Refinery29*, April 23, 2014: https://www.refinery29 .com/en-gb/2018/04/197127/women-silent-era-hollywood-prominent -directors-writers.

Anna Carey, "Female Films: Where Did the Women Go?", *The Irish Times*, February 20, 2021: https://www.irishtimes.com/culture/film/female-films-where-did-the -women-go-1.4483236.

Noami McDougall Jones, "When Hollywood's Power Players Were Women," *The Atlantic*, February 9, 2020: https://www.theatlantic.com/culture/archive/2020/02 /naomi-mcdougall-jones-wrong-kind-of-women-excerpt/606277/.

Pamela Hutchinson, "Leading Ladies: The Women Who Helped Build Hollywood," *The Guardian*, March 7, 2016: https://www.theguardian.com/film/filmblog/2016 /mar/07/women-pioneers-of-early-cinema-alice-guy-blache-mary-pickford.

Phillipa Snow, "Paris Hilton Is the Greatest Performance Artist of Our Time," *i-D*,

May 16, 2019: https://i-d.vice.com/en_uk/article/j5wgad/paris-hilton-is-the
-greatest-performance-artist-of-our-time.

Molly Haskell, *From Reverence to Rape: The Treatment of Women at the Movies*
(Chicago: University of Chicago Press, 1987).

Jude Doyle, *Dead Blondes and Bad Mothers: Monstrosity, Patriarchy and the Fear of
Female Power* (New York and London: Melville House Publishing, 2019).

Mary Beard, *Women & Power: A Manifesto* (London: Profile Books, 2017).

Gabrielle Moss, "The Legacy of '90s Teen Girl Murder Films," RogerEbert.com,
March 10, 2022: https://www.rogerebert.com/features/the-legacy-of-90s-teen
-girl-murder-films.

Nathan Rabin, "The Bataan Death March of Whimsy Case File #1: Elizabethtown,"
The AV Club, January 25, 2007: https://www.avclub.com/the-bataan-death
-march-of-whimsy-case-file-1-elizabet-1798210595.

Nathan Rabin, "I'm Sorry for Coining the Phrase 'Manic Pixie Dream Girl,'" *Salon,*
July 15, 2014: https://www.salon.com/2014/07/15/im_sorry_for_coining
_the_phrase_manic_pixie_dream_girl/.

THE BITCH

Laurie Penny, *Bitch Doctrine: Essays for Dissenting Adults* (London: Bloomsbury,
2017).

Laura Bradley, "Was *Girlboss* Netflix's First Truly Terrible Show?" *Vanity Fair,* June
26, 2017: https://www.vanityfair.com/hollywood/2017/06/girlboss-netflix
-canceled-one-season.

Whitney Stine (with Bette Davis), *Mother Goddam* (New York: Hawthorn Books,
1974).

Paula S. Bernstein, "Having Some Fun with the Barbara Stanwyck Role," *The New York
Times,* October 23, 1994: https://www.nytimes.com/1994/10/23/movies/film
-having-some-fun-with-the-barbara-stanwyck-role.html.

Roger Ebert, "To Die for Review," RogerEbert.com, October 6, 1995: https://www
.rogerebert.com/reviews/to-die-for-1995.

Janet Maslin, "THE LAST SEDUCTION; A Femme Fatale Who Lives Up To the
Description," *The New York Times,* October 26, 1994: https://www.nytimes
.com/1994/10/26/movies/film-review-the-last-seduction-a-femme-fatale-who
-lives-up-to-the-description.html.

Mark Kermode, "Love Fool: Peter Berg in 'The Last Seduction,'" *Sight & Sound
Magazine,* December 1994: https://archive.org/details/Sight_and_Sound_1994
_12_BFI_GB.

Kim Newman, "The Last Seduction Review," *Empire,* December 6, 1998: https://
www.empireonline.com/movies/reviews/last-seduction-review/.

Richard Schickel, "Wretch on a Sexual Rampage," *Time,* November 14, 1994: https://
content.time.com/time/subscriber/article/0,33009,981817,00.html.

David Denby, "Sex and Sexier," *The New Yorker*, April 25, 2016: https://www
.newyorker.com/magazine/2016/05/02/what-the-hays-code-did-for-women.

Vincent Canby, "Passion in the Ancien Regime: 'Dangerous Liaisons' on Screen," *The
New York Times*, December 21, 1998: https://www.nytimes.com/1988/12/21
/movies/review-film-passion-in-the-ancien-regime-dangerous-liaisons-on
-screen.html.

Scott Myers, "Great Character: Bridget Gregory ('The Last Seduction')," *Go into the
Story* (blog), March 22, 2013: https://gointothestory.blcklst.com/great-character
-bridget-gregory-the-last-seduction-36950642ee4f.

"Glenn Close Breaks Down Her Career, from 'Fatal Attraction' to '101 Dalmatians,'"
Vanity Fair, YouTube, November 25, 2020: https://www.youtube.com/watch?v
=X6Rw59-6gkA&ab_channel=VanityFair.

Sophie Gilbert, "Is Television Ready for Angry Women?"*The Atlantic*, June 2018:
https://www.theatlantic.com/magazine/archive/2018/06/marti-noxon
/559115/.

Jia Tolentino, Trick/Mirror: Reflections of Self Delusion (London: 4th Estate, 2019).

Pamela Hutchinson, "The Bitch Is Back," Tortoise Media, May 26, 2019: https://
www.tortoisemedia.com/2019/05/26/cultural-history-of-the-bitch/.

Jo Freeman, "The BITCH Manifesto," 1968: https://www.jofreeman.com/joreen
/bitch.htm.

Daniel Daddario, "Lena Headey on Playing Cersei on Game of Thrones: 'I Admire
Her,'" *Time*, July 10, 2017: https://time.com/4773785/lena-headey-cersei
-game-of-thrones/.

Diahann Carroll Interview: https://interviews.televisionacademy.com/interviews
/diahann-carroll.

THE MEAN GIRL

Naomi Fry, "'Heathers' Blew Up the High-School Comedy," *The New Yorker*, March
27, 2019: https://www.newyorker.com/culture/touchstones/an-appreciation-of
-the-dark-comedy-heathers.

Stephen Holden, "FILM REVIEW; Back to Their Old Tricks, but a Whole Lot
Younger," *The New York Times*, March 5, 1999: https://www.nytimes.com/1999
/03/05/movies/film-review-back-to-their-old-tricks-but-a-whole-lot-younger
.html.

Rose McGowan, "Exclusive: Rose McGowan Loves That Jawbreaker RemakesAre
Coming, but Warns That 'No One Will Ever Be Me,'" *Refinery29*, February 19, 2019:
https://www.refinery29.com/en-us/2019/02/224526/rose-mcgowan-jawbreaker
-20th-anniversary-new-tv-show.

Brady Langmann, "It's Time to Accept That Otis Milburn Is the Villain of Sex
Education,"*Esquire*, September 28, 2021: https://www.esquire.com/entertainment
/tv/a37709652/otis-milburn-asa-butterfield-sex-education-villain/.

THE ANGRY WOMAN

Jess Zimmerman, "A Fury's Battle: How Our Culture Demonizes Women's Anger and Protects Abusers," *Lit Hub,* March 11, 2021: https://lithub.com/a-furys-battle -how-our-culture-demonizes-womens-anger-and-protects-abusers/.

Humintell Admin, "Why Angry Men Are More Influential Than Angry Women," *Humintell,* October 29, 2015:https://www.humintell.com/2015/10/why-angry -men-are-more-influential-than-angry-women/.

Roxane Gay, "Who Gets to Be Angry?" *The New York Times,* June 10, 2016: https:// www.nytimes.com/2016/06/12/opinion/sunday/who-gets-to-be-angry.html.

Angelica Jade Bastién, "Emerald Fennell Explains Herself," *Vulture,* January 22, 2021: https://www.vulture.com/2021/01/promising-young-woman-ending-emerald -fennell-explains.html.

Angela Jade Bastién, "What Jessica Jones Understand about Female Rage," *Slate,* March 19, 2018:https://slate.com/culture/2018/03/jessica-jones-season-2-female -rage.html.

Arielle Richards, "Bimbofication Is Taking Over. What Does That Mean for You?" *Vice,* February 22, 2022: https://www.vice.com/en/article/4aw4kd/bimbofication -is-taking-over-what-does-that-mean-for-you.

Soraya Chemaly, "The Power of Women's Anger," *TED,* February 28, 2019: https:// www.youtube.com/watch?v=wMt0K-AbpCU&ab_channel=TED.

Janice C. Simpson, "Moving into the Driver's Seat," *Time,* June 24, 1991: http:// content.time.com/time/subscriber/article/0,33009,973249-2,00.html.

THE SLUT

Christina Newland, *She Found It at the Movies: Women Writers on Sex, Desire and Cinema* (London: Red Press, 2020).

Madonna, *Sex* (New York: Warner Books, Maverick, Callaway, 1992).

Morgan Sung, "Bimbos Are Good, Actually," *Mashable,* December 5, 2020: https:// mashable.com/article/bimbo-tiktok-meme-feminism.

P.A., "Madonna Stays Mum on Sex," *The Sydney Morning Herald,* September 15, 2003: https://www.smh.com.au/entertainment/music/madonna-stays-mum-on-sex -20030915-gdhe68.html.

Priya Elan, "Looking Back at Madonna and Sex," *The Guardian,* April 25, 2012: https://www.theguardian.com/music/shortcuts/2012/apr/25/looking-back-at -madonna-sex.

Emily Nussbaum, "Difficult Women," *The New Yorker,* July 22, 2013: https://www .newyorker.com/magazine/2013/07/29/difficult-women.

Angelica Jade Bastién, "Kathleen Turner Made the Modern Femme Fatale," *Vulture,* April 8, 2022: https://www.vulture.com/2022/04/kathleen-turner-made-the -modern-femme-fatale.html.

THE TRAINWRECK

Jude Doyle, *Trainwreck: The Women We Love to Hate, Mock, and Fear...and Why* (New York and London: Melville House Publishing, 2017).

Lib Tietjen, "'Let's Get Drunk and Make Love': Lois Long and the Speakeasy," *Tenement Museum Blog*, n.d.: https://www.tenement.org/blog/lets-get-drunk -and-make-love-lois-long-and-the-speakeasy/.

Nisha Gopalan, "'Splat!': The Oral History of Sex and the City's Most Shocking Episode," *Vulture*, June 6, 2018: https://www.vulture.com/2013/12/sex-and-the -city-oral-history-splat-episode.html.

Katy Steinmetz, "How the Meaning of 'Hot Mess' Has Changed through History," *Time*, April 2, 2014: https://time.com/46267/hot-mess-history-amy-schumer/.

Marianne Eloise, "2007: The Year Dumb Bro Comedy Died," *Little White Lies*, September 9, 2017: https://lwlies.com/articles/frat-pack-comedy-2007-blades -of-glory-hot-rod/.

Guelda Voien, "The Most Shameful Thing a 30-Something Woman Can Say? I Watch 'Girls,'" *Observer*, February 10, 2017: https://observer.com/2017/02/the -most-shameful-thing-a-30-something-woman-can-say-i-watch-girls/.

Christina Dugan Ramirez, "Lena Dunham Discusses Girls' 'Unlikable' Characters— and Reveals Why She's 'Really Proud of' Her Costars," *People*, December 15, 2016: https://people.com/celebrity/lena-dunham-discusses-girls-unlikable-characters -what-makes-her-really-proud/.

De Elizabeth, "The Girls of 'Girls' Were Unlikeable, and That Is What I Will Miss Most," *Teen Vogue*, April 14, 2017: https://www.teenvogue.com/story/hbo-girls -unlikeable.

Phoebe Hurst, "The Evolution of the 'Messy Woman,'" *Vice*, August 8, 2019: https://www .vice.com/en/article/zmjeew/animals-film-emma-jane-unsworth-interview -messy-women.

Kate Stables, "Animals Review: Two Friends' Clash of Millennial Hedonism and Romantic Yearning," *Sight & Sound Magazine*, August 8, 2019: https://www2 .bfi.org.uk/news-opinion/sight-sound-magazine/reviews-recommendations /animals-sophie-hyde-holliday-grainger-alia-shawkat-end-party-loving-female -friendship.

David Ehrlich, "Trainwreck Review," *Little White Lies*, August 14, 2015: https:// lwlies.com/reviews/trainwreck/.

Jason Reitman, "INTERVIEW: Jason Reitman Made Unmakeable Young Adult for $12 Million," *Indiewire*, interview conducted by Anne Thompson, December 5, 2011: https://www.indiewire.com/2011/12/interview-jason-reitman-made-unmakeable -young-adult-for-12-million-183880/.

Alison Herman, "'Girls' Deserved What It Got. But It Also Deserved Better," *The Ringer*, April 15, 2022: https://www.theringer.com/tv/2022/4/15/23026177 /girls-hbo-pilot-10-year-anniversary-lena-dunham.

THE CRAZY WOMAN

Gary Nunn, "The Feminisation of Madness Is Crazy," *The Guardian*, March 8, 2012: https://www.theguardian.com/media/mind-your-language/2012/mar/08/mind-your-language-feminisation-madness.

Richard Corliss, "Cinema: Killer! Fatal Attraction Strikes Gold as a Parable of Sexual Guilt," *Time Magazine*, November 16, 1987: http://content.time.com/time/subscriber/article/0,33009,965968-5,00.html.

The Film Programme, BBC Radio 4, September 20, 2018: https://www.bbc.co.uk/programmes/b0bk1sq8.

Susan Faludi, *Backlash: The Undeclared War against Women* (London: Vintage, 1993)

Lana Del Rey, "Lana Del Rey: 'I Wish I Was Dead Already,'" *The Guardian*, interview conducted by Tim Jonze, June 12, 2014: https://www.theguardian.com/music/2014/jun/12/lana-del-rey-ultraviolence-album.

Tom Meltzer, " The Best TV of 2013: No 6—Orange Is the New Black (Netflix)," *TheGuardian*, December 17, 2013: https://www.theguardian.com/tv-and-radiotvandradioblog/2013/dec/17/best-tv-2013-orange-is-the-new-black-netflix.

Rayne Fisher-Quann, "Standing on the Shoulders of Complex Female Characters," *Internet Princess*, February 6, 2022: https://internetprincess.substack.com/p/standing-on-the-shoulders-of-complex?s=r.

THE PSYCHO

Luxurious Editorial, "Books That Defined the Decade, according to a Professional Storyteller,"*LuxuriousMagazine*,December27,2019:https://www.luxuriousmagazine.com/five-books-that-defined-the-decade/.

Christina Radish, "Rosamund Pike Talks GONE GIRL, Shooting "That Scene", and More at SBIFF", Collider, February 4, 2015: https://collider.com/rosamund-pike-gone-girl-interview/.

Gillian Flynn, "I Was Not a Nice Little Girl…", *Powell's Books Medium*, July 17, 2015: https://medium.com/@Powells/i-was-not-a-nice-little-girl-c2df01e0ae1

Vincent Canby, "A Writer Who Really Suffers", *The New York Times*, November 30, 1990: https://www.nytimes.com/1990/11/30/movies/review-film-a-writer-who-really-suffers.html.

Sharon Stone, *The Beauty of Living Twice* (London: Allen & Unwin, 2021).

Hannah Giorgis, "Killing Eve and the Riddle of Why Women Kill," *The Atlantic*, May 28, 2018: https://www.theatlantic.com/entertainment/archive/2018/05/killing-eve-and-the-riddle-of-why-women-kill/561074/.

Interview with Julia Ducournau, *The Final Girls Podcast*: https://podcasts.apple.com/mk/podcast/bonus-interview-with-julia-ducournau-titane-writer/id1484614975?i=1000546240222.

Roger Ebert, "Basic Instinct Review," RogerEbert.com, March 20, 1992: https://www.rogerebert.com/reviews/basic-instinct-1992.

Rita Kempley, "Basic Instinct Review," *The Washington Post*, March 20, 1992: https://www.washingtonpost.com/wp-srv/style/longterm/movies/videos/basic instinctrkempley_a0a2a8.htm.

James Fox, "Gender and Homicide," Crime and Justice Research Alliance, n.d.: https://crimeandjusticeresearchalliance.org/rsrch/gender-and-homicide/.

Amanda L. Farrell, Robert D. Keppel, and Victoria B. Titterington, "Testing Existential Classifications of Serial Murder Considering Gender: An Exploratory Analysis of Solo Female Serial Killers," *Wiley Online Library*, May 20, 2013: https://onlinelibrary .wiley.com/doi/abs/10.1002/jip.1392.

Mike Aamodt "Serial Killer Statistics," *Radford University*, September 4, 2016: http://maamodt.asp.radford.edu/serialkillerinformationcenter/projectdescription.htm; https://www.independent.co.uk/news/uk/crime/women-murders-men-ons-sarah-everard-b1815779.html.

Cody Cottier, "Female Serial Killers Exist but Their Motives Are Different," *Discover*, December 3, 2020: https://www.discovermagazine.com/mind/female-serial-killers-exist-but-their-motives-are-different.

Xan Brooks, "Gone Girl Unleashes Battle of the Sexes at New York Film Festival," *The Guardian*, September 14, 2014: https://www.theguardian.com /film/2014/sep/27/gone-girl-battle-of-sexes-new-york-film-festival-premiere #:~:text=Flynn%20said%3A%20%22I%20see%20Amy,stories%20that%20she's %20pulled%20together.

Oliver Burkeman, "Gillian Flynn on Her Bestseller Gone Girl and Accusations of Misogyny," *The Guardian*, May 1, 2013: https://www.theguardian.com/books /2013/may/01/gillian-flynn-bestseller-gone-girl-misogyny.

Beatrice Loayza, "Misery at 30: A Terrifying Look at theToxicity of Fandom," *The Guardian*, November 30, 2020: https://www.theguardian.com/film/2020/nov/30 /misery-at-30-terrifying-look-toxicity-fandom-kathy-bates.

Justin Sayles, "The Bloody Bubble," *The Ringer*, July 9, 2021: https://www.theringer .com/tv/2021/7/9/22567381/true-crime-documentaries-boom-bubble-netflix-hbo

Jia Tolentino, "The Pleasurable Patters of the Killing Eve Season Finale," *The New Yorker*, May 27, 2018: https://www.newyorker.com/culture/on-television/the-pleasurable-patterns-of-the-killing-eve-season-finale.

Mary Gaitskill, "In Charm's Way," *BookForum*, Sep/Oct/Nov 2013 Issue: https://www.bookforum.com/print/2003/gone-girl-s-sickening-worldview-12173.

THE SHREW

Lizzie Skurnick (ed.), *Pretty Bitches: On Being Called Crazy, Angry, Bossy, Frumpy, Feisty, and All the Other Words That Are Used to Undermine Women* (New York: Seal Press, 2020).

Lane Brown, "In Conversation: Vince Gilligan on the End of Breaking Bad," *Vulture*, May 12, 2013: https://www.vulture.com/2013/05/vince-gilligan-on-breaking-bad.html.

Marion Johnson, "Mad Men, Megan Draper and the Skyler White Effect," *The Huffington Post,* June 3, 2013: https://www.huffpost.com/entry/mad-men-feminism _b_3005489.

Anna Gunn, "I Have a Character Issue," *The New York Times*, August 23, 2013: https://www.nytimes.com/2013/08/24/opinion/i-have-a-character-issue.html.

Anne T. Donahue, "Even If You Hated Skyler White on Breaking Bad, She Changed TV Forever," *Marie Claire*, August 10, 2018: https://www.marieclaire.com /culture/a22676549/skyler-white-breaking-bad-strong-female-lead.

Mark Ehrman, "CLIQUES: The Importance of Hating Brenda," *The New York Times*, February 7, 1993: https://www.latimes.com/archives/la-xpm-1993-02-07-tm -1357-story.html.

Zosha Millman, "Shalita Grant Can't Wait for People to Hate Her in YOU," *Bustle*, October 14, 2021: https://www.bustle.com/entertainment/shalita-grant-you-season -3-sherry-interview.

THE WEIRDO

Emily Nussbaum, "Requiem for Daria," *Slate*, January 21, 2002: https://slate.com /culture/2002/01/requiem-for-daria.html.

Abraham Riesman, "The Hidden Story of Harley Quinn and How She Became the Superhero World's Most Successful Woman," *Vulture*, February 5, 2020: https:// www.vulture.com/2014/12/harley-quinn-dc-comics-suicide-squad.html.

Charles Pulliam-Moore, "The Suicide Squad's 'Harley Vision' Will Tap Into Birds of Prey's Flights of Fancy," *Gizmodo*, July 26, 2021: https://gizmodo.com/the -suicide-squads-harley-vision-will-tap-into-birds-of-1847263709.

Angelica Jade Bastién, "Emerald Fennell Explains Herself," *Vulture*, January 22, 2021: https://www.vulture.com/2021/01/promising-young-woman-ending-emerald -fennell-explains.html.

Michael Wilmington, "Nothing Bewitching about The Craft's Tale of Student Sorcerers," *The Chicago Tribune,* May 3, 1996: https://www.chicagotribune.com/news/ct-xpm -1996-05-03-9605030190-story.html.

Rita Kempley, "Poor Little Witch Girls," *The Washington Post*, May 3, 1996: https:// www.washingtonpost.com/wp-srv/style/longterm/movies/videos/craft .htm#kempley.

Roger Ebert, "The Craft," *RogerEbert.com*, May 3, 1996: https://www.rogerebert.com /reviews/the-craft-1996.

INDEX

ABOUT THE AUTHOR

© Ella Kemp

Anna Bogutskaya is a film programmer, writer, and broadcaster based in London. In the past, she was the Film and Events Programmer at the BFI, where she curated many seasons and created the Woman with a Movie Camera Summit. She programs for the BFI, the Edinburgh International Film Festival, and Fantastic Fest. As a writer, she has contributed to *BBC Culture, Sight & Sound, Little White Lies, BFI, Tortoise, TimeOut, The Guardian, NME, MUBI, Vulture,* and *i-D,* among other outlets. She is the co-founder of horror film collective The Final Girls and hosts the podcast of the same name.

ANNABOGUTSKAYA.COM

TWITTER: @ANNABEMENTED   INSTAGRAM: @ANNABEMENTED